# THE
# DESERT
# RATS

# THE DESERT RATS

### The History of the 7th Armoured Division 1938 to 1945

*by*

## Major-General G. L. Verney,

### DSO, MVO

With a New Introduction by General Sir John Hackett
With a Foreword by Field Marshal Sir John Harding

**Greenhill Books, London**
**Presidio Press, California**

This edition of *The Desert Rats: The History of the 7th Armoured Division*
first published 1990 by Greenhill Books, Lionel Leventhal Limited,
Park House, 1 Russell Gardens, London NW11 9NN
and
Presidio Press,
31 Pamaron Way, Novato, Ca.94949, U.S.A.

**Lionel Leventhal**
**Celebrating 30 years of military publishing**
**1960-1990**

British Library Cataloguing in Publication Data
Verney, G. L. (Gerald Lloyd)
The Desert Rats: The History of the 7th Armoured Division.
1. World War 2. North African campaign. Army operations during
North African campaign of World War 2 1940–1943. Great Britain.
2. World War 2. Western Europe campaigns. Army operations 1943–1945.
Army operations during Western European campaigns of World War 2.
Great Britain.
Army. Eighth Army. Seventh Armoured Division.
I. Title        940.5423

ISBN 1–85367–063–4

Publishing History
*The Desert Rats: The History of the 7th Armoured Division* was first
published in 1954 (Hutchinson & Co.) and is reproduced now
exactly as the original edition, complete and unabridged.
For this edition a new Introduction by General Sir John Hackett
has been added.

# CONTENTS

Foreword by Field Marshal Sir John Harding,
G.C.B., K.B.E., D.S.O., M.C.                    *Page* 11

Preface                                                  13

Prologue                                                 17

*Chapter* I   The First Offensive                        21

II   Operation "Battleaxe"                               49

III  Operation "Crusader"                                65

IV   Retreat and Defence                                 99

V    Alamein to Tunis                                   127

VI   Italy                                             162

VII  Normandy                                          180

VIII From Normandy to Belgium                           211

IX   The Low Countries                                  247

X    The Advance into Germany                           265

Epilogue. The Greatest Day                              281

*Appendices*

1. Orders of Battle                                     283

2. Roll of Senior Commanders and Staff Officers         291

3. The Earliest Days                                    295

4. A Few Statistics                                     299

5. The Story of the Divisional Sign                     301

6. Bibliography                                         303

Index                                                   305

THIS HISTORY
IS DEDICATED TO
THE OFFICERS,
WARRANT OFFICERS,
NON-COMMISSIONED OFFICERS
AND
PRIVATE SOLDIERS
OF THE 7TH ARMOURED DIVISION
WHO GAVE THEIR LIVES IN THE WAR
1939 TO 1945

# LIST OF PLATES

Appearing between pages 154 and 155

Crusaders going into Action

Light Tanks of the 1st Royal Tank Regiment

German PZ KW IIIs knocked out at Sidi Rezegh

25-pounders of the 4th R.H.A.

Headquarters, 4th Armoured Brigade

Another Prisoner for a Jock Column

The R.H.A. in Action near Acroma

Forward from Alamein

1st/6th Queens in Tobruk

The 11th Hussars enter Tunis

In Action near Vesuvius

Cromwells of the 4th C.L.Y. leaving the Normandy beaches

A Cromwell AA Tank of the 4th County of London Yeomanry landing in Normandy

Forming up for Operation "Goodwood"

The road into Aunay

Welcome for the 1st/6th Queens at Ste Margueritte de Viette near Lisieux

Liberation of Gournay en Bray

Entry into Holland

An 8th Hussar "Dingo" competing with an icy road

The 1st Battalion Rifle Brigade at the German village of Masendorf

The 3rd R.H.A. lead the Victory Parade in Berlin

# MAPS

Appearing between pages 11 and 12
North Africa
Central and North-West Europe

| 1. | The Battle of Sidi Barrani | *Page* 26 |
| 2. | Cyrenaica and Western Egypt | 34 |
| 3. | The Battle of Beda Fomm | 40 |
| 4. | Operation "Battleaxe" | 54 |
| 5. | (*a*) Operation "Crusader" | 64 |
| 5. | (*b*) Operation "Crusader" | 82 |
| 6. | May and June 1942 | 102 |
| 7. | The Battle of Alam Halfa | 120 |
| 8. | The Battle of Alamein | 128 |
| 9. | Southern Italy | 164 |
| 10. | The Crossing of the Volturno | 172 |
| 11. | Normandy | 182 |
| 12. | The Battle of Villers Bocage | 190 |
| 13. | Operation "Goodwood" | 202 |
| 14. | The Battle of Mont Pincon | 212 |
| 15. | The Advance to the Seine | 222 |
| 16. | The Advance to Ghent | 230 |
| 17. | The Low Countries | 246 |
| 18. | The Advance into Germany | 268 |

# INTRODUCTION

by

## GENERAL SIR JOHN HACKETT

WHEN General Verney's history of the 7th Armoured Division was first published in 1954 the foreword was written by the best-loved of all generals in our time, who was also 7th Armoured's most famous commander. This was John Harding – the late Field Marshal Lord Harding of Petherton. It is with some diffidence that I follow him, as a founder member of the ramshackle little force sent out into the Western Desert in 1935 for the war with Italy that never broke out (officially known as The Mobile Force though sometimes less formally referred to as The Immobile Farce) which was the basis of the formidable fighting instrument late to be knocked into shape by Hobo,* to become perhaps the best known of all British Divisions in the Second World War. I was also its last commander (save for a successor put in to disband it) when it was killed off by unimaginative Whitehall warriors in 1958. Its early story is one of endless inadequacies in almost everything an armoured division needs and of huge difficulties triumphantly overcome in the unique blend of enthusiasm, resource and light-hearted comradeship which made Seventh Armoured stand out on its own, a focus of pride and affection for all who ever wore the Desert Rat. It is hard to see any good reason for its disbandment. The argument that you may not have a seventh of anything if there are fewer than six others can be dismissed with contempt. The division's very prestige may have played a part in its undoing. We shall never know. I personally particularly mourned the demise of the 7th Armoured Division Signal Regiment. Brigades, Regiments, Battalions and other units moved in and out, but the Signals Regiment was always there at the very heart and centre, a divisional shrine whose transformation

---

* Major-General P. C. S. Hobart

9

into no more than a numbered nonentity was sheer iconoclasm. The rat lives on (though some would have liked to see that go too) as the sign of the 7th Armoured Brigade, but much else worth keeping has been lost in a triumph of tidiness over commonsense which even in the military corners of Whitehall can have had few equals. What lives on, above all, is the incomparable spirit of what we in the Middle East used to call *The* Armoured Division during all the months when the British army *had* only one. The republication of Gerald Verney's admirable book, a record most carefully researched and written, will do much to help its memory survive.

1990

# FOREWORD

by

### FIELD MARSHAL SIR JOHN HARDING
G.C.B., K.B.E., D.S.O., M.C.

*Chief of the Imperial General Staff*

THIS book contains the story of the exploits of the 7th Armoured Division during the Second World War. It is an epic of courage and endurance, a thrilling tale of many a hard-fought battle in broiling heat, in bitter cold, in blinding rain or mud, often against heavy odds. Through it all there runs a single theme of stern determined service by a devoted band of warriors bound together by a steadfast belief in their cause, and by their comradeship in arms.

The Desert Rats, as the Division came to be called from its now famous sign, twice fought their way across the Western Desert and were twice forced back before the tide was turned for good at the Battle of El Alamein. From there it fought its way with others to Tunis, up Italy, and from Normandy to the Elbe. The Division can rightly claim a record second to none in the annals of British arms, and every single man who ever served in the Division has a share in that proud claim.

The Division still holds its place in the ranks of the British Army. Today it serves in Europe where it stands on guard against aggression. Whatever the future may hold one thing is certain: 7th Armoured Division will foster and uphold the spirit of service and comradeship for which it has always been famed. I trust that all who read this book will be inspired and encouraged to go forward into the future with that same indomitable spirit.

*John Harding*

*F.M.*

SARDINIA

ITALY

M E D

TUNIS

Cap Bon

Medjez
el Bab

SICILY

Enfidaville

Kairouan        Sousse

Fondouk

T U

Malta

Sfax

Gafsa

N

Akarit

Gabes

I

Maretho

Medenine

S

Ben Gardane

Zouara        TRIPOLI

Foum
Tatahouine

I

Homs

Tarhuna

Misurata

A

Buerat

T R I P O L I T A N I A        Sirte

Nofilia

MARBLE ARCH

N.

L I B

0    50    100    150    200    250 MILES

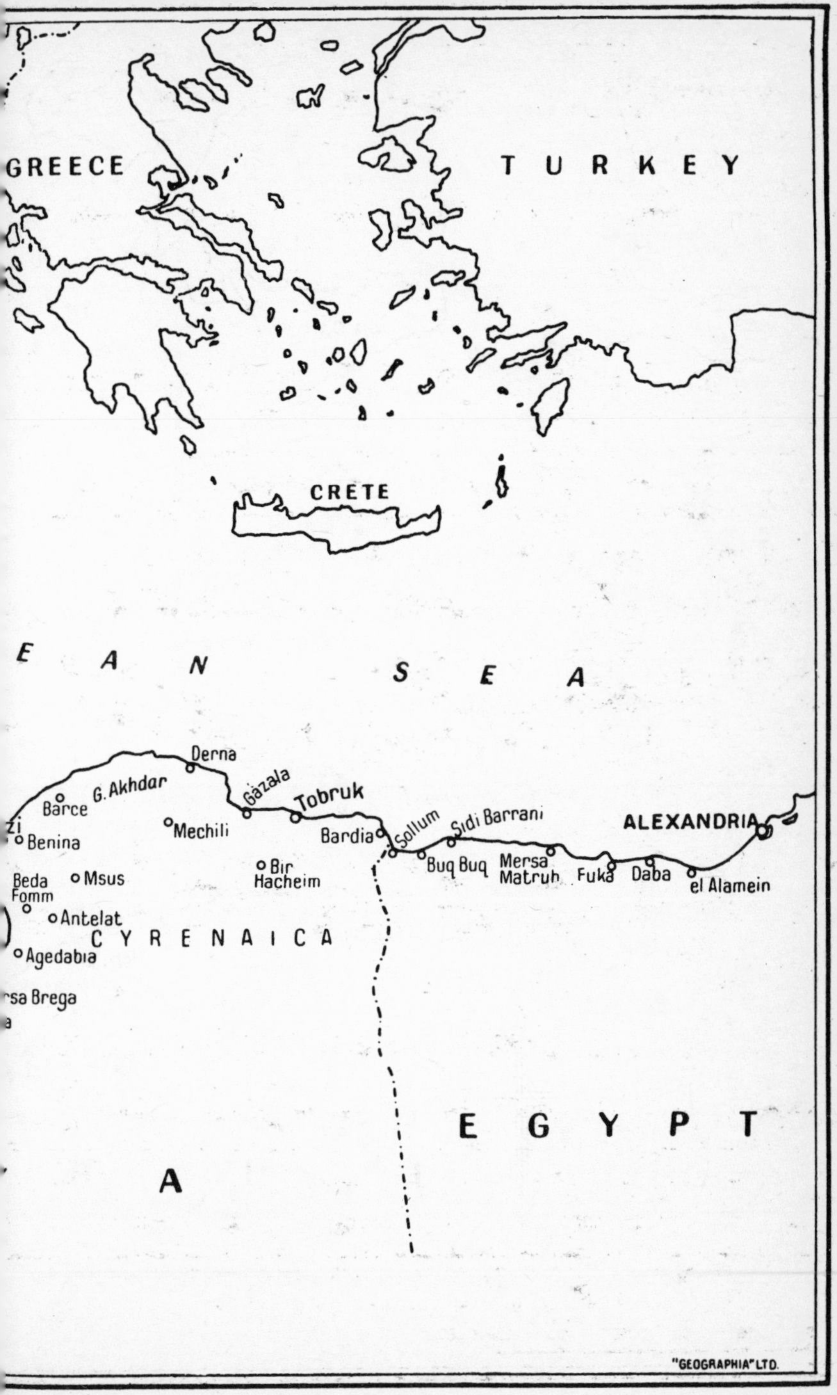

GREECE

TURKEY

CRETE

E A N S E A

Derna

G. Akhdar

Gazala

Tobruk

Barce

Zi

Benina

Mechili

Bardia

Sollum

Sidi Barrani

ALEXANDRIA

Beda
Fomm

Msus

Bir
Hacheim

Buq Buq

Mersa
Matruh

Fuka

Daba

el Alamein

Antelat

C Y R E N A I C A

Agedabia

rsa Brega

a

E G Y P T

A

"GEOGRAPHIA" LTD.

# PREFACE

THE story of the 7th Armoured Division is a long one, for it covers the whole period of the war and much of the development of armoured warfare as well.

The problem with which I have been confronted has been to compress this long tale into the covers of a book that is neither unwieldy in size nor extortionate in price. I have tried to select from the records those events which are of greater historical importance and abiding significance, and to direct the light more on those actions which will one day be emblazoned on Standards, Guidons and Colours as "Battle Honours".

There were long periods when, although the whole Division was in the forward area, only a portion was in contact with the enemy; such, for instance, is the time between June and November in 1941. Many were hazardously and actively fighting, and leading the arduous life of the Jock Column. That they find scant attention paid to their doings does not mean that their good work is, or was, unappreciated or forgotten; if it were not for what they did, the tale of the Desert War would be far different.

Those readers who have themselves engaged in battle need no reminding of the important part played by what are collectively known as the Supporting Arms and Services. In war we would not survive a day without them, and their praise is often on our lips, but one has only to read the average Divisional or Regimental History to realize that when war is done they suffer the fate of the blameless vestal, "the world forgetting, by the world forgot". I have tried to say something about what we all owe to them—it is inadequate, I know; few of them get a mention more than once, but we must remember that they were always there. Such renown as came to the Division we justly and gratefully share with them.

My task has been made very much easier on account of Brigadier Carver's short history written after the fall of Tunis, which covers the whole of the African Campaign, and of the other short history, covering the Italian and North-West European Campaigns, written by Captain the Hon. Martin Lindsay and Captain M. E. Johnston. These books have provided me with a sure road on which to tread, and my gratitude to the authors is all the greater because they have given me permission to make the fullest use of their works.

My other sources of information have been papers loaned by individuals to which I refer later, Regimental Histories, and War Diaries. I wish to express my thanks to the authors of the Histories; their books are recorded in Appendix 6, together with those other books to which I have had access.

When one considers the conditions under which the War Diaries were written—fatigue, discomfort, uncertainty, danger—one can only marvel at the devotion of the Adjutants and Intelligence Officers who compiled them. Inevitably, there are blank patches, and sometimes two units or two formations give differing accounts of the same event—who would expect otherwise? Often, too, they verge on the side of being too terse and uninformative—one gathers that the unit is still in being but little more. Possibly it is invidious to single out one above all the others, but no one who reads it can fail to be impressed by the magnificent and moving writing in the War Diary of the Support Group for November 1941. The author was Captain (later Lieutenant-Colonel) I. H. D. Whigham, Rifle Brigade, probably assisted occasionally by the Brigade-Major, Major J. L. Corbett-Winder, K.R.R.C., also later a Lieutenant-Colonel. How the Brigade Staff found time during the turmoil of the Battle of Sidi Rezegh to write such a detailed and thrilling account of all that was happening when they were likely to be overwhelmed at any moment and their Commander and others were winning Victoria Crosses, I cannot imagine.

I would have liked to include fuller details of casualties, but to untangle them from the Middle East records has proved an impossible task; even later records are not always complete. Similarly with decorations; as it was clearly impossible to get a full list or to find out who was entitled to what decoration at any one time, I have thought it better to disregard them altogether except for the Victoria Cross. In the Index I have aimed at showing the rank that I believe the individual reached on the last day of the war.

For the last two and a half years of the war the Division included the 131st Infantry Brigade, and for most of that time it was composed of Battalions of the Queens Royal Regiment, the correct designations of which were the 1st/5th, 1st/6th and 1st/7th. For simplicity I have abbreviated them to what we always knew them by in the war, 5th, 6th and 7th Queens. I hope the Regiment will forgive me.

The Illustrations are all from the Imperial War Museum, and I would like to record my debt to the gentlemen there who took endless trouble to find what I wanted.

Always a vexed question is Maps. Unfortunately, they are a very expensive item in publication, but luckily this is not a text book on strategy or tactics, and I have felt that readers do not require detailed maps with lots of little arrows in lots of colours. I have probably erred on the austere side. I have tried to abide by the principle that every place mentioned in the text should be on the appropriate map. Occasionally this has not been possible unless one was prepared to provide a map of very large size with very much detail; where a place is mentioned in the text and is not included on the appropriate map, a note has been made and a description of its approximate location given.

This book could never have been written if I had not had the greatest encouragement and almost overwhelming practical help from nearly every senior officer who served in the Division. They have lent me papers, many of great personal or historical value; they have answered questions; they have read drafts; they have entertained me at their homes or clubs; even the busiest ones, like Sir John Harding at the head of Army affairs, or Generals Erskine and Hinde, fighting a Campaign in East Africa, have appeared delighted to turn aside from their tasks and give me their time whenever I have asked. The list of them is too long for insertion. Sir Winston Churchill, too, has kindly permitted me to quote from a speech he made in Berlin in July, 1945.

Brigadier Dudley Clarke and his publishers, Messrs. Michael Joseph, have kindly allowed me to quote from the *History of the 11th Hussars*, and Brigadier Carver and the editors and publishers of the *Royal Armoured Corps Journal* have permitted a quotation from an article in that publication.

The 7th Hussars generously lent me the proofs of the Regimental History by Brigadier G. M. O. Davy which was in process of production, and all the Royal Horse Artillery Regiments lent me records, some, like those of the 3rd R.H.A., being of immense interest and help.

Brigadier Latham and his Staff in the Historical Section of the Cabinet Office gave me a lot of assistance in my research and I am most grateful for all the time they devoted to my demands.

Finally, I have to thank Brigadier Wingfield, a former Commander of the 22nd Armoured Brigade, for taking so much trouble to read my drafts and for advising on them, and my son who has also read the drafts and made many helpful suggestions.

I am well aware that I must have failed from time to time to produce a balanced narrative that has done justice to all portions of the Division. To those who feel that they, or their Regiments or Battalions or Corps, have not had fair mention, I can only express my regrets and, misquoting the words of the Prime Minister uttered on a not inappropriate occasion, I would urge them to take consolation from the fact that, at least, they can always say with pride:

"I marched and fought with the 7th Armoured Division."

G. L. V.

# PROLOGUE

*September, 1938 to May, 1940*

THE war clouds gathered thickly over Europe in September 1938 and it appeared that the war against Germany which many had foreseen was about to break out. Since Italy was a close ally of Germany it was to be expected that she would immediately take part in hostilities; her task clearly would be to attack the Suez Canal, the vital life-line of the British Empire. There were large numbers of Italian troops not only in Cyrenaica on the Western frontier of Egypt, but also on the frontiers of the Sudan and of British East African territories. The threat to the security of Egypt and the Canal was no single one.

The most immediate menace was that from the west. To counter it Headquarters British Troops in Egypt assembled at Mersa Matruh, 170 miles west of Alexandria, a Mobile Force composed of units forming the Cairo Cavalry Brigade, whose commander, Brigadier H. E. Russell, took command. The Regiments concerned were the 3rd Regiment Royal Horse Artillery, the 7th, 8th and 11th Hussars, the 1st Royal Tank Regiment, No. 5 Company Royal Army Service Corps and the 2nd/3rd Field Ambulance. This Force was the nucleus of the future 7th Armoured Division. Co-operating with them was the 2nd Field Company, Royal Engineers, under Major R. N. Maclaren.

Their equipment was lamentable, old and out of date. The Artillery had 3·7 howitzers towed by lightly-armoured vehicles. The 7th Hussars had various sorts of old light tank and no ammunition for their heavy machine-guns. The 8th Hussars had Ford 15-cwt. trucks armed with medium machine-guns.

The 11th Hussars had Rolls-Royce armoured cars of First War vintage and some Morris light armoured cars. The 1st Royal Tanks had brought from England a few months before all the light tanks available, but these had been in service for so long that the potential mileage capacity of their tracks was nearly exhausted and the only new tracks available did not fit properly.

17                                                                                    B

With the settlement at Munich the crisis died down and the Force returned to Cairo in October. Here they were joined by the 1st Battalion King's Royal Rifle Corps whose commanding officer was Lieutenant-Colonel W. H. E. Gott.

Meanwhile, soon after their arrival at Mersa Matruh, Major-General P. C. S. Hobart had arrived from England by air with orders to form a Mobile Division. It would have been difficult to find an officer better qualified for the task, for he possessed great experience, enthusiasm, energy and determination. He had to compete with considerable difficulties in his efforts to get his command equipped. In his periodical reports suggesting changes in organization and equipment General Hobart displayed prophetic powers, for the organization that was adopted by the time of the Invasion in 1944 and the weapons, vehicles and other equipment with which the troops were then supplied had almost all been suggested in his reports of 1938 and 1939.

Throughout the winter problems that were likely to face the young Division were studied, and in March 1939 the troops went out to the Desert again for training. This was far from being an adequate introduction to imminent war, for the tanks were strictly limited in the number of miles they were permitted to cover and there was a marked shortage of wheeled vehicles. Nevertheless much was accomplished, and during the summer back in Cairo indoor exercises and conferences probed every aspect of the rôle and administration of an Armoured Division in Desert warfare, an almost unknown study in the Army till then.

As his right-hand man General Hobart had Major C. M. Smith, R.A.S.C., and together they evolved the administrative basis on which the Division was to fight successfully in the coming war.

During this period there was some re-equipment. The 7th Hussars received new light tanks and the 8th Hussars were given the Light tanks discarded by the 7th. The 3rd R.H.A. were equipped half with 25-pounder guns and half with 37-mm. anti-tank guns. More Morris armoured cars were issued to the 11th Hussars on a scale of one per Troop and two in Regimental and each Squadron Headquarters; these were the only wireless cars in the Troops.

By August 1939 it was apparent that war was likely to break out in a matter of a very few weeks, and the Division moved out once again to the Western Desert. It was a very different formation this time—true, the equipment was not of the best nor the most modern, but the officers and men were far more highly trained, and General

Hobart had besides imbued them with that most valuable of all qualities, confidence in their comrades and in their own abilities.

The Order of Battle was:

*The Light Armoured Brigade* (Brigadier H. E. Russell)—
7th, 8th and 11th Hussars.
*The Heavy Armoured Brigade* (Lieutenant-Colonel H. R. B. Watkins)—
1st and 6th Royal Tank Regiments.
*Pivot Group* (Lieutenant-Colonel W. H. B. Mirrlees)—
3rd R.H.A., F Battery 4th R.H.A., 1st K.R.R.C.

As soon as it became clear that Italy was not going to join in hostilities when war with Germany began, training was resumed and much valuable work was done before the Division returned again to Cairo in December. By then, General Hobart had returned to England. His departure came as a rude shock to the Division. To his country the General's services had been considerable, to the Division he had formed and trained they were immeasurable, and the long record of success in the years that followed stands as a tribute to their first commander.

In December 1939 Major-General M. O'Moore Creagh arrived to take command. More exercises were carried out and the flow of new equipment improved slightly. More changes in organization also took place; the Light Armoured Brigade became the 7th Armoured Brigade and the Heavy Armoured Brigade became the 4th. The name of the Pivot Group was changed to the Support Group, and this necessitated a change in tactics. The Support Group was commanded, first by Colonel E. S. B. Williams, then by Brigadier Gott. A second Motor Battalion, the 2nd Battalion Rifle Brigade, came from Palestine, and joined the K.R.R.C. and the 3rd and 4th R.H.A. in the Support Group. Brigadier J. A. L. Caunter took command of the 4th Armoured Brigade.

When it became apparent towards the end of April that Italy was going to come into the war, the 11th Hussars and the Support Group were moved out to Mersa Matruh. In the middle of May Divisional Headquarters and the 4th Armoured Brigade followed. For another month the Division continued training intensively and certain surreptitious reconnaissances of the Italian frontier posts were carried out by squadron leaders of the 11th; these had to be done with great discretion as there were strict orders that in no circumstances was action to be taken that might be considered provocative. The area covered by the 11th Hussars was so great that they found it necessary to re-organize their transport on a double-echelon basis; otherwise they could not maintain themselves, for the distance from Regimental Headquarters to Squadrons was 60 to 80 miles. A welcome reinforcement about this time was the arrival of volunteers from Southern Rhodesia; some went to the Rifle Regiments and fifty-five who went to the 11th were formed into Scout Troops in Ford cars; they all proved to be a great asset to their new Regiments.

Most of the Division was in a concentration area at Gerawla and had just held a highly successful "mechanized Hunt Meeting" complete with "bookies" and a Lance-Corporal dressed up as the Duchess of Gerawla to give away the prizes, when news came of the fall of France and Italy's entry into the war.

The Division formed part of the Western Desert Force under Lieutenant-General R. N. O'Connor. The only other troops in the Force were the Cairo Infantry Brigade who garrisoned Mersa Matruh and a small contingent of the Royal Air Force under Air Commodore Collishaw, the forerunners of the famous Desert Air Force. The Division had under command No. 208 Squadron which was led by Squadron Leader Brown. A very close and valuable association was established and, in spite of their limited equipment, they performed great work and earned the admiration of the troops for their courage and skill.

On that day when the Division concentrated at Mersa Matruh for the first time for active operations, with the 11th Hussars forward at Sidi Barrani, little could they have imagined what a long hard road they were about to tread. It would have seemed a wild nightmare to imagine that this was the first step in a journey that was to stretch for several thousand miles right across North Africa, through part of Italy, across France and the Low Countries, and that the final order, "Halt, Dismount", would be given only in Berlin six years later.

# THE
# DESERT
# RATS

CHAPTER I

*June, 1940 to February, 1941*

# THE FIRST OFFENSIVE

*Reference Maps—Front Endpaper. No. 1, page 26. No. 2, page 34.
No. 3, page 40*

## *The Rival Forces*                                    *June 1940*

GENERAL SIR ARCHIBALD WAVELL had become Commander-in-Chief Middle East in July 1939. Under him, General Sir Henry Maitland Wilson commanded the British Troops in Egypt. The most immediate danger they faced was the Italian Army on Egypt's western frontier. This was estimated to consist of nine Divisions in Tripolitania and five more in Cyrenaica with a total strength of 215,000 men.

Against them there were only the 7th Armoured Division, the infantry brigade in Mersa Matruh already referred to, and the 4th Indian Division newly arrived in Egypt. The 6th Australian Division had reached the Middle East in February and the New Zealand Division had followed soon afterwards, but these Dominion Forces, although of splendid material, were still in need of training and so were not available for operations on the outbreak of the Campaign.

The actual strength that could be deployed was not as good as it seemed on paper; the 7th Armoured Division was not yet ready to come forward as the 8th Hussars had not completed training on their new tanks, and the 4th Indian Division was short of one infantry brigade. There was a great shortage of field and medium artillery and practically no anti-aircraft artillery, this last a serious deficiency in view of the strength of the Italian air force. Worst of all, there was a grave shortage of motor transport of every kind, a shortage that was destined to handicap operations most seriously right up to the autumn of 1942.

Wavell's policy, since it was plain that he could not hope to adopt the offensive for some time to come, was to maintain a strong screen of troops well forward carrying out offensive patrolling, but prepared to give ground when forced to do so. At least, there was plenty of room in the Desert.

## Desert Conditions

The ground over which the campaigns of the next two and a half years were to be fought consists of a sandy coastal plain which for the most part is about thirty miles wide; it is broadest at its eastern end, but near the frontier at Sollum it narrows to a few hundred yards where the Escarpment comes down to the sea. The Escarpment is several hundred feet high and to the south of it is the Desert proper, rocks and sand, few tracks, occasional wells and "going" that varies from good to impassable. Much of the area is covered with scrub and this, together with the hills, depressions and ridges, gives variety to the scenery.

The nature of the ground was such as to throw a great strain on most types of motor vehicle. To make matters worse, the repair facilities were of the most slender and there was as yet no organized system of recovery for damaged or broken-down vehicles. A railway line from Alexandria ran as far west as Mersa Matruh, 125 miles short of the frontier, but this was run by the Egyptian State Railways. There were only two proper motor roads in Egypt, those from Cairo to Alexandria and from Cairo to Suez. There was no suitable transport in Egypt that could be requisitioned. It is well for those who may feel inclined to be critical of the fighting during the first two years of the Desert Campaign to reflect on the immense difficulties, on the transport side alone, that faced commanders and troops. That so much was achieved with so little is to their everlasting credit.

The climate ranges from great heat by day, especially in the summer, to extreme cold at night. The contrast between the heat of the day at any time of the year and the sharp drop in temperature at night-fall is most trying, but the most severe trial is the Khamseen, a hot wind blowing from the south, which whirls up huge clouds of dust and sand, fills every crevice and makes life almost unbearable, for it is impossible to cook or carry on any other activity, and visibility is reduced to a few yards.

Water was always short. The daily ration for a man was one gallon for all purposes, but sometimes this had to be cut to half a gallon; occasionally it was so tainted as to be almost undrinkable. Rations were bully beef and biscuits, with an occasional issue of tinned meat and vegetables, for it was seldom possible to provide fresh food.

For the first year of the war in the Desert it was very difficult for anyone to adhere to the time-honoured custom of the British Army of making issues of food from a ration scale. Although these scales existed, they were quite valueless for the simple reason that the food did not exist. At one period all troops were issued with as much as eight ounces of jam and eight ounces of rice per day in order to produce a reasonably balanced diet. During the first campaign it was not unusual to have bully beef for all three meals each day— fried for breakfast, cold for lunch and stewed for supper. This last meal was always good as it was flavoured invariably with a tomato purée which was captured from the Italians at Sidi Barrani.

Except for the desert sores which developed from the smallest scratch, it was not an unhealthy life. There was a certain amount of sandfly fever and jaundice; it is an odd fact that the officers seemed to be more prone to jaundice than the private soldiers. The effects of this trying climate were, however, to make themselves felt towards the end of the war among those who had endured them for long.

The whole of the Desert west of the Cairo-Alexandria road from Siwa and the Sand Sea in the south to the coast in the north and to Sollum and the frontier in the west had been carefully reconnoitred before war broke out—the 11th Hussars had been pioneers at this work—and as a result a "going" map had been made; this showed the nature of the surface and the type of vehicle that could traverse it.

The tactical plan aimed at stopping an enemy advance at Mersa Matruh, and here was positioned the main infantry force. Forward of this area General Creagh was to maintain a force that was to give warning of the approach of the enemy and do all it could to hinder his progress. This force was composed of the 7th and 11th Hussars with Captain R. F. L. Chance's company of the 1st K.R.R.C., all under command of Brigadier Caunter.

*Into Action*                                    *June 11th, 1940*

At one o'clock on the morning of June 11th war was declared against Italy. The 11th Hussars with the Support Group immediately went into action. The orders given to Lieutenant-Colonel J. F. B. Combe, commanding the 11th, were to penetrate the frontier wire, to dominate the areas between Fort Capuzzo and Fort Madalena, to harass the Italian communications back towards Bardia and Tobruk, and to delay any Italian advance. With few casualties, raids and ambushes collected two hundred prisoners in the first

week and destroyed tanks and wheeled vehicles. On June 14th Fort
Capuzzo was captured by a force consisting of the 7th Hussars, less
one squadron, a company of the K.R.R.C. and a Troop of the Royal
Engineers, all under the command of Lieutenant-Colonel G. Fielden
of the 7th Hussars. This operation was completely successful and
took only a few hours; sixteen officers and over 200 other    iks were
taken prisoner and the Fort demolished. On the same day the Fort
at Madalena, after being bombed, surrendered to the 11th Hussars.
Much damage had also been inflicted on the defended camp at
Sidi Azeiz. Traffic between Bardia and Tobruk was ambushed, and
the only Italian reaction was to suspend movement on this road.

On June 16th was fought the first tank-*v.*-tank battle of the
Campaign, when an Italian force with twelve light tanks and thirty
lorries carrying infantry, which had been located and pinned down
by Second-Lieutenant W. H. V. Gape's Troop of the 11th Hussars,
was surrounded and destroyed by a mixed tank squadron of the 7th
Hussars under Major Seymour-Evans, and Major A. G. Miller's
squadron of the 11th, supported by anti-tank guns of the Royal
Horse Artillery. At a cost of no British casualties, an Italian infantry
battalion with two companies of tanks and a motor artillery battery
were wiped out. More than the material results was the fillip given
by this action at Ghirba to morale throughout the Middle East.
Besides this, the successes of the first week's fighting had gained
valuable time for General Wavell and had caused Marshal Graziani,
the Italian commander-in-chief, grossly to over-estimate the strength
opposed to him.

At the end of June the 7th Armoured Brigade relieved the 4th
in the area of Sidi Sulieman. However, the wear and tear on the
vehicles, and in particular on the tracks of the tanks, made it advisable to conserve forces, so the Division was concentrated in an
area south of Mersa Matruh, leaving the Support Group and the
11th Hussars to watch the frontier and to patrol forward. They
were strengthened by the 3rd Battalion Coldstream Guards under
Lieutenant-Colonel J. Moubray; they had been hurriedly re-fitted
to be a motorized battalion. Although the Italians had re-occupied
Fort Capuzzo with a strong force, long-range patrolling and harassing continued, the 11th Hussars voyaging far into enemy-held
territory. Signs mounted that the Italians were preparing for some
more ambitious operation than the recapture of their frontier
positions, but their only really hostile activity was maintained by
their air force, to oppose which the R.A.F. had no resources, for the

few fighters available had to be employed escorting the light reconnaissance planes whose daily sorties were so important.

In July Lieutenant-Colonel Smith, who had so successfully organized the administrative system of the Division, left for another appointment. His place was taken by Lieutenant-Colonel J. L. C. Napier, Royal Tank Regiment, who had hitherto been G.S.O.2.

*The Italians Advance*                                                *September 13th*

On September 13th the long-awaited Italian advance began. Neither the time nor the direction came as a surprise, and their actions followed those that had been forecast by General Wavell's Staff long before. The 3rd Coldstream were positioned along a twelve-mile front, with a company on the top of Halfaya Pass, and they had artillery and the machine-guns of the Royal Northumberland Fusiliers under command. To the south were the remainder of the Support Group.

The withdrawal was carried out as planned; the enemy advance was held up repeatedly by mines, and great execution was done by the artillery. To everyone's surprise the Italians halted in the area of Sidi Barrani, eighty miles short of Mersa Matruh which was the key to the British position. By then, the Coldstream were back in the Matruh garrison and the Division was so placed as to be able to operate on the south flank of the Italians if they renewed their advance.

The enemy had suffered some 3,500 casualties against 150 British. They had shown no great tactical skill or enthusiasm. General Wavell's principal worry was the state of British tanks and transport. By now the Mediterranean was virtually closed, and it took many weeks for supplies to arrive by the Cape route. Nevertheless, orders were issued for an offensive operation, and this took place in December.

In the meantime, much patrolling and harassing of the Italians took place, and it was during this phase of the Campaign that "Jock Columns" first made their appearance. They were named after Lieutenant-Colonel J. C. Campbell, 4th R.H.A., and were small columns of all arms: armoured cars for reconnaissance, 25-pounders for hitting, and infantry companies for the protection of the guns and for doing night work. Their task was to probe into the enemy's back areas and attack any suitable target that presented itself. It was the work of these columns that established that moral superiority over the Italians which was to assist so greatly in the gaining of the victories of the next few months.

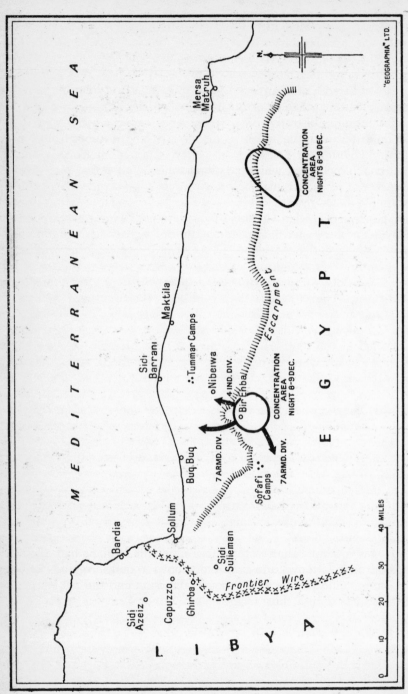

Map No. 1.—The Battle of Sidi Barrani, December 8th to 10th, 1940

During this period the Division received substantial reinforcements. The 3rd Hussars with light tanks and the 2nd Royal Tank Regiment with cruisers arrived and thus doubled the tank strength of the Division. The 1st and the 106th R.H.A. also came, the latter being composed half of anti-tank guns and half of anti-aircraft. The Order of Battle at the end of November 1940 is given in Appendix I.

On the administrative side, repair and recovery arrangements had improved with the arrival of three Brigade Workshops from the Cavalry Division in Palestine, and they operated in front of the Divisional Workshops which adjoined railhead at Fuka, forty-five miles east of Mersa Matruh. Even with this addition there were still less than a dozen recovery vehicles in the Division and only five that were capable of towing Cruiser tanks, and the total number of men still fell far short of what were needed. On the other hand, tank crews were experienced and well trained, and their standard of maintenance was a high one. The Ordnance also set up a Vehicle Reception Park for the inspection of all vehicles passing into the hands of the Division, either on first issue or after repair. A most important addition was a Divisional Reinforcement Camp. This had been conceived by Colonel Smith and was commanded by Major V. H. Jones, 14th/20th Hussars. Its task was to accommodate men on their way forward or back, and the crews of vehicles in Workshops.

*The Offensive Begins*                    *December 9th, 1940*

*Reference Map—No. 1, facing page 27*

The Italians were spread over a wide front holding defended camps which were not mutually supporting. The gaps between them offered a tempting weakness and there appeared to be no depth in their dispositions. General O'Connor's plan was to attack through the open centre, leaving small forces to contain the defended localities on the flanks.

It was reckoned that east of the frontier the Italians had about 75,000 troops with over 200 guns and about 120 tanks. Against them O'Connor could pit the 7th Armoured Division and the 4th Indian Division, less than a third of the enemy in numbers, and a total of 275 tanks.

The outline plan having been accepted, the details were worked out by General O'Connor with the two Divisional Commanders concerned, Generals Creagh and Beresford-Peirse. In view of the great numerical superiority of the enemy, the only hope of success lay in obtaining surprise and this was no easy matter in the open Desert against a greatly superior air force and in a country containing not only neutrals but also large numbers of enemy nationals.

The first essential was to keep knowledge of the coming attack from all but a very few senior officers. The next essential was to make sure that the gap in the centre of the Italian area through which the attacking troops were to advance remained open. This was at Bir Enba where, about the middle of November, the Italians tried to establish a defended camp; this was prevented. The Enba area was eighty miles from Mersa Matruh, and surprise could not be obtained unless the troops could be moved forward this distance unknown to the enemy.

Gradually the patrolling by the 7th Armoured Division and other units of the Army built up an accurate picture of the Italian defences, including mines, trenches and wire. Though strongly outnumbered, the R.A.F. increased their photographic efforts, but the demands of the operations in Greece, which had been invaded by the Italians in October, had left them very weak; they had to face some 500 Italian aircraft with only four bomber and three fighter squadrons. By destroying aircraft on their airfields it was hoped to reduce the inferiority under which the R.A.F. laboured, and by attacking Italian troops on the ground it was hoped to throw the enemy air force on the defensive.

The situation as regards tanks and vehicles was still unsatisfactory. There was a shortage of several thousand trucks and lorries. The range of tanks was still limited by the amount of wear in their tracks which were supposed to be good for about 1,700 miles in all. Every tank commander, therefore, had a continuous worry as to how much further his tanks would be able to go before their tracks wore out and they became immobilized. This naturally had a limiting effect on the future plans of all commanders, for the greater their success and the further they travelled the smaller would their tank force become and the weightier their administrative problems. Such great distances were covered in the Desert Campaigns that much more serious supply and replacement difficulties arose than in any European theatre of war.

The enemy's dispositions were estimated to be as follows: Maktila and Sidi Barrani contained 7,500 troops, Nibeiwa Camp 2,500, the Camps at Tummar 7,000 and Sofafi Camps 7,000. Despite the rough handling they had had some months before, morale was described as good.

The British plan was for both Divisions to concentrate in the Enba area. Thence, while the 7th Armoured Division protected the south and west flanks, the 4th Indian was to strike north for Sidi Barrani overcoming the camps en route by attacks from the flanks and rear. While this was going on the Matruh force was to make feint attacks against Maktila. The 4th Indian Division was to be supported by the "Infantry" tanks of the 7th Royal Tank Regiment (Lieutenant-Colonel R. Jerram) which was an independent Regiment for the close support of infantry. Slow moving but heavily armoured, these tanks were to play a most important part in the assaults on the various defended positions of the enemy.

In view of the fact that these operations were to continue successfully for two months and to cover a thousand miles, it is interesting to recall that their original scope was not intended to embrace more than a few days' fighting. At that time it was considered that the endurance limit of the Division as a whole was twelve hours, and that of the 11th Hussars and Support Group 72 hours; it was hoped that the 11th could get to Sollum. Fortunately, General Wavell was "offensive-minded" and was served by commanders of similar calibre; all were determined to press their advantages and successes to the limit.

Gradually the troops were moved forward to the concentration area south-west of Matruh. Thence the move to Enba had to be carried out in daylight, but fortunately the weather was hazy and there was a sand storm which prevented reconnaissance by the hostile air force. Soon after nightfall on December 8th all was ready, and only then did the troops learn that this was not just another exercise but the "real thing".

*The First Five Days*          *December 9th to 13th*

At dawn on December 9th the attack began. The 4th Indian Division soon overcame the resistance at Nibeiwa Camp and moved on to attack the Camps at Tummar.

The task allotted to the 7th Armoured Division was to cut off the Italians in Sidi Barrani. Led by "B" Squadron of the 11th Hussars (Major Miller) with "C" Squadron (Major P. Payne Gallwey) to watch the west flank, the 4th Armoured Brigade moved forward and they were soon astride the main coast road west of Sidi Barrani. By dark resistance in the Tummar area had ceased and Sidi Barrani was safely isolated. By the evening of the 10th Sidi Barrani had fallen, with what were described as "acres" of prisoners, of which the 2nd Royal Tanks had taken 16 officers and 1,300 men. They destroyed over fifty guns, but lost Major J. B. Brown killed.

General O'Connor's orders for the next day were for the Division to secure Buq Buq where it was thought the enemy might make a stand. General Creagh therefore decided to send the 7th Armoured Brigade up for this task and to pull the 4th Brigade back to Enba. Reports from the 11th Hussars had already indicated that the Italians might be preparing to abandon Buq Buq, so a squadron was ordered to patrol well to the west at first light and to report the positions of the Italian flanks. At 9.30 a.m. Second-Lieutenant A. Reid-Scott's Troop eluded a Blackshirt Division and entered Buq Buq, the Italians having slipped out during the night and made off for Sollum.

However, a short distance west of the village an Italian force of almost the strength of a Division had taken up a position among sand dunes and mud flats. "C" Squadron of the 11th Hussars who were watching them, were soon joined by the 3rd Hussars under Lieutenant-Colonel W. G. Petherick, and early in the afternoon "B" Squadron of the 11th also came up. Brigadier Russell was held up owing to his tank being damaged and he ordered Colonel Combe to take charge of the attack. With Lieutenant-Colonel T. G. Watson of the 8th Hussars and the R.H.A. battery commander, a plan was made for the cruiser tanks of the 8th to attack frontally while the 3rd Hussars pressed in from a flank. The latter Regiment was equipped with light tanks but had a cruiser squadron of the 2nd Royal Tanks in place of their own "B" Squadron which was serving with the 2nd Tanks.

The leading squadron, "C" of the 3rd, was soon held up by the fire of twenty or thirty guns at point-blank range. "A" Squadron passed behind them to attack the enemy's left flank; they moved at speed in line-ahead and then wheeled into line-abreast and charged. The salt-pan on which they found themselves could carry the weight of their tanks so long as they kept moving fast, but the moment they slowed down they became stuck. As soon as they appeared in sight they met the full force of many guns, but they covered all but three hundred of the thousand yards separating them from the Italian artillery. Immobilized though they were, the tanks fought back desperately and fired thousands of rounds at the enemy until, one by one, they were knocked out. Still the crews of the disabled tanks fought on until their vehicles caught fire.

Meanwhile, "B" Squadron of the 3rd Hussars, who were with the

2nd Royal Tanks, also attacked the Italian flank. Captain Marsh led two Troops in a charge through the gun positions, silencing and destroying at least twenty-four. The enemy broke and fled, leaving three or four thousand prisoners in British hands and fifty-eight field guns with many dead. The cost to the attackers had not been light; the 3rd Hussars suffered particularly severely. Major W. V. Ritson and two of his officers of "A" Squadron, Second-Lieutenants Hartigan and O'Sullivan, had been killed and three officers wounded; seventeen N.C.O.s and men were casualties and thirteen tanks had been lost.

The surviving Italians collected themselves together in the rough ground of the salt marsh and resumed their retreat. The 11th Hussars did their best to cut them off but they were badly impeded by the state of the ground. Nevertheless by the end of the day a couple of Troops of "B" Squadron of the 11th found themselves embarrassed by no less than 7,000 prisoners. The total of prisoners in this area amounted to 14,000, with sixty-eight guns and much booty.

While all this fighting was going on, the Support Group was dealing with the Italian forces in the Sofafi area, and the 4th Armoured Brigade were preparing to pursue along the Escarpment and across the frontier into Cyrenaica. On the evening of December 13th this Brigade advanced in two columns with, as usual, the armoured cars of the 11th Hussars ahead of them. At dawn they crossed the frontier, and not long afterwards were in position on the coast road about twenty miles west of Bardia.

*Administrative Problems*                      *December 14th to January 3rd*
A pause ensued while the 6th Australian Division were brought forward for the assault on Bardia. By the 15th all Italian troops were over the frontier and the total of prisoners exceeded 38,000 and included one Corps and four Divisional Commanders, 240 guns, 70 tanks and much petrol and equipment. Already the Prime Minister was able to say that the events of the past week "constituted a victory of the first order". It was, indeed, the first victory gained by the Army in the war. In his message to General Wavell, Mr. Churchill said: "the Army of the Nile has rendered glorious service to the Empire and our cause."

About this time the Support Group were joined by the 1st Free French Motor Company, a gallant band under the leadership of Commandant Foliot who had all escaped from Syria; they were not able to communicate with their families for fear of the reprisals which the Vichy sympathizers would exact.

During the 14th the enemy carried out 18 bombing and 23 dive-bombing attacks on a composite column of the 4th Armoured Brigade known as "Birksforce", which was operating under the command of Colonel H. L. Birks, the Brigade second-in-command. Three men were killed and 23 wounded, and an armoured car and four other vehicles destroyed. On the 16th Sidi Omar was taken by the 7th Hussars and the 2nd Royal Tanks, supported by the 4th R.H.A., with nearly 1,000 prisoners and a fine store of food and wine. However, the tank strength of the Division was decreasing, and by the 18th the 4th Brigade had been reduced to 31 cruisers and 55 light tanks and the 7th to 28 cruisers and 53 light tanks.

A curious incident occurred on the 24th when a Bedouin family of six men and two women with twelve sheep and a camel were apprehended. As the Italians had evacuated all Bedouin this was considered suspicious. It was discovered that a telephone wire led from their encampment to a disused enemy position. About this time there was a very cold spell, and it is recorded that at Divisional Headquartersthe milk was frozen in the jugs at breakfast. On Christmas Eve there was a full rum ration and in the evening carol singing by the men of the 6th Royal Tanks. On Boxing Day the water ration was cut to half a gallon per man per day, but this was so salty that it was almost undrinkable. On the 27th the 1st R.H.A. fought a naval action, scoring several hits on an enemy warship and forcing her to go out to sea. The Divisional Commander made the signal, "Splice the main brace", which was duly honoured, and an endless correspondence then ensued as to who should pay for the extra rum consumed—the answer has not yet been found.

The capture of the coast road eased the administrative situation considerably. It had been calculated that a lorry could cover 250 miles on a road for the same amount of petrol that it would need to cover only a hundred miles in the Desert. The petrol problem was aggravated by the method of supply, for it was sent forward in flimsy four-gallon drums, rightly described as "expendable". So great was the leakage from the poor quality of the tins and from evaporation that one per cent was lost for every ten miles it was carried. It was not long before the Force had gone so far that the tins arrived half empty. This appalling wastage is an example of the consequences of the pre-war policy of doing things "on the cheap", and a heavy responsibility for lives lost and money squandered rests on the shoulders of those individuals who permitted this state of affairs. Fortunately much of the petrol captured from the Italians was in more robust containers. In 1942, the type of container adopted was the German "jerrican" with which the world is now familiar.

The supply situation limited the number of troops that could be maintained in the forward area and it was not possible to supply two infantry Divisions. Accordingly, General Wavell withdrew the 4th Indian Division and replaced them with the less experienced 6th Australians. The Indians, immediately after the capture of Sidi Barrani, were moved to the Sudan whence they played a prominent part in the successful Abyssinian Campaign.

The feeding and evacuation of the vast numbers of prisoners threw a heavy additional strain on the Lines of Communication, but this was eased by the Navy who took many back by sea. Nevertheless, heavy calls were made on transport and on the always slender supplies of food and water.

Within the Division, despite the forward dumps that had been built up, improvisation was always necessary in order to keep the forward troops supplied. On occasions, the transport of the infantry battalions had to be diverted from troop-carrying to reinforcing the supply echelons. It would be difficult to exaggerate the important part played by the officers and men of the Supply Columns. Months after this Campaign was over, General O'Connor wrote: "I can say with certainty that I have never met a more efficient body of men than those of the 7th Armoured Division R.A.S.C. They never failed the troops on any occasion, and in spite of every difficulty such as execrable going and continual dust storms, their maintenance was kept up to a very high state of efficiency at all times, and this efficiency was fully appreciated by all the other units of the Division who depended on them for their supplies." One can pay no higher tribute than to say that they kept up this standard throughout the war.

At the end of December there were considerable water difficulties; the journeys of the water-carrying vehicles became longer and longer with the result that they arrived later and later every day. The water in most of the coast towns was salty, but the situation was improved when it was found that the water at Bir Rigeit, which had been deliberately salted before the retirement in September, had apparently not been affected. A few days later, however, this water suddenly began to show signs of salt and the problem again became acute. It was solved by using ships, and the water so brought was

C

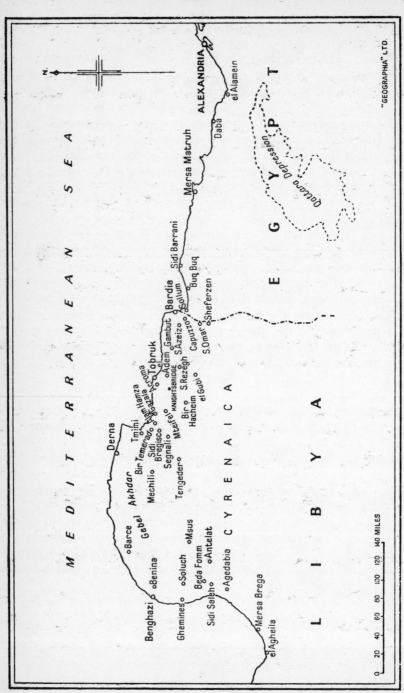

Map No. 2.—Cyrenaica and Western Egypt

stored in large tanks at Capuzzo whence it was taken forward by lorry.

During the pause before the assault on Bardia the Armoured Corps Ordnance Field Park arrived, and at last there was a proper organization for the issue of vehicles and spare parts.

*The Advance Resumed*          *January 3rd to 31st*

Meanwhile the 7th Armoured Division had been positioned so as to isolate Bardia from communication with the west. The Support Group and the 11th Hussars were astride the coast road with the 4th and 7th Armoured Brigades to the south and south-west. In order to curtail the activities of the Italian air force, the airfield at Gambut had been harassed continuously by the armoured cars of the 11th Hussars. On December 20th the key point of its defences, known as the Colonel's House, had been occupied by the 11th, whose History records that the Colonel had evidently departed in something of a hurry but that his time there had not been without amorous diversion. The Italians then abandoned the airfield.

On January 1st the Western Desert Force was re-named the XIIIth Corps. On the 3rd the Australians began their attack on Bardia and the town fell on the 5th, yielding 45,000 prisoners, 462 guns and 129 tanks.

Immediately Bardia had fallen it became the task of the 7th Armoured Division to carry out a similar enveloping movement at Tobruk. The Support Group again moved to cut the coast road, while the two Armoured Brigades were positioned to the south, south-west and west. The 11th pushed patrols out to the Gebel Akhdar and Mechili; the latter place was found to be held.

Another pause followed while the 6th Australian Division was moved up for the attack on Tobruk, together with the "I" tanks of the 7th Royal Tank Regiment, now sadly reduced in numbers. Like Bardia, it had been expected that the town would be stoutly defended, but it surrendered on January 22nd, the day after the attack began, with another 30,000 prisoners, 236 guns and 87 tanks. Again the Support Group assisted the attack by a feint attack from the west and artillery support.

By this time mechanical troubles had reduced the tank strength of the Division to about fifty cruisers and ninety-five light tanks. Consequently, the 8th Hussars in the 7th Brigade and the 6th Royal Tanks in the 4th Brigade were dismounted, and their tanks redistributed to the other Regiments.

As soon as it was evident that the attack on Tobruk was succeeding, the 4th Armoured Brigade moved off to Mechili where they arrived on January 23rd. Here a sharp action was fought on the next day but the enemy withdrew under cover of darkness and made good his escape. The Italians withdrew into the Gebel Akhdar followed by the Support Group over difficult going.

Another pause ensued while the Australians drove the enemy out of Derna and the administrative staff tried to solve some of their ever-increasing problems and build up supplies. The 4th Brigade was near Mechili with the 11th Hussars patrolling between them and the Australians at Derna; the remainder of the Division was then near Mechili.

During the course of the next two weeks the three Light Recovery Sections were gradually brought forward and concentrated at Mechili. All three had, of course, been overburdened with work, collecting and repairing the many tanks that had fallen by the way-side. A Field Supply Depot was established by Corps about thirty miles south-west of Mechili and gradually built up; at the time it was the most forward unit of the Division. As usual, water was a problem. The Water Tank Company brought some forward daily; other water was discovered in various wells and cisterns round Mechili, but some of this had been oiled and was unusable.

### THE BATTLE OF BEDA FOMM
*Reference Map No. 3, facing page 41*

"Forward, Forward, let us range."

As the beaten remnants of the Italian Army streamed back towards Benghazi, indications appeared that it was Marshal Graziani's intention to abandon Cyrenaica altogether. Two alternatives now faced the British commander. One was to devote the maximum strength to pursuing the Italians along the coast; the other was to use the more mobile portion of the Corps to try to cut off the enemy as they marched south from Benghazi.

The direct pursuit had certain obvious advantages—the lines of communication could be concentrated and full use could be made of the Navy, both for active support with their guns and for easing the administrative difficulties. Against this, the natural features of the country, with the mountains pressing close down to the sea, between Derna and Benghazi would assist delaying actions by the

Italians; even with only a half-hearted resistance, the advance would be slow and costly, and many Italians would escape.

The alternative course would entail despatching the 7th Armoured Division, in strength as great as circumstances would permit, across 150 miles of Desert, almost all of which was unknown and all of which was unmapped. The supply difficulties were obvious and there might well be serious trouble over water shortage. They would also, of course, be out of touch with the rest of the Corps and they would lose the direct benefits that the Navy had been affording to the Army. In addition, there was always the possibility that a force astride the main road south of Benghazi might be attacked from behind by reinforcements from Tripolitania. Account had to be taken, too, of the physical state of the vehicles in the Division. They had always been few in numbers and now those that were still running were by no means in good shape, not because the efforts of their crews had failed but from sheer wear and tear.

But a glittering prize was offered, for if the enemy retreat from Benghazi could be cut off it would mean the complete destruction of the Italian Tenth Army with all that that stood for not only materially but morally. Such a victory would resound throughout the world to encourage the Empire, now standing alone with Greece against the Axis Powers, and to influence those neutrals whose opinions were still unsettled.

*Preliminary Moves*                                        *February 4th*
General Wavell flew up to the forward area for consultations with Generals Wilson, O'Connor and Creagh, and the decision was made to take the bold course and try to cut off the Italians south of Benghazi. Accordingly, orders were given for the Division to advance to Msus, and early on the morning of February 4th they started, the 11th Hussars being in the lead, followed by the 4th Armoured Brigade. The main column was led by the tanks, with the artillery and the 2nd Rifle Brigade behind.

Difficulties soon arose. The maps proved to be most inaccurate, and contact with the various supply echelons was almost impossible as the officers in command were not able to pinpoint their positions with accuracy. Soon after leaving the Field Supply Depot beyond Mechili there was a stretch of appallingly bad ground.

The original orders had directed the Division to go west after leaving Msus, but information came in that the enemy withdrawal from Benghazi had already started, so General Creagh decided to depart from the letter of his instructions and to strike south-west in order to trap more Italians. This was a bold decision and one that was to have far-reaching consequences in the coming battle—indeed, it was to make the difference between great success and overwhelming victory. As soon as the alteration was reported to General O'Connor he appreciated its great importance and immediately approved.

So bad was the going and so slow the progress that it was decided to send the wheeled vehicles ahead, that is, the Rifle Brigade and a detachment of artillery. Under Colonel Campbell, they were ordered to join Colonel Combe and his 11th Hussars who were already many miles in front. The artillery consisted of "C" Battery 4th R.H.A. with 160 rounds per gun; under command, they had three guns of the 155th Light Anti-Aircraft Regiment, R.A., under Second-Lieutenant Straker, and a section of the 106th Anti-Tank Regiment, R.H.A. With the Rifle Brigade were eight anti-tank guns of the 106th R.H.A. under Major Burton.

*February 5th*

The organization of the "Flying Column" which had been ordered on the 4th took a considerable time. The units comprising it had to be filled up with petrol and given extra petrol lorries so as to ensure that they could complete the march. To make up the petrol requirements of the R.H.A., lorries carrying reserve ammunition had to dump their loads and be reloaded with petrol. Special wireless communications had to be arranged and the Rifle Brigade had to be extracted from the rear of the column.

Colonel Campbell reached the 11th Hussars Headquarters early in the morning, accompanied by Lieutenant-Colonel J. M. L. Renton who commanded the Rifle Brigade, but difficulties had arisen over the release of that Battalion from command of the 4th Armoured Brigade, and they, with their artillery, did not get on the move until 8 a.m. Another trouble arose when it was found that a portion of the 4,000 gallons of petrol earmarked for Colonel Combe's new command (which was known as "Combeforce") had been diverted to the Armoured Brigade.

The going continued to be extremely bad; tracked vehicles here were less handicapped than wheeled, with the result that the armour caught up with, and were at one time held back by, the Flying Column in front of them. This stretch of bad going lasted for about twenty miles and must be one of the longest stretches of almost impassable country that a mechanized force has ever been ordered to cross. So soon as the going improved, the wheeled column, of course, speedily went away from the tracked portion of the Division, and in view of subsequent events the decision of the Divisional Commander to reorganize his order of march, even though it cost much time, was amply vindicated. During the day orders were received from General Creagh that speed was of more importance than anything else. Consequently halts, and the length of each halt, were cut down to the minimum. A hot following wind caused radiators to boil and thus created an additional anxiety over water supplies. There were several attacks by the Italian air force. The rough going caused the carriers of the Rifle Brigade to use an excessive quantity of petrol, and eventually they ran right out of fuel and were able to take no part in the battle, a matter that might well have had serious consequences.

Apart from the bad going, additional delay was caused in an area that had been strewn with "thermos bombs". These were small bombs dropped by aircraft, and they lay unexploded until they were touched or moved. Once past the rough ground and the bomb area, the Flying Column moved at high speed. There was no time to spare.

"C" Squadron of the 11th Hussars led the advance under Major Payne Gallwey. Also under command of Colonel Combe were the R.A.F. Armoured Car Squadron and Major A. P. C. Crossley's Squadron of the King's Dragoon Guards in place of the 11th Hussars "B" Squadron which was operating with the Australians. ("A" Squadron of the 11th was with the Support Group.) Msus was soon cleared of the enemy, and the leading squadron reached the coast road near Sidi Saleh during the morning of the 5th. They were soon joined by the rest of the Regiment and the column that Colonel Campbell was bringing forward.

"Combeforce" amounted to less than 2,000 men with twenty guns of various types but no tanks. It says much for the skill of the Rifle Brigade drivers and fitters that out of 140 trucks only one failed to complete the journey.

*Sidi Saleh*                                     *February 5th*
The K.D.G.'s Squadron was positioned to the south in order to give warning if an attack should develop from Tripolitania, and hardly had the main force arrived astride the road when, at 2.30 p.m., the first column of retreating Italians was engaged. This

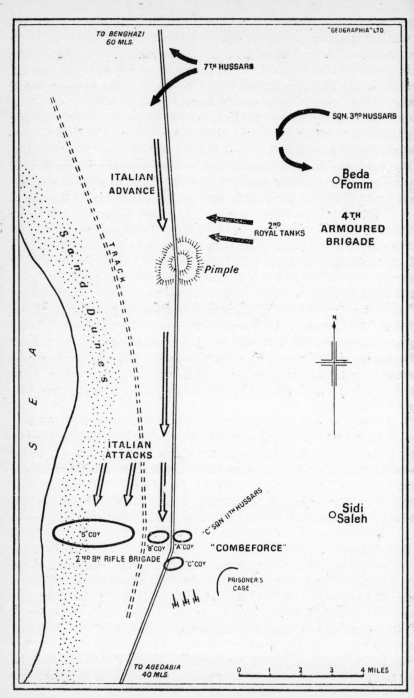

Map No. 3.—The Battle of Beda Fomm, February 5th to 7th, 1941

was estimated to consist of 20,000 men and they had both tanks and guns. The first blow fell upon a single company of the Rifle Brigade, that of Major T. C. H. Pearson, which was covering the main road. The appearance of the British in front of them when they were thought to be several hundred miles away had such a demoralizing effect on the Italians that they seemed to become paralysed. Instead of co-ordinating their efforts and launching a carefully planned attack—for they were always in such overwhelming strength that they could easily have outflanked the British positions—they merely attacked frontally from time to time while on the road behind them there piled up a monumental traffic block.

The Riflemen and the artillery shattered the first attack. This was largely due to the actions of Captains Cook and Warden, who moved across an open slope under heavy fire in order to obtain better observation from which to silence the enemy's guns. The momentum of the Italian advance caused them to fan out towards the sand dunes between the road and the coast, with the result that "B" Company (Major T. C. Sinclair) had to be brought up to the left of "A" Company. They were well supported by Major Goschen's guns. However, by dark the artillery ammunition situation was becoming critical; they had been in action almost continuously since their arrival, and the 4th R.H.A. were already down to only thirty rounds per gun. The supply of more ammunition was problematical.

During the night a skilful patrol under Lieutenant M. H. Mosley with a couple of anti-tank guns operating to the west had succeeded in giving the enemy the impression that the position was more extended and held in greater strength than it really was. By midnight on February 5th, therefore, the road was blocked at Sidi Saleh and the force there, though lamentably weak, had shown that much more than ill-planned frontal attacks would be needed to shift them.

*Beda Fomm*                                        *February 5th*

Meanwhile, the 4th Armoured Brigade column, consisting of the 7th Hussars, the 2nd Royal Tanks with "B" Squadron 3rd Hussars, one battery of the 4th R.H.A. under Major H. C. Withers, the rest of the 106th R.H.A. and two Troops of the 3rd R.H.A., one with "B" Squadron 7th Hussars and one with the 1st Royal Tanks, a total strength of only twenty Cruisers and thirty-six Light tanks, was pushing on as hard as it could go. On the 4th they had advanced until midnight despite the inaccuracies of the map and the inevitable exhaustion that driving under such conditions imposes on the crews.

On the 5th the advance was resumed at 7 a.m. There was delay in the thermos bomb area, but then the going improved and a better speed was maintained. About noon there was a halt for an hour; then they pushed on, arriving in the area of Antelat about 4.30 p.m. Here Brigade Headquarters intercepted a message from the 11th Hussars to Division replying to an enquiry from the latter as to where the Armoured Brigade could best help; the 11th reported good tank going to Beda Fomm whence the tanks could attack on the flank an unending stream of lorries that was coming down the Benghazi road. Accordingly Brigadier Caunter ordered the 7th Hussars to move as fast as possible to the road at Beda Fomm, the Cruisers of the 2nd Royal Tanks with the R.H.A. battery to move to Beda Fomm itself.

At 5.15 p.m. "B" Squadron of the 7th Hussars reported Beda Fomm clear, and just after 6 p.m. "B" and "C" Squadrons surprised the enemy having an evening meal. "B" shot up the column while "C" hunted the escaping vehicles towards the west. However, darkness was falling and put a stop to the operations but not before Lieutenant Murray-Smith had set alight an Italian petrol lorry whose lurid flames served as a useful landmark through the night.

Meanwhile the 2nd Royal Tanks (Lieutenant-Colonel A. C. Harcourt) engaged the enemy with "A" Squadron, under Major M. J. Woollcombe, until dark, when they pulled back a short distance. The rest of the Regiment leaguered at Beda Fomm and "A" Squadron spent the night near the scene of their action. During the night they were approached by two Italian tanks. Trooper E. Hughes climbed onto the turrets of these tanks and forced their surrender at the point of his pistol.

The task given to the 3rd Hussars had been to block the tracks north and north-west from Antelat, and during the night, which was wet with strong winds, they remained in those positions. The 7th Hussars had been withdrawn to Beda Fomm, and their orders for the next day were that they and the 2nd Royal Tanks, who appeared to have struck a more strongly defended portion of the Italian column than had the 7th, should keep the road blocked, supported by the battery of the 4th R.H.A. It should be remembered that at this stage, although it was fairly certain that the enemy were evacuating Cyrenaica, it was not known how many of their troops had managed to get away from Benghazi and past the position held by Colonel Combe's force.

*Sidi Saleh*                                                    *February 6th*

The night had been fairly quiet; there had been no attack but several hundred Italians had come into the lines and been taken prisoner. With the 4th Armoured Brigade safely established to the north and north-east, the right flank could be disregarded and it was evident that if the Italians tried an outflanking movement it would have to be to the west. Accordingly Colonel Renton extended his left and Colonel Campbell moved another section of his guns to that area. Shortage of food, ammunition and petrol were already causing anxiety, and the supply lorries were not getting through. Further requests for more artillery ammunition brought the soldierly answer that the utmost economy must be exercised and that every round must pay a one hundred per cent dividend. All was quiet to the south.

About 10.45 a.m. the first serious Italian attack came in; three columns, each of about 300 vehicles, came down the main road, the track to the west of it and along the coastal area. Two were halted at once and they surrendered as soon as they were engaged by the anti-tank guns and small arms fire, but the third, on the main road, had tanks and guns and it took an hour's fighting before they, too, gave up. Three or four other similar attacks were made during the day and the enemy showed a certain amount of determination, but the Rifle Brigade and their supporting artillery in their three and a half miles long position held firm. The toll of prisoners began to mount into thousands and already included one General and his staff.

Away to the south the K.D.G. squadron was also becoming embarrassed by prisoners, and their wireless batteries were getting low. They had met a certain amount of opposition, but there was still no serious threat from that direction.

About 9 p.m. a further attack was launched against the Riflemen by three columns supported by tanks; the enemy had managed to avoid a small minefield. Casualties were caused among some of the gun crews and the position was pierced, with the result that the close support that had been so admirably supplied by the gunners temporarily became limited. Nevertheless, the line still held and the enemy within the area, about five hundred, were rounded up. An hour later, two more guns of the 106th R.H.A. arrived and were immediately placed at Colonel Renton's disposal. Their appearance was most timely and greatly strengthened the anti-tank defences about the main road. More mines were laid and the leading vehicle of the next attack was blown up with the result that another 150 prisoners were roped in. At midnight a column moving across the front was broken up and at 4 a.m. on the 7th two medium tanks were captured in the sand dunes area owing to the enterprise of Platoon-Sergeant-Major Jarvis and Rifleman O'Brien.

*Beda Fomm*                                           *February 6th*
    Throughout the day, the 2nd Royal Tanks with "A" and "C" Squadrons, the latter under Major J. H. C. Richardson, were engaged with enemy columns and tank attacks. Major Withers' "F" Battery pounded the Italian tanks and transport as hard as they could and without ceasing. The enemy launched their attacks with groups of tanks varying in number from twenty to forty, but they were met by the British from hull-down positions and most skilful use of fire and movement in the broken ground. Every attack cost the Italians ten or a dozen tanks, but the British tanks were dwindling too and there were frequent pauses for replenishment of ammunition. The Regiments and the Brigade handled this matter with great skill so that there was never a time when the front was not covered by at least a few tanks.
    The 7th Hussars, now commanded by Lieutenant-Colonel F. W. Byass (Colonel G. Fielden had been seriously wounded shortly before), about eight miles further north, were similarly involved and they fought with great skill against enemy columns moving south. Their orders were to report enemy movements and they carried out their task magnificently, sending back throughout the long day clear and accurate reports of enemy columns advancing, thus enabling the successive enemy attacks to be anticipated with extreme accuracy. The total number of Italian tanks they reported amounted to 107, which was somewhat different to the couple of dozen which had been supposed to be the total enemy strength.
    The 3rd Hussars, meanwhile, with a Troop of "D" Battery 3rd R.H.A., had been ordered to an area about four miles north of Beda Fomm and they reached their position shortly before 11 a.m. Soon after noon they came under heavy shell-fire and reported that they were engaging about thirty enemy tanks. In the column of lorries ahead of them were more tanks. It appeared, therefore, to Brigade Headquarters that apart from the forty or so tanks that had already been knocked out there were at least another sixty coming on. The Cruiser strength of the Brigade was now reduced to nine, but good news arrived that the 1st Royal Tanks from the 7th Armoured Brigade were on their way to help.

For the 4th Brigade the crisis of the battle was reached about midday when, for various reasons, only six tanks remained in action in the Pimple area; some had been knocked out, others had broken down, some had had to pull out to replenish. It was fortunate that the Italians lacked the ability and initiative to take advantage of the situation. During the afternoon two squadrons of the 1st Royal Tanks, under Majors N. C. B. Fellows and L. G. Hynes, came into action against the enemy tanks, and their arrival averted what might have become a critical situation.

About 2.20 p.m. an attack was launched against the enemy columns, and an hour or so later it was reported that the enemy tanks were trying to make off towards the north-east. During the remaining hours of daylight—it became dark about six—the battle still remained evenly balanced, for there were few British tanks left and they were greatly outnumbered by the Italians. By now, the 7th Hussars had found the tail of the enemy force and were moving south down the main road with no enemy behind them. At the south end of the area, the 2nd Royal Tanks, who were reduced to seven Cruisers including the two of their Regimental Headquarters, were facing more than twice their number advancing at them, with another thirty and some artillery beyond.

North of the 2nd Tanks, the 1st Tanks were pursuing about twenty Italian tanks in a north-westerly direction. The squadron of the 3rd Hussars, now reduced to only three tanks, were also moving north-west in order to gain touch with the retreating enemy.

Night drew down the curtain on an extraordinary sight. For several miles round the Pimple were knocked-out tanks, tanks abandoned or ditched, burning or burned-out lorries and cars, dead and dying Italians and all the flotsam and jetsam of modern war. Very large numbers of Italians were wandering about looking for somebody to whom to surrender, and the only aggressive movement, if it can be termed aggressive, was that of a considerable force trying to make a detour between the main road and the sea. It was clear that they would soon be arriving in front of Colonel Combe's force, so warning was sent to him. The Brigade leaguered for the night north and south of Beda Fomm. Including the tanks of the 1st Royal Tanks, the state of the Brigade that night was 39 tanks undamaged, 48 hit by gun-fire, eight others knocked out, one un-hit but burned out and eight out of action from unknown causes, a total of 101 tanks.

The Support Group had been advancing further to the north,

pressing forward to Ghemines with a view to taking the Italians in the flank and rear. During the day the Australians captured Benghazi.

### Beda Fomm                                                    February 7th

All was quiet during the night. At dawn the 7th Hussars pushed patrols north and north-west; the 2nd Royal Tanks were ordered to move south to assist Combeforce. The Support Group were now coming down from the north and soon gained touch with the 7th Hussars. The 2nd Tanks reached Sidi Saleh just too late to take part in the final stages of the battle. At 11 a.m. General Virginio, the Chief of Staff of the Italian Tenth Army, arrived at Headquarters 4th Armoured Brigade with the Army staff.

### Sidi Saleh                                                   February 7th

At 6.30 a.m. the Rifle Brigade Battalion Headquarters was heavily shelled and shortly afterwards two large columns attacked with tank and artillery support. The road column managed to penetrate both the forward and the reserve company areas, and before they were halted one tank had got as far as Battalion Headquarters where it was knocked out. This was a critical moment, but the resolution of the infantry and the accurate fire of the artillery surmounted the crisis. The lorries following the tanks were stopped by heavy fire from all arms, and then surrendered. With the failure of this effort the heart went out of the enemy. All down the column the white flags began to go up. General Bergonzoli, known to the world as "Electric Whiskers", gave himself up to Major Pearson, and with his surrender the battle was over and the Italian Tenth Army had ceased to exist.

As at Beda Fomm, the battlefield presented an astonishing sight. Besides the knocked-out tanks that covered a wide area, the main road for fifteen miles was blocked by battered and destroyed guns and vehicles all in the utmost confusion.

To the staunch fighting qualities of the Rifle Brigade and their supporting gunners under Colonel Combe's overall command was added the skilful fighting of the armour and especially the accurate gunnery of the 2nd Royal Tanks from hull-down positions. The fighting of the Armoured Brigade held much weight off the slender defences at Sidi Saleh, and their battle has been described as a text-book example of an armoured battle, Cruiser tanks using their mobility and fire-power to deal with enemy tanks, light tanks screening the flanks and front and Horse Artillery to deal with the enemy infantry. But all this would have been in vain if it had not been for the Rifle Brigade and their Gunners who stood firm and fought it out and held the head of that immense column. Between them, these two forces of Colonel Combe and Brigadier Caunter under General Creagh's direction beat the very heart out of the enemy and totally destroyed his Army.

Later victories on a greater scale have eclipsed the Battle of Beda Fomm and memories of those days have become dim. At the time, this victory, which still has no equal for completeness and smallness of cost, brought a great glow of good cheer into the blackness of the Allied night. Unhappily the territory it gained, the great Italian colony of Cyrenaica, was soon to be lost again, for by February it had become necessary to send substantial military and air forces to Greece in order to attempt to hold back the German invasion of that country which was clearly impending and was launched on April 6th.

Nothing, however, could alter the material fruits of the victory, the complete destruction of the Italian Army with a total of prisoners at Sidi Saleh of over 20,000, with six Generals, 216 guns, 112 tanks, 1,500 lorries and an immense quantity of arms, equipment and stores of all kinds, not to mention the toll of dead. All this was gained at a cost to the 7th Armoured Division of nine killed and fifteen wounded.

Despite almost incredible difficulties of terrain and supply, the Division had advanced in thirty hours across 150 miles of almost un-mapped Desert, without the benefits of air support—indeed, in the face of a much more powerful air force than their own—at high speed into what was, literally, the unknown. There, out-numbered, short of water, food, ammunition and petrol, with no prospect of support or reinforcement, they had out-fought and conquered an Army more than ten times their strength trying desperately to escape from the trap in which they were caught. Small wonder that they felt pride in their achievement.

It is difficult for those accustomed to the lavish scales of 1944-45, especially in transport, wireless and air support, to appreciate the problems that faced the Desert fighters in those early days. What was achieved with such meagre and unreliable resources ought never to be forgotten.

In two months the Army of the Nile, as the Prime Minister said, had advanced 700 miles and destroyed an Army of more than nine

Divisions, and had captured 130,000 prisoners, 400 tanks and 1,290 guns. The Army that achieved this had never consisted of more than two Divisions, of which one was always the 7th Armoured, nor more than 33,000 men, had always been short of every type of transport, equipment and other supplies considered necessary for modern war; they had endured extremes of heat and cold, dust, flies, sand storms and mirages; they were always short of water and lived on a monotonous diet. Their only advantage lay in the command of the sea by the Royal Navy, their own high morale, and the courage and skill of their commanders.

*After the Battle*                                    *February 8th to 28th*
As soon as the battle was over, the 11th Hussars pushed on to Agedabia and then to el Agheila. Behind them came the Support Group who went to Mersa Bregha. By now the Division could muster only twelve Cruisers and forty light tanks. Two of the Light Recovery Sections were moving up, and the Divisional Workshops opened five miles south of Benghazi. Water, for once, was plentiful, but the feeding, watering and evacuation of the thousands of prisoners threw an immense additional strain on the administrative services.

On the 14th the coming of the Germans was heralded by an attack by aircraft bearing the ominous black crosses; one was brought down by the 11th Hussars and the pilot captured by Lieutenant J. A. N. Crankshaw. The return of the Division to Egypt then started, led by the 11th Hussars. They had a sad parting from the R.A.F. Armoured Car Company which had joined them from Palestine at a time when the losses of their own vehicles had begun to assume serious proportions, and they had operated together most happily for the past four months.

The K.D.G.s took over from the 11th, and the Division as a whole was relieved by the 2nd Armoured Division. The 3rd Hussars were left behind with all the light tanks that could be collected; so also were the 1st R.H.A. and the 6th Royal Tanks—the latter being mounted in captured Italian tanks.

The rest of the Division, flushed with victory and bedecked with captured flags, drove into Cairo before the end of the month, the speedometers of the 11th Hussars registering 922 miles for the return journey.

## CHAPTER 2

*April to October, 1941*

# OPERATION "BATTLEAXE"

*Reference Maps—No. 2, page 34. No. 4, page 54*

*The Strategical Situation*          *February and March, 1941*

AFTER the rout of the Italians and the destruction of their Army, General O'Connor was anxious to push on to Tripoli; so far as enemy forces went, there was little to oppose him. Such an advance would, however, require the fullest possible support from the Royal Navy and the R.A.F., particularly the former as the land lines of communication were far too extended for the limited amount of transport available.

Unfortunately political and strategical considerations prevented any exploitation of the victory. The British Government was committed to a policy of assistance to Greece and, apart from that commitment, was loth to adopt any course that would entail the abandonment of the Balkans, the coming occupation of which by the Germans was clearly foreshadowed. In mid-February the R.A.F. had had to send further reinforcements to Greece so the Corps in Cyrenaica was left almost without air support. At the same time directions were sent to Wavell, firstly not to advance beyond Cyrenaica; secondly, to hold that colony firmly; thirdly, to send land and air forces to Greece in as great a strength as possible; and finally, to press on with attacks on the islands of the Dodecanese. On March 1st the Germans invaded Bulgaria and an invasion of Jugo-Slavia was imminent.

Properly to understand the events of the next sixteen months, it is necessary to record this strategic background, for people are still apt to question how it was that such resounding victories could have been succeeded by such grave reverses. Distant though these other places were, the campaigns that had to be fought there had a long-lasting effect on the Desert war. Before many more months

had passed, there were to be the additional commitments of a
revolt in Iraq and a small war in Syria. No military commander
has ever had to face such a multitude of problems as those that
confronted Wavell, and there can be few men who would have
surmounted them with such a degree of success.

## The Tactical Situation

The 6th Australian Division, by now experienced and successful,
was sent to Greece together with the New Zealand Division and
the 1st Armoured Brigade from the 2nd Armoured Division. The
7th Australian Division was also earmarked for Greece, but the
development of events in the Desert resulted in their going instead
to Tobruk, in the defence of which they played an important part
until almost the end of the siege.

For the protection of the extensive Province of Cyrenaica there
were left only the remainder of the 2nd Armoured Division and
the 9th Australian Division. Both these formations were in a
lamentable state of under-equipment—tanks worn out or out of
date, spare tracks that did not fit, insufficient wireless communications, battered lorries and trucks and too few even of these, some
regiments even mounted in captured Italian tanks—so the sorry
tale runs. One of the consequences of the shortage of transport was
that recourse had to be had to dumping; not only did this restrict
the liberty of action of commanders, but it often entailed the
destruction of valuable stores and commodities when retreat was
forced on the troops.

Apart from all these handicaps, the armoured and motorized
troops who had had several years' experience in the Desert and
nearly a year's fighting there, were now back in Egypt for badly-
needed rest, re-fitting and re-training. Through sheer inexperience
and ill-equipment, those who were about to face the violent German
onslaught were ill-fitted for the ordeal. When one takes into account
the conditions under which they had to fight, one can only admire
the stout resistance they put up.

Besides the complete re-organization of the force, there were
changes in the high command. General Wilson was appointed
Governor and Commander-in-Chief of Cyrenaica, General
O'Connor was brought back to take his place in command of the
British Troops in Egypt, and Lieutenant-General P. Neame, V.C.,
came to be the new commander of the XIIIth Corps. However,
when the Greek crisis arose, General Wilson went to command in

that country and General Neame combined the command of Cyrenaica with that of the Corps.

For some time prior to the end of March there were many indications of the build-up of a German Army in Tripolitania, and there was much German air force activity from the middle of February onwards. Wavell was greatly handicapped by the absence of any Intelligence organization across the frontier—in the original war plans this work had been allotted to the French. Such reports as came in were of doubtful reliability and in addition, the transfer of so many aircraft to Greece, combined with a much increased and more efficient enemy air activity, resulted in a serious reduction in British strategical reconnaissance. Wavell's defensive plan envisaged a delaying action back to Benghazi, but as he realized the weakness of the XIIIth Corps the commander was authorized to abandon the town if necessary and to hold the high ground to the east.

*The Germans Advance*                                    *March 31st, 1941*

Early in February the German High Command had decided to form an Afrika Korps consisting of the 5th Light and the 15th Panzer Divisions, the commander to be General Erwin Rommel. At the end of March Rommel was ready to move forward from Tripolitania although his 15th Panzer Division had not yet arrived, and on the 31st his advance began, the force comprising the 5th Light Division and two Italian Divisions, the Ariete and the Brescia. On April 3rd, by which time his Headquarters were at Agedabia and the British forces in front were retiring, he took the decision to follow up closely and to endeavour to re-take Cyrenaica.

The German offensive had not been going for long when General Neame was forced to order a withdrawal to the line Derna–Mechili. Already petrol was short and there was some confusion in the retiring transport columns. On April 6th Rommel's forces were reported to be moving by way of Mechili as well as along the coast, and at the same time the news was brought to Wavell that General O'Connor (who, with Brigadier Combe, had hurried to the forward area when the attack started) and General Neame had been cut off by a German column in the darkness and made prisoner. In O'Connor the Army lost the most able and experienced senior officer in the Desert, and in Combe one of the most outstanding of the younger senior officers. Both escaped from their prison camp three years later and again commanded formations in battle before the war was over.

*Divisional Moves*

For the Division, returned from the Tripolitanian frontier, the fleshpots of Cairo had proved a pleasant change from Desert life, but G.H.Q. had been hard up for troops, and the officers and men of the Division were soon engaged in a wide variety of tasks. General Creagh was employed to organize an Armoured Corps Branch of the Staff, and in March was actually in Turkey, the Motor Battalions to guard the Suez Canal and the Tura Caves, while personnel of the Armoured Regiments found themselves manning anti-aircraft defences in merchant ships. There was no reserve of tanks with which to re-equip the Division and as a fighting formation it rapidly disintegrated.

When the seriousness of the German advance was realized certain portions of the Division were sent forward. The first to go were the 1st Battalion K.R.R.C. under Lieutenant-Colonel S. C. F. de Salis who moved forward on March 29th. By April 7th they were engaged with the advancing enemy near Derna and during the following week they carried out a fighting withdrawal. The next to leave Cairo, on April 5th, were the 11th Hussars under Lieutenant-Colonel W. I. Leetham. When the warning order had come thirty-six hours before they had been in process of re-equipping with Marmon-Harrington armoured cars, and they were able to assemble only a Headquarter Squadron (Major K. Alexander) and two sabre Squadrons under Majors Payne Gallwey and A. V. C. Robarts, Major W. Wainman's Squadron remaining behind for the time being.

On April 13th the Support Group Headquarters moved to Mersa Matruh. By this time the Germans had completed the investment of Tobruk where the 1st R.H.A. and the 1st Royal Tanks remained for the siege. On the 14th Brigadier Gott's force was close to the enemy at Sollum and he took over command of all troops operating in the area on the 16th with the title "H.Q. Mobile Force". On the previous day, the 3rd Battalion Coldstream Guards, who were temporarily forming part of the Support Group and were positioned at Halfaya Pass, carried out a raid on the barracks above Sollum.

By this time the bulk of the 2nd Armoured Division had been destroyed, and outside Tobruk there was little left but the scattered remnants of this Division and such troops of the 7th as were sufficiently equipped to be sent forward. On April 30th the 2nd Battalion Rifle Brigade under Lieutenant-Colonel A. S. G. Douglas joined the Support Group.

*April and May*

The build-up of the German forces went ahead more quickly than had been expected and they made rapid progress in getting the port of Benghazi in working order. Even so, there was bound to be a pause while they accumulated supplies and there was reason to hope that the concentration of the 15th Panzer Division had been delayed by the sinkings of some of the ships used for carrying them from Italy.

It was clearly important for Wavell to seize this opportunity to counter-attack, but unfortunately the re-equipment of the 7th Armoured Division was proceeding very slowly indeed. A special tank-carrying convoy was being rushed through the Mediterranean, but when they arrived, having sustained a loss of about a quarter of the tanks they contained, much work had to be done in the workshops to make the tanks fit for the Desert. In addition, the repair of the older tanks was also going on very slowly. The prospects of an early British offensive depended on the time by which the 7th Armoured Division could be got ready for battle, but by the beginning of May there were still only two squadrons of Cruiser tanks and two of "I" tanks in the forward zone, though it was hoped to have sufficient armour ready by the middle of June. It should be remembered that the tank crews had to become accustomed to new types of tank, that the guns had to be calibrated and the reinforcements trained—one cannot just draw a new tank from the stores and go off to battle.

For any future offensive the possession of Halfaya and Capuzzo was of much importance, so an attack was launched on May 15th and the enemy positions at the top of the Halfaya Pass were occupied and Capuzzo taken. In the evening, however, a strong German counter-attack re-took Capuzzo and the Coldstream were left with a precarious hold on Halfaya. Rommel appreciated as well as anyone else the threat that this pointed at his forces investing Tobruk, so on May 26th he attacked and captured the commanding ground overlooking the positions of the Coldstream. Another heavy attack was put in next morning and the Coldstream were ordered to withdraw, which they did in good order though with losses amounting to over one hundred.

On May 14th Divisional Headquarters had moved to el Hammam, about 35 miles west of Alexandria. By the 26th they had in the Western Desert the 11th Hussars and one squadron of the Royals, who had just been converted into an armoured car

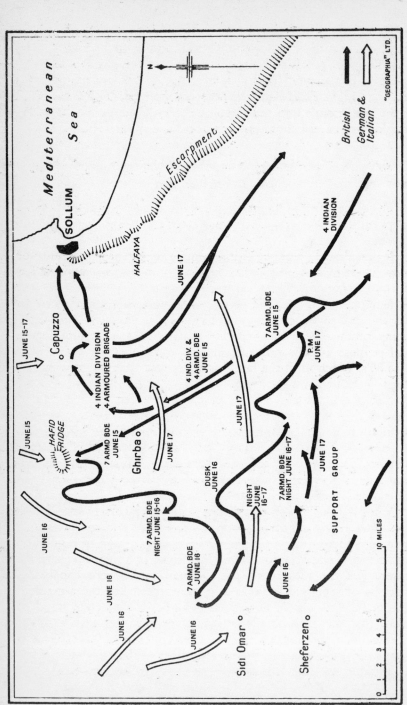

Map No. 4.—Operation "Battleaxe", June 15th to 17th, 1941

regiment; the 7th Armoured Brigade, consisting of the 2nd and 4th Royal Tanks; the Support Group, of the 1st K.R.R.C., 2nd Rifle Brigade, 4th R.H.A. and a battery of the 3rd R.H.A.; one squadron of the 7th Hussars; four R.A.S.C. Companies, the 13th and 15th Light Field Ambulances, and the Ordnance Field Parks of the 7th Brigade and the Support Group. The remainder of the Division was at el Hammam or in the Cairo area.

## OPERATION "BATTLEAXE"

### June 15th to 17th, 1941

The object of this Operation was defined as "to defeat the enemy troops in the Western Desert and to drive them back west of Tobruk."

It was thought that the British would have a preponderance of tanks; there is still considerable variance in the figures given for the tank strengths of the two sides. It seems probable that the Germans put into the field rather more than two hundred tanks, and the British between 180 and two hundred. In addition, the enemy produced for the first time the redoubtable 88-millimetre dual purpose anti-aircraft and anti-tank guns, hereinafter referred to as 88's, which until the last day of the war were to prove such a thorn in the sides of their opponents.

The troops employed, under the command of Lieutenant-General Sir Noel Beresford-Peirse, consisted of the 4th Indian Division, now back from the successful Abyssinian Campaign, supported by the 22nd Guards Brigade, and the 7th Armoured Division, composed of the 7th Armoured Brigade, the thickly-armoured "I" tanks of the 4th Armoured Brigade (Brigadier A. H. Gatehouse), and the Support Group.

Many of the Cruiser tanks were the new Crusaders armed with the 2-pounder gun; great things were expected of them. Unhappily their high speed was not matched by a high degree of reliability, and the gun was to prove most inefficient in range and striking power. For the most part, the German tanks were capable of knocking out the British tanks at 2,000 yards, while the 2-pounder guns of the latter were not effective beyond six or eight hundred yards. The only alternative way of dealing with German tanks was by using the 25-pounder field guns, the crews of which were devoid of armour protection.

Fighting in the Desert resembled in many respects Naval

warfare. Attack from the flanks or rear could quickly be met by armoured vehicles that manœuvred as easily as ships, and the decision then rested with the side that had the better gun and the better armour. Unlike warships, however, tanks are not capable of carrying more than a few hours' supply of ammunition, fuel, water and food, so in all actions much turned on the ability of the supply services to re-victual the fighting troops. Since the supply columns had no effective anti-tank defences of their own, the liberty of action of commanders was often limited by the necessity of detaching armoured troops for the protection of transport columns or supply dumps. It is well that critics should bear in mind the dominating factors of gun power, armour and supply as they were in those days.

## The Plan

The 4th Indian Division was to attack Halfaya, Sollum and Capuzzo, having the "I" tanks of the 4th Brigade under command in the initial stages. The 7th Armoured Division was to move by bounds parallel with the Indians. As soon as the latter could dispense with the "I" tank Brigade they were to come under command of the 7th Division. This intended organization of a Cruiser Brigade with an "I" tank Brigade was a novelty, and, although it increased the hitting power of the Division, it gravely affected the mobility of the Division as a whole, for the speed of the "I" tank was but five miles per hour. The idea was to surprise the enemy by drawing him onto the "I" tanks which were to be concealed in hull-down positions. As events turned out, the 4th Armoured Brigade were never to come under command of the 7th Armoured Division, but the freedom of action of the latter was somewhat curtailed by the anticipation that they were going to do so. The later stages of the plan envisaged the capture of Bardia, the relief of Tobruk and an advance to the line Derna–Mechili.

Within the Division, the plan was for the 7th Brigade to form the main striking force with the 11th Hussars, while the Support Group, operating in columns of all arms, was to protect the left flank and rear of the Division by working southwards from Sidi Omar.

## June 15th

The advance began at 2.30 in the morning. Both the first two bounds were secured without opposition and a small party of the enemy was seen to withdraw. About 7.45 the 7th Brigade began to go forward to the third bound, Hafid Ridge. Visibility was down to about fifty yards and it was difficult for the troops to know when they had reached their objective. Unknown to them, the Ridge actually consisted of three ridges, so when they reached the first they reported that they had gained their objective. However, patrols pushed forward to get contact with the enemy immediately met very heavy fire from tanks, anti-tank guns and artillery, and it appeared that the enemy was deployed in strength on two more ridges.

The leading Regiment was the 2nd Royal Tanks and the Commanding Officer, Lieutenant-Colonel R. F. E. Chute, immediately deployed his second squadron, that of Major J. R. D. Carlton, to carry out an attack on the left flank of the leading squadron, Captain J. K. W. Bingham's. Although they destroyed thirty lorries and ten guns the opposition proved too strong for them. The 6th Royal Tanks under Lieutenant-Colonel M. D. B. Lister were then sent up to assist. They met very heavy fire and soon after midday were themselves attacked by about forty tanks which they held off.

In the evening the 6th Tanks attacked again. "A" Squadron, moving in line-ahead, had what was described as "a good broadside shoot" on an enemy concentration and definitely destroyed nine tanks, but "B" Squadron, although they managed to reach the second ridge, lost half a dozen tanks at once. When night fell the losses of the Brigade amounted to nineteen tanks destroyed and twenty-two out of action through enemy action or mechanical failure. In addition, Colonel Chute had been wounded. It was reckoned that they had been engaged with 75 enemy tanks, of which they claimed thirteen destroyed.

During the day the 4th Indian Division captured Capuzzo, but the situation in the evening at Sollum and Halfaya was obscure.

*June 16th*

General Creagh was expecting to have the 4th Armoured Brigade back under his command early in the morning, and in conjunction with the commander of the 4th Indian Division had arranged to attack the Hafid position and an enemy out-flanking manœuvre that appeared to be developing. However, at dawn the Germans attacked Capuzzo and put such pressure on the Indians that it was not possible to release the 4th Brigade. In addition to three separate attacks on Capuzzo during the day, the enemy began to move down the wire in the direction of Sidi Omar. The 7th Armoured Brigade engaged this movement in co-operation with the Support Group and all available artillery. The Support Group and the 6th Royal Tanks attacked the head and the 2nd Tanks the flank, all doing much damage to the transport. This successful action forced the enemy to withdraw in the direction of Ghirba, but there were no reserves with which to follow up, an unfortunate consequence of having only two Regiments in the Armoured Brigade and no Divisional Reserve. By noon the 6th Royal Tanks were reduced to only sixteen tanks in running order, and not long afterwards they had only nine.

By now it was becoming apparent that the enemy was carrying out a wide turning movement intended to encircle the 4th Indian Division. This was confirmed by the 11th Hussars, and soon after-wards a tactical reconnaissance aircraft dropped at Divisional Headquarters an excellent sketch-map showing the enemy lined up along the wire from Sidi Omar to Sheferzen. An enemy advance in the evening, taking advantage of the setting sun behind him to disturb his adversaries' fire, was met and halted by the 7th Brigade and the Support Group. In the action that followed twenty-one enemy tanks were claimed as destroyed at a cost of seven knocked out and sixteen damaged.

In the evening the Indians reported that they held Capuzzo and the barracks at Sollum, and that as they were dug into anti-tank localities they could release the 4th Armoured Brigade in the morning. A plan was accordingly made for this Brigade to attack the German turning movement frontally while the 7th Brigade attacked the flank and the Support Group the rear. The enemy were now in considerable strength, while the 7th Brigade were reduced to about twenty-five tanks and the 4th Brigade were also very weak.

*June 17th*

However, early in the morning the 4th Indian Division reported further fierce attacks and considered that if the 4th Brigade were withdrawn Capuzzo could no longer be held. Under these circum-stances there was no alternative but to countermand the move of the Brigade. All the 7th Armoured Division could do was to try to slow down the German advance and inflict as many casualties as possible. Both the 7th Brigade and the Support Group continued to engage the enemy and caused heavy losses to his columns. The situation was becoming serious when General Wavell, who had a

habit of turning up at critical moments, arrived at Divisional
Headquarters with General Beresford-Peirse. Having studied the
situation the Commander-in-Chief gave the order to withdraw,
and as soon as the Indians has broken off their action this order was
put into effect, the Support Group and the 11th Hussars remaining
in contact. The enemy showed no inclination to follow up—he had
had enough.

The two Armoured Brigades and the Support Group claimed a
bag of ninety enemy tanks, about fifty lorries and thirty guns of
various types, but their own losses were very serious. The 7th
Brigade had lost 29 tanks, and the 4th, who had most skilfully
covered the retirement of the Indians and the Guards Brigade, had
had to abandon about sixty tanks. This was partially due to the fact
that there were no recovery vehicles capable of lifting this type of
tank and the crews had had little time for maintenance, or indeed
for rest either. Fortunately the losses in men were comparatively
light. It is recorded that of the 52 tanks with which the 6th Royal
Tank Regiment began the battle, only five were present throughout
the operations.

Although the results of this battle were disappointing, the
vindication of the operation lies in the fact that for the next five
months the Germans were unable to advance or carry out any
offensive operations except at Tobruk.

The War Diary of the 7th Armoured Brigade summed up the
month of June in these words—"this concludes a very successful
but unfortunate month. The 72-hour battle on the 15th, 16th and
17th taught us a lot. Everybody in the Brigade fully realizes their
marked superiority when fighting the Hun, but let us hope and pray
that next time we face him the Brigade is of three complete Regiments, not one and a half as in this case. Throughout the month
the health and spirits of the men under genuinely trying conditions
in the frontier area were excellent. The presence of German
armoured troops, active patrols and superiority in the air made us
constantly on the alert, and the men stood this severe strain in a
spirit that is beyond praise. Our drinking water was at times
undrinkable. N.A.A.F.I. stores were non-existent and flies were
very persistent."

*The Summer of 1941.*

The next four months were a comparatively quiet time in the
Western Desert. For the British, further operations were impossible

until the losses in tanks had been made good. The workshops in the
Delta were greatly overloaded with vehicles needing repair and
with new equipment of all kinds requiring adaptation to Desert
conditions. There were reinforcements to be absorbed, and old and
new units to be trained. Consideration had to be given to the
plans to be adopted if the enemy launched an offensive, and it is
of interest to recall that troops were brought to an area near a
small railway station called el Alamein where defensive positions
were dug; this was less than sixty miles from Alexandria and seemed
an absurdly long way back.

The Division suffered a sad loss when the Rev. E. J. Dodge,
the Senior Chaplain, was killed on June 23rd by a bomb dropped
from a German aircraft. Mr. Dodge had been with the Division
since the early days when there had been only one Chaplain in
each Brigade. It had been his policy, contrary to that of the War
Office, who then considered that the place for Padres was the
waggon-lines, to encourage his subordinates to move and live in
the place where the strain was greatest, the front line. That this
was the right policy no one who remembers the work done by
these men will doubt, and as time went on and the number of
Chaplains in the Army increased so it became the custom for them
to operate always in the forward area, to the very great benefit
of their "parishioners". At the time of his death Mr. Dodge had
been ordered back to the Delta for a rest, and he had just handed
over his appointment to the Rev. S. M. F. Woodhouse, who, after
serving in the Retreat to Dunkirk, had come out to the Desert with
the 3rd Hussars; after arrival, he had become Chaplain to the
Support Group. By the time Mr. Woodhouse took over the number
of Chaplains in the Division had been increased by the arrival of
sixteen, and it then became possible to allot three to each Brigade
and some to the Divisional Troops. One of the qualifications of the
Chaplain, and one that he had not been taught at home, was that
he should be capable of desert navigation; without that, he would
soon have got lost going round his parish.

Changes took place in the higher command which resulted in
the departure of General Wavell. It was felt that he was a tired man,
for, to use the Prime Minister's words, "we had ridden the willing
horse to a standstill". He was given the highly important post of
Commander-in-Chief in India, of which country he was to become
Viceroy a few years later. He was succeeded in the Middle East
Command by General Sir Claude Auchinleck, and command of

the Army of the Nile, soon to be re-named the Eighth Army, went to Lieutenant-General Sir Alan Cunningham, the conqueror of Italian East Africa and Abyssinia.

Matters were not easy for Rommel. On June 22nd the Germans had invaded Russia and it was inevitable that the Desert war should become a "side-show". If Rommel wanted to carry the fighting further east an undefeated Tobruk constituted a menace to his rear. Another threat came from Malta; the Afrika Korps alone required over 40,000 tons of stores per month and there were large numbers of Italian troops to be supplied as well. The Navy took a steady toll of shipping making the voyage to North Africa from Italian ports, but their resources were gravely strained by having to maintain the garrisons of Malta and Tobruk after suffering heavy losses in the evacuations from Greece and Crete.

During the summer the German 5th Light Division was re-organized as the 21st Panzer, and a new Division, the 90th Light, was formed of four infantry battalions with unusually strong artillery support. By the start of the next British offensive, in November, Rommel's command was to be made up of three German Divisions and six Italian Divisions, two of them partially armoured.

In the 7th Armoured Division the armoured units were being re-equipped and re-trained, and the open Desert on the left flank of the Army was watched by a "Forward Group" under Brigadier Gott. Their tasks were to keep watch, to harass the enemy whenever an opportunity occurred and in the early stages to prevent the German salvage parties from recovering damaged vehicles left on the battlefield. In those days, before "recovery" had been properly organized and when both sides were suffering from an acute shortage of vehicles of all sorts, this salvage assumed much importance; it was the perquisite of the winner.

The tasks of the Forward Group were carried out for the most part by Jock Columns. For them it was a period of discomfort and hardship, intense heat, flies which made life unbearable, monotonous food, permanent water shortage, scant news from home—for the mail service was still bad—and none of the amenities of civilization. From time to time there would be clashes with small enemy columns, and day and night there was need for the strictest vigilance.

About 4.30 in the morning each column would break up its leaguer and spread out over an area of several square miles or move to a new area; the 25-pounders and the anti-tank guns would take up firing positions, and the carrier platoons and observation posts spread out on an approximate patrol line. There they would stay till after sun-down. During the middle of the day when the sun was fully up the landscape would blur and shake with the heat, and mirages would appear. Neither side could then move with safety. Sometimes the armoured cars of the enemy would approach and engage in a short action. The columns could never relax, and by the time they returned to leaguer after dark everybody would be dropping with fatigue. For the officers and N.C.O.'s, then, there would be routine correspondence to be dealt with, the inevitable returns to be made up and the details of the wireless codes and frequencies for the next day to be noted. By the time this business was finished there were not many hours left for sleep.

A column could neither capture ground nor prevent the enemy from seizing it, so its military value was limited, but for an Army at a time of material weakness it served a useful purpose for it was an economical method of covering a wide front and it constituted a harassment to the enemy. The lessons learned by the men of these columns were to prove of value in later battles.

*Changes*

In August the 4th South African Armoured Car Regiment, who had distinguished themselves in Abyssinia, began to relieve the 11th Hussars, and the 2nd R.H.A. (Lieutenant-Colonel L. Bolton) took the place of the 4th R.H.A. In September General Creagh left in order to take command of an Armoured Group in England; of his successes with the Division it is not necessary to speak, but it is interesting to note that until the end of the war no Divisional Commander was to have so long a tenure of the appointment as he. Brigadier Gott was promoted to take his place and command of the Support Group was assumed by Brigadier Campbell. Brigadier Russell was appointed to the staff in Cairo and his place in command of the 7th Armoured Brigade was taken by Brigadier G. M. O. Davy. Towards the end of September the King's Dragoon Guards joined the Division and patrolled in an area to the south of the South Africans.

At the end of October the 4th Armoured Brigade came forward, composed now of the 8th Hussars and the 3rd and 5th Royal Tanks, and equipped with the American light tank known as the Honey or General Stuart. At this time the 7th Brigade was equipped with Crusaders mainly, but they still had a few older Cruiser tanks.

When the 11th Hussars returned they had the new Humber armoured cars. The final addition to the Division in the forward area was the 22nd Armoured Brigade who had arrived ahead of their own 1st Armoured Division from the United Kingdom.

The Order of Battle on November 1st, 1941, is shown in Appendix I.

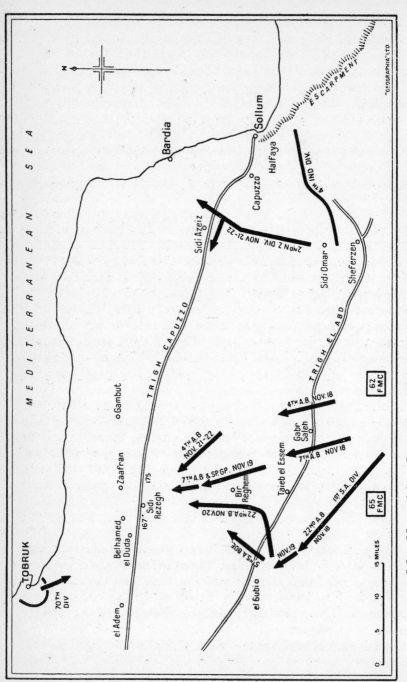

Map No. 5 (a).—Operation "Crusader", November 18th to 22nd, 1941

## CHAPTER 3

November and December, 1941

# OPERATION "CRUSADER"

*Reference Maps—No. 2, page 34. No. 5 (a), page 64. No. 5 (b), page 82*

THE intentions of this Operation were to destroy the enemy's armour and to re-capture Cyrenaica. The relief of Tobruk would follow naturally on the defeat of the Germans. The forces available to General Auchinleck comprised the newly-named Eighth Army of two Corps, the XIIIth under Lieutenant-General A. R. Godwin-Austen, and the XXXth under Lieutenant-General C. W. M. Norrie. The 7th Armoured Division formed part of the latter Corps. The Army Commander was Lieutenant-General Sir Alan Cunningham. Seventy miles away lay the garrison of Tobruk with a strength of five infantry brigades and one armoured brigade.

The R.A.F. had been built up to a total of over a thousand aircraft, and the British tank strength amounted to more than seven hundred tanks, of which half were Cruisers. Against them the enemy could put into the field about five hundred, two-thirds of which carried guns heavier than those in the British tanks. In addition, the enemy were stronger in anti-tank guns, both in quantity and quality.

## The Plan

The plan was for the XIIIth Corps, which contained the bulk of the infantry, to hold the enemy's fixed defences on the line from Halfaya to Sidi Omar, and to outflank them from the south with the New Zealand Division, while the armour of the XXXth Corps moved more widely round the south flank, either to destroy Rommel's armour or to prevent it from interfering with the XIIIth Corps. The garrison of Tobruk was to make a sortie when the right moment came.

Very elaborate security measures were taken and the plans for keeping secret the forthcoming operations were carefully drawn up, and as a result complete surprise was gained. The railway line was extended over fifty miles west of Mersa Matruh; water was brought by a pipe-line from Alexandria almost as far as railhead, and over 25,000 tons of supplies of every kind were accumulated in dumps in the forward area. Sea and air attacks were launched by the Navy and the R.A.F., and the latter provided detailed and accurate information of the enemy's dispositions.

In order to conceal the tanks they were equipped with a camouflage structure which caused them to resemble lorries when viewed from above. These were known as "sunshades" and were retained until the last minute. Thanks to these and other measures adopted, the Army was able to concentrate in the forward area without the Germans discovering what was afoot. They were themselves assembling for an assault on Tobruk which had been planned for November 23rd and Rommel was in Rome when the British attack began. The enemy air reconnaissance had failed to detect the Eighth Army's preliminary moves and heavy rain on the eve of the offensive put their landing-grounds out of action temporarily.

The task of the 7th Armoured Division was to advance to the airfields at el Adem and Sidi Rezegh, and, as usual, the 11th Hussars were to be in the van. On the night before the battle, says their History, "there was no moon and the bitter November cold had given way to milder weather. As the crews of the forward squadrons swallowed their tots of rum and snatched what sleep they could beside their loaded cars, small parties of infantry and sappers moved past them in the dark to cut gaps in the fence ahead. Over all, there hung the tension of the eve of battle. Some of the regiments were fresh from England and to them it was the first time, but for the majority of the Eleventh the waiting brought mostly reminders of early fighting round this very spot—all the Desert was scarred with the dregs of war."

*November 18th, 1941*

The Division advanced at 6 a.m., the tank strengths being 4th Armoured Brigade 166, 7th Brigade 129 and 22nd Brigade 158. Shortly before noon the Brigades filled up at various dumps which had been made beforehand, and, except for light screens of enemy armoured cars which withdrew without fighting, there was no hostile movement; there was also no interference by the German air force, for the advance was well covered by the R.A.F. When darkness fell about 5.30 p.m., two Brigades had reached the objectives ordered for the first day. Both the 4th on the right and the 7th in the centre were over the Trigh el Abd, while on the left the 22nd Brigade, who had been slightly delayed by difficulties in finding their re-fuelling places, were about six miles short of their objective and twenty miles south-east of el Gubi.

*November 19th*

On the left, the 22nd Armoured Brigade were engaged all day against the tanks of the Italian Ariete Division at el Gubi. The first contact was made about noon by the 2nd Royal Gloucestershire Hussars (Lieutenant-Colonel N. A. Birley) who came up against strong defences, and soon afterwards the 4th County of London Yeomanry (Lieutenant-Colonel W. G. Carr) were also involved. During the course of the next few hours the R.G.H. made some progress and the 3rd C.L.Y. (Lieutenant-Colonel Jago) were brought up on their right. By dusk, however, it was plain that an attack by tanks alone could not gain the position and the action had to be broken off. The heaviest losses had fallen upon the R.G.H. who numbered six officers, including Colonel Birley wounded, and 42 rank and file as their casualties, and the tank strength of the Regiment was reduced to nineteen. The Brigade claimed 45 enemy tanks destroyed but had lost about the same number themselves.

In the centre, the 7th Armoured Brigade were in action all the morning and were somewhat impeded by bad going. Early in the afternoon they were ordered to move forward towards Sidi Rezegh airfield. As the field came into view the 6th Royal Tanks (Lieutenant-Colonel M. D. B. Lister), who were leading, raced on at full speed over good hard ground. Three enemy aircraft hurriedly took off and two of them made low-level attacks on the tanks, but nineteen were captured on the ground together with eighty prisoners and much transport.

The 4th Armoured Brigade were heavily involved. The 3rd Royal Tanks (Lieutenant-Colonel A. A. H. Ewin) had moved north in pursuit of a German reconnaissance unit, and by the early afternoon were on the Trigh Capuzzo. At about the same time a German Battle Group moved south with the intention of reaching the frontier wire. The enemy were lucky enough to find a gap in the armoured car screen and they ran onto the 8th Hussars

(Lieutenant-Colonel D. S. Cripps). The Germans were estimated to number about a hundred tanks, and their advance was preceded by dive-bombing and machine-gun attacks which were mostly concentrated on Regimental Headquarters. The enemy tanks opened fire at a range of 1,500 yards where they were immune from the guns of the British tanks. The 5th Royal Tanks (Lieutenant-Colonel H. D. Drew) came to the aid of the 8th and the battle raged until dark when it was broken off, by which time the 8th Hussars had lost twenty tanks.

*November 20th*

The 4th Armoured Brigade was early engaged with the same German Battle Group as they had met the night before. This time the enemy moved across their front and a running fight ensued, as a result of which the Group turned away to the north. The 4th Brigade then resumed their position near Gabr Saleh.

The 7th Armoured Brigade established themselves early in the day on the Sidi Rezegh airfield, and the Support Group were ordered to join them. At 10.30 a.m. the latter arrived and took over the area. There was a large number of German anti-tank guns on the western side of the airfield, and it was soon evident that the enemy were not going to loosen their hold without a fight.

The area of Sidi Rezegh had two claims to importance, one the airfield, the other the ridge to the north. Occupation of this ridge would deprive the enemy of the use of the Trigh Capuzzo and thereby sever his communications with the bulk of his forward troops at Sollum and Capuzzo and to the south. Further, it over-looked the enemy troops investing Tobruk. It was indeed, "ground vital to the enemy", as the text-books put it.

Despite a certain amount of opposition, "D" Company of the 1st K.R.R.C. (Major R. F. L. Chance) succeeded in taking up a position on the edge of the escarpment to the east of the airfield, and the 6th Field Regiment established an Observation Post with them. "C" Company (Major E. G. V. Northey) took up a defensive position to the south of the airfield and spent the day digging-in in hard ground, being shelled from time to time. It was clear by the evening that the enemy were in strong positions north-east of "D" Company and north and west of "C" Company. There were signs of an impending attack, but patrols during the night had nothing to report.

General Norrie considered the prospects of a link-up with the

Tobruk garrison to be good, so the code word was sent for a break-out to begin at dawn on the 21st.

Meanwhile the 15th and 21st Panzer Divisions appeared near the 4th Armoured Brigade, and after a certain amount of man-œuvring halted to refill with petrol and ammunition. The threat to the 4th Brigade was such as to cause orders to be sent for the 22nd Brigade to be transferred from el Gubi to join the 4th. Before they could do so, however, the 15th Panzer attacked with about a hundred tanks and a fierce fight followed until dark, by which time the 4th Brigade had been reduced to 98 tanks, a decrease of 68 since they had crossed the wire. The excellent support of the 3rd R.H.A. under Colonel Wilson had played no small part in holding off the enemy attacks, though at one time there was much anxiety over ammunition supply.

The 22nd Brigade were unable to re-fuel until noon as their supply lorries had great difficulty in reaching them. It was not until nearly dark that they got up to the 4th Brigade and the Brigade was in action only for a short time.

During the day the 11th Hussars had had one squadron on an observation line before the defences of el Adem. Two other squadrons were near el Gubi, and when the 22nd Brigade moved to close with the 4th, one squadron, Major Wainman's, acted as flank and rear guard.

The fighting had been spread over a wide area and when night fell the Desert was covered with small parties of both sides, unsure of their positions and anxious to make contact with their parent units. As a result, there was some worry over the movements of the supply columns and there were many false alarms for the resting troops. So far the actions of the Germans had been designed to menace the flanks of the main British armoured force. Rommel's intention now was to concentrate his armour, and he hoped to meet the opposing armour in small groups so that he could defeat them in detail.

*The Battle of Sidi Rezegh—First Day*                    *November 21st*

During the night Rommel had realized that he was faced with a major effort to disrupt his whole position, and that this was no mere reconnaissance in force. He therefore ordered General Cruewell with the Afrika Korps (15th and 21st Panzer Divisions) to concentrate against the British forces in the Sidi Rezegh area as early as possible on the 21st. These Divisions had spent the night

only a short distance to the north and north-east of Gabr Saleh,
near where the 4th and 22nd Armoured Brigades had also leaguered.
Before first light the German force set off in a north-westerly direction.

This movement was detected and the 4th and 22nd Brigades
followed up with a view to launching an attack. Unfortunately
the enemy, although mounted in slower tanks, had the start of
them and got away with no more than slight losses to the rear
of the columns. Unluckily, also, both Brigades had to stop and
re-fuel, the 4th on account of the short range of their light tanks
and the 22nd because of the difficulty they had had in contacting
their supply columns the night before.

Meanwhile, at 8.30 a.m. the 1st Battalion K.R.R.C. under
Lieutenant-Colonel S. C. F. de Salis, with "A" Company of the
2nd Rifle Brigade (Major T. C. Sinclair), and the 6th Royal Tanks
less one squadron, and supported by the 4th R.H.A. (Lieutenant-
Colonel J. C. Currie) and the 60th Field Regiment (Lieutenant-
Colonel A. F. Hely), attacked the edge of the escarpment north of
the airfield.

In support of the attack the artillery fired a barrage which
was closely followed by the Carrier Platoons moving at top speed.
Behind them came the infantry of the Motor Platoons on foot.
The artillery fire and the clouds of dust that it raised enabled the
Carriers to get to close quarters while the defenders still had their
heads down. In certain areas, however, the defences were further
back than had been anticipated, and the Carriers of the right-hand
company, "D", suffered severely, five out of the seven being hit and
the Platoon Commander, Second-Lieutenant R. F. Paine, being
killed. The Carriers of "A" Company (Captain H. A. Hope) in the
centre also met heavy fire, but they manœuvred to their right, dismounted and fought it out on foot, taking thirty prisoners and
overcoming all opposition.

The infantry in the middle of the enemy position still remained
comparatively unharmed and it was their fire that caused losses
to the men of the Motor Platoons advancing on foot across the
open ground of the airfield. There was about 2,000 yards to go,
the ground was perfectly open and afforded little cover, even to
men lying down. The dust from the barrage and from the fast-
moving Carriers ahead gave much assistance in the early stages,
but as the infantry reached the north side of the airfield they came
under heavy fire and the advance was slowed down. Great gallantry

was shown by many officers and men as the attack was pressed home. Rifleman J. Beeley ran forward firing his Bren gun from the hip and wiped out the crews of an anti-tank gun and two machine-gun posts before being killed. He was posthumously awarded the Victoria Cross.

Colonel Lister of the 6th Royal Tanks led his Headquarters and two tank squadrons across the Trigh Capuzzo. In a valley north of the airfield they encountered very strong enemy gun positions and immediately began to suffer losses. Nevertheless several tanks reached the escarpment beyond the Trigh. Since they clearly could not hope to maintain their positions they withdrew, but only about six tanks got back from this very gallant venture. The losses were severe—the Commanding Officer, the second-in-command, two squadron leaders and four other officers were missing, together with many tank crews.

By noon the whole escarpment had been taken, with seven hundred prisoners, German and Italian, and great quantities of arms and booty. The battle cost the K.R.R.C. the lives of three officers and twenty-six rank and file, with five officers and fifty rank and file wounded. It became clear to Colonel de Salis that he had not the strength to occupy and hold the whole extent of the position taken, so he closed his companies in towards Point 167 where they reorganized and adapted the trenches for themselves—it was too hard to dig, so sandbags and stones were used. Rations were brought up during the evening and the troops were able to have their first meal for twelve hours. Artillery Observation Posts were immediately established and the guns shelled the enemy's main road for the rest of the day.

While the Riflemen were engaged in their successful battle the 7th Armoured Brigade, to the south of them, became involved with the Afrika Korps. At about 8 o'clock news was received of the imminent approach of the German armour from the south-east, and, leaving the one remaining squadron of the 6th Royal Tanks to support the infantry, the 7th Brigade turned to face the coming assault. The brunt of this fell upon the 7th Hussars who were struck by a hail of fire. Both the tanks carrying the rear-link wireless to Brigade Headquarters were knocked out, in "C" Squadron Major J. Congreve had his wireless microphone shot away so only part of his squadron received his orders to move, and in "B" Squadron Major Younger's tank was disabled and he himself wounded—in a few moments only two tanks of this squadron were left in action.

Not long afterwards a shell struck the turret of the Commanding Officer's tank and Colonel Byass was killed.

Major Fosdick took over command, the Regiment being by this time reduced to only twelve tanks, several of which had already been hit. By now they were cut off from the remainder of the Brigade and surrounded, but they fought their way out under the dust raised by all the shelling and the black clouds of smoke billowing up from the numerous burning tanks which covered the battlefield. It was not until next day that the survivors were able to rejoin their Brigade, for they ran out of petrol, and it was only by good fortune and much skill on the part of the officer in command of the petrol lorries that they were replenished.

The 2nd Royal Tanks under Lieutenant-Colonel R. F. E. Chute were attacked by about fifty tanks. Others that had passed through the 7th Hussars fell upon Battalion Headquarters and "S" Company of the Rifle Brigade where they came up against the two-pounder anti-tank guns of the 3rd R.H.A. under Lieutenant G. Ward Gunn and the 25-pounders of the 60th Field Regiment. Both these German attacks were beaten off, and the Panzers drove on to the escarpment east of the Support Group and rallied there to refill with petrol and ammunition. It was plain that this was only a temporary pause and that a new attack would shortly develop.

This was preceded by dive-bombing attacks and unusually heavy artillery support. In the Rifle Brigade Headquarters two of the three vehicles were at once set on fire, and five Crusader tanks coming to their support were knocked out almost as soon as they appeared. There then remained only the two 2-pounder anti-tank guns, portées on Chevrolet chassis, under Lieutenant Ward Gunn, and a Bofors anti-aircraft gun under Lieutenant P. McSwiney, all without armour protection and all out-ranged by the German guns. On this small party of British gunners the enemy concentrated all their fire—artillery, mortars, machine-guns and tanks—but the crews fought back and picked off the German tanks one by one. The Bofors was knocked out and one 2-pounder destroyed; on the other all the crew were killed or wounded. Together with Major B. Pinney, the Battery Commander, and with Sergeant Gray acting as loader, Lieutenant Ward Gunn got this last gun into action again. Despite the flames from the burning vehicle which might have exploded the ammunition at any moment, they went on fighting. After firing a few more rounds, Lieutenant Ward Gunn was killed and the gun so badly damaged as to become unusable.

Gunner Turner drove the portée out of action with the gun still in flames, and the dead and wounded on the back of his vehicle. Another gun was fitted and the portée then drove back into action. Sad to relate, Major Pinney was killed the next day. The posthumous award of the Victoria Cross was made to Lieutenant Ward Gunn, and if Major Pinney had been similarly honoured it would have been richly deserved.

While this was going on, the guns of the 60th Field Regiment went on firing despite a mounting toll of casualties, and the men of the Rifle Brigade were pinned down in their shallow trenches, but again the enemy were beaten back. The whole area had been under incessant artillery fire and the vehicles of the forward transport echelons had become scattered as they moved about to avoid either accurate enemy shelling or approaching enemy tanks. In the Aid Post Captain Foster of the R.A.M.C. had continued to go about his work regardless of the shells falling round him or the solid shot that from time to time ricocheted past. General Gott had earlier realized that the 7th Armoured Brigade had been too badly knocked about to be capable any more of giving adequate support to the position, and he had ordered the 4th and 22nd Brigades forward. The former were held up by a German anti-tank gun screen and the latter were delayed owing to some confusion in the orders.

Between 3 and 4 o'clock in the afternoon the Germans attacked again. By this time the 7th Armoured Brigade could muster only forty battle-worthy tanks, mostly those of the 2nd Royal Tanks, but help was coming from the other two Brigades. About 5 p.m., when the light was beginning to fail, the enemy were within a thousand yards of the Support Group Headquarters which was being shelled and was also getting the "overs" from the tank battles. Brigadier Campbell, who had been in all the thickest part of the fighting all day on foot or in his car, led forward the dozen surviving tanks of the 6th Royal Tanks, standing up in his car and holding aloft his blue scarf. Within five minutes seven of these tanks were blazing wrecks, but this gallant effort checked the enemy and held them long enough for darkness to fall and put an end to their assaults.

In spite of the weight of their attacks, the Afrika Korps had failed to shake the hold of the Support Group on Sidi Rezegh airfield or the escarpments to north and south of it. On the other hand, Rommel had severely battered the 7th Armoured Brigade and had held off the other two Armoured Brigades for most of the day.

General Gott had halted the advance of the 5th South African Brigade about ten miles south of Sidi Rezegh in order to prevent them from getting involved in the tank battles, and the 70th Division, coming out from Tobruk, had not advanced far enough to affect the main engagement. For these successes the price Rommel had to pay was the denuding of his frontier positions of their mobile troops, with the consequence that the 4th Indian Division had enveloped Sidi Omar and the New Zealanders had reached Bardia and cut the communications of the enemy troops in the frontier zone. Rommel's rapid concentration of his armour (although he inflicted much damage on the British armour) was not going to turn out to be, in the long run, such a very good move after all.

*The Battle of Sidi Rezegh—Second Day*                    *November 22nd*
     When day dawned the defenders on the ridge could see, to the north, about three miles from them, a large concourse of enemy vehicles, including about eighty tanks. Brigadier Campbell was with the guns of the 60th Field Regiment, who were by then short of both officers and men, and he himself helped to turn the trails of the guns so as to engage this target which light of the new day revealed. The fire thus quickly brought down caused the Germans to disperse, but they soon struck back. Shortly after 9 a.m. the Brigadier was again in his car flying his blue scarf and leading forward a squadron of the 2nd Royal Tanks. There had been more losses among the officers, including a Battery Commander, Major Sir H. B. Shiffner, and Brigadier Campbell perched himself on the wing of a derelict Italian aircraft and directed the fire himself. The Regiment was still bringing fire down on the main road and the German artillery made every effort to knock out their observation posts.
     Soon after 1 p.m. the German tanks moved off at high speed to the west. They swung round the edge of the ridge, turned east and attacked the flank and rear of the position occupied by Colonel de Salis' force. Such anti-tank weapons as the troops possessed proved completely ineffective. "B" Company of the Rifle Brigade, under Major Viscount Garmoyle, were soon involved. "A" and "C" Companies of the K.R.R.C. were overwhelmed though Second-Lieutenant O. H. Newton's Platoon held out till dark. Once again, the 60th Field Regiment made desperate efforts to hold the attack and again Brigadier Campbell was there helping to turn the guns in the new direction.
     "D" Company were at first somewhat better off as they were

further away and had some support from tanks, but as a result of this they soon found themselves in the middle of a tank-*v.*-tank battle. The Commanding Officer rallied such men as could be gathered together and they took up a position in a wadi, but they had not been there long when a wave of German half-track carriers appeared and they were overwhelmed too. Only a handful of officers and men rallied at main Battalion Headquarters that night; they included some anti-tank guns and their crews who had been ordered back by Colonel de Salis just before the end.

While the German attack on the forward troops was in progress the 22nd Armoured Brigade, numbering 79 tanks, arrived and was faced with the task of keeping the enemy off the remainder of the Support Group and the gun positions. "The Regiments fought magnificently," says the War Diary, "and though greatly out-numbered and out-ranged, fought on and never gave the Germans an opportunity to close with the Support Group or the artillery." Brigadier Campbell, who had been driving about the battlefield all the morning in his un-armoured motor-car, then appeared on the scene to guide the 4th Armoured Brigade into the fight. In his open staff car with Major R. A. Eden, the commander of "M" Battery, and with a portée of the Battery on each side, he led the tanks into action. The 3rd Royal Tanks and the 5th Royal Tanks were at once closely engaged, but their Light tanks were quite unsuitable for fighting against the German tanks and it was beyond their powers greatly to influence the battle. Nevertheless Brigadier Campbell was among them on foot directing their fire and inspiring them by his wonderful example. At 4.30 p.m. he was wounded, fortunately not badly, and was brought back to his Headquarters on the back of a tank.

By then there was nothing for it but to give the order for the survivors of the Support Group and the Armoured Brigades to withdraw. Troop by Troop the Artillery retired; the last Troops of the 60th Field and the 3rd R.H.A. seemed doomed with the advancing German infantry almost on them, but they continued firing. A small force of British tanks appeared and halted the enemy long enough to enable the guns to get away. The 22nd Brigade had but thirty-four tanks left, and they were formed into a composite Regiment under Colonel Carr and moved at once to support the South Africans while Brigade Headquarters joined the Support Group Headquarters.

For the unfortunate 4th Armoured Brigade the troubles of the

day were by no means over, for soon after dark, just as the Brigade
was about to form leaguer, a large force from the 15th Panzer
Division came upon them. The area was illuminated with flares
and about thirty tanks with a large number of infantry charged
into the assault. Most of Brigade Headquarters were killed, wounded
or captured and a similar fate befell the 8th Hussars whose War
Diary describes November 22nd as "a disastrous day". After three-
quarters of an hour of close-quarter fighting only six tanks were
left, and they were withdrawn by Major P. Sandbach and Captain
Threlfall. The Commanding Officer, Colonel Cripps, was taken
prisoner. In a report some days later, the Medical Officer, Captain
J. Heycock, said,"sparks then began to fly—machine-gun, tommy-
gun and tank shot poured into the leaguer from all sides, and
German soldiers rushed in with tommy-guns. A splendid fight was
put up, but the whole leaguer was full of Germans." Captain
Heycock collected the wounded and tried at intervals through the
night to persuade the Germans to take them to a hospital. Early in
the morning they were removed in a captured A.C.V., but soon
afterwards they came under the fire of our own tanks and were
transferred to an ambulance. This, luckily, ran into a party of
New Zealanders who rescued them from the enemy.

About 10 p.m., while the 8th Hussars' fight was still going on,
the 5th Royal Tanks came up to help, but they ran into another
enemy force and were involved in confused fighting at a range of
only a hundred yards. After inflicting some loss, the enemy withdrew.

This night action had resulted in the loss of many Headquarter
vehicles, and communications, both to the Brigade from Division
and within the Brigade itself, were interrupted for many hours.

The situation at midnight was that the remains of the Support
Group were in a position south of the airfield, and the 4th Brigade,
much scattered, was near them. Six miles to the south-west were the
7th Brigade, now reduced to twelve tanks, protecting the rear of the
Division. The 22nd Brigade had about forty tanks and were three
miles west of the 7th, and a couple of miles further south were the
South Africans who had themselves been engaged with strong
enemy forces and had sustained heavy losses.

The 70th Division had made some progress towards el Duda
during the day, but their operations had again not been near
enough to influence the 7th Armoured Division's battle. The
XIIIth Corps had continued their advance, and during the night

22nd/23rd the 6th New Zealand Brigade with a squadron of "I" tanks made an exhausting march and reached a point fifteen miles east of Sidi Rezegh where they ran into the main Headquarters of the Afrika Korps, capturing most of the operations staff.

For his actions on these two days Brigadier Campbell was awarded the Victoria Cross. The citation, after mentioning what has been narrated above, concluded "throughout these two days his magnificent example and his utter disregard of personal danger were an inspiration to his men and to all who saw him. His brilliant leadership was the direct cause of the very heavy casualties inflicted on the enemy. In spite of his wound, he refused to be evacuated and remained with his command where his outstanding bravery and consistent determination had a marked effect in maintaining the splendid fighting spirit of those under him."

*November 23rd*

This was a day of hard, confused and scattered fighting. The German plan envisaged a move of the 15th Panzer Division, with the tank Regiment of the 21st Panzers under command, to join up with the Italians at el Gubi. The combined force was then to move north-east and, like a line of beaters, drive the British onto the positions of the 21st Panzers.

There was a heavy morning mist which did not clear until 7 a.m. Soon afterwards the 15th Panzers started their movement and very shortly ran into the right rear of the 7th Armoured Division, the tail of the 5th South African Brigade and the head of the 1st South African Brigade. The combination of the mist, the disorganization of command resulting from the events of the previous evening and the fact that the Germans appeared from an unexpected direction led to the British being surprised. However, the enemy also were surprised, for they had expected to pass to the south of their opponents.

The Germans were engaged by whomever was nearest, the whole battle taking place in the middle of a vast assembly of "soft" vehicles belonging to every formation, many of which became scattered, thus adding to the confusion. The Support Group tried to withdraw south, but by no means all were able to get away. Among those lost was Captain Foster who had so distinguished himself during the two previous days, and with him went two Chaplains who were helping with the wounded. As the Support Group column moved south a German column moved parallel with them; there was shelling but no direct attack. "The Command vehicle as it withdrew under shell-fire resembled a London bus as, perched on the roof, were a dozen officers and men of the 22nd Brigade who had had their tanks knocked out the previous day and had been picked up during the night."

The Desert was covered by scores of vehicles all moving at their best speed. Brigadier Campbell, with what was left of his Support Group, "C" Squadron of the 11th Hussars and a dozen tanks of the 7th Hussars, performed tremendous feats in rallying the scattered drivers. He himself directed artillery fire when the forward observation officer was wounded. The 7th Hussars were closely engaged. Major Younger had his tank hit, and in the confusion of the dust and shelling and the burning vehicles they were probably fired on by both sides. That evening, their War Diary recorded "a bad end to a bloody day".

Meanwhile, the Germans shook themselves clear of the mêlée and rallied to the south-west, but one effect of their attack was to stop the move of the 1st South African Brigade who had intended to join the 5th Brigade. This proposed move was soon made more difficult by the appearance from the west of the Ariete Division who contented themselves with an observation rôle and did not attack. In the middle of the afternoon, however, the Germans, with a minimum of preparation, began what can only be described as a charge against the south flank of the 5th South African Brigade, and immediately a battle of intense ferocity broke out.

The 22nd Brigade went to the help of the South Africans. Major Walker's squadron of the 4th C.L.Y. went in again and again in efforts to hold the enemy back. "C" Battery of the 4th R.H.A. and the South African artillery poured in their fire, and then Colonel Carr led a squadron of the R.G.H. in what was described as "a glorious charge across the enemy's advance, every tank firing its hardest". By 4.30 the enemy were inside the South African leaguer. Colonel Carr's composite Regiment rallied and charged through, throwing the German right into disorder and enabling the main part of the South Africans to get away. "The final rush through the camp was thrilling. Colonel Carr was at the head. Towards the end his tank was set on fire, and he and Major Kidston got on to other tanks and went on. Major Kidston had his new tank knocked out and had to spend the night in the enemy's lines, getting out next morning on Lieutenant Melville's tank."

The losses of the 22nd Brigade, who had already been reduced to no more than a small composite Regiment, were proportionately severe, and about ten tanks were left on the field of battle. Thirty or forty enemy tanks had, however, been destroyed. Captain Rosekilly, the Technical Adjutant of the 4th C.L.Y., had been salving tanks in the leaguer when the action began, but he remained there throughout the battle and afterwards salved 150 lorries, found drivers, conducted them out through the enemy infantry and handed them over to the 1st South African Brigade; he then went back to try to salve more tanks.

During the night many stragglers found their way back. Amongst others were five tanks of Major Wilson's squadron of the 3rd Royal Tanks and five tanks of the 5th Royal Tanks, which had been surrounded and had run out of ammunition. Until dark, the crews hid, leaving the tanks to look like derelicts. During the night petrol was brought up, and by the aid of flares and wireless they were guided back.

Another aspect of the day's fighting is recorded in the annals of the 3rd R.H.A.: "At about 3 p.m. a force of sixty or eighty tanks was seen approaching from about 1,500 yards away; there was heavy artillery support and a smoke screen. The enemy concentrated their fire on two Troops, one of 'D' Battery and one of 'J', and one by one all the guns were knocked out except one of 'J',s which managed to withdraw in flames. Many casualties were sustained, but throughout the night survivors trickled back. Special praise is due to Major Stewart of 'D' Battery who, though wounded several times, rallied the guns again and again. Inexorably the enemy forces pressed on. All the remaining guns of the Regiment—four from 'D', four from 'J', and six from 'M'—now lined up on the left, the guns hub-cap to hub-cap, presenting a defiant wall of guns. The Regiment retired slowly at about two miles an hour engaging the enemy all the way. Each time a gun was hit the survivors would pile on to the next gun salvaging the precious ammunition. Finally, dark came and the action was broken off, leaving the sky lit with blazing tanks and vehicles. The Regiment claimed thirteen tanks for certain."

When night fell the 5th South African Brigade had ceased to exist as a fighting formation. About 2,300 men had returned to our lines out of the 5,700 of which the Brigade had consisted, but the bulk of the equipment of the Brigade had been lost. What was left of the 7th and 22nd Armoured Brigades were leaguered a short distance south of the Sidi Rezegh airfield, with the 4th

Brigade south-east of them. At Gabr Saleh were the Support Group, now greatly depleted in numbers. Heavy as had been the losses of the Division during the past three days, the enemy had suffered heavily too, particularly in officers, and on the 23rd alone they lost seventy tanks, a loss that was to have a considerable effect on the future course of the operations.

During the day the New Zealanders had got to within six miles of Sidi Rezegh and were at Point 175. The 4th New Zealand Brigade, who had captured the landing ground at Gambut, were at Bir Chetla, ten miles to the east of their colleagues.

## Reflections

So ended the first phase, and the fiercest, of Operation "Crusader". For the 7th Armoured Division it had been a gruelling time and the remembrance of much gallantry on the part of many individuals and units did nothing to atone for the long list of casualties. The Division had drawn on to itself the full might of Rommel's armour, both sides had suffered severely, but, although the Division had been worsted tactically, or perhaps it would be more correct to say technically, it proved to be a short-lived satisfaction to the enemy, for his losses had been such that he could not for much longer stand against the attacks of the Eighth Army. As General Gotts aid after the battle, "The Germans never again massed such quantities of heavy tanks nor did they ever attack our armoured forces with such ferocity."

For the men of the Division the most disheartening recollection about the past operations was the misfortune that had befallen the armour. Everyone had seen the British shot bouncing off the German tanks, and the enemy knocking out the Crusaders and Light tanks at ranges far beyond the limits of the miserable 2-pounder gun that the War Office had been so extremely ill-advised to adopt as the principal armament against German tanks. Even outside the armour there was no anti-tank gun that could worry a German tank except at point-blank range. It is pitiful to contemplate the situation in which the infantry had to be placed, deprived of a single weapon with which to protect themselves against what was known long before the war to be Germany's principal arm. Not even an adequate telescopic sight was available.

We had had more tanks than the enemy, the operation had been brilliantly prepared, full surprise had been achieved, the country favoured tank action and the side with the most tanks, and the troops had fought with much gallantry. Yet we had been driven back on the south flank because the Army was supplied with tanks and guns of markedly inferior type to those of their opponents.

### "CRUSADER"—SECOND ROUND

*November 24th to December 1st, 1941*

*Rommel's "Raid".*

Despite the success won by the German tanks against the British armour, Rommel's position on the morning of the 24th was not an easy one. Along the Trigh Capuzzo he was faced by the advancing New Zealanders; to the south was the bulk of the British tank force, battered but capable of a come-back if left quiet for a few days to refit. Behind him was the 70th Division endeavouring to fight its way out of Tobruk towards the relieving troops. In the frontier zone the Germans and Italians were being attacked by strong forces that might prove a serious menace. Rommel had the strength to inflict at least a severe reverse against any one of these opponents, but it seems probable that he was not fully aware of the extent of his tank losses on the previous day, and also that he mistakenly thought he had completely eliminated the XXXth Corps.

He made a daring decision, though hardly a wise one in view of his lack of reserves—to drive through the XXXth Corps area to the frontier and beyond, creating as much havoc as he could, with the intention of so damaging the Lines of Communication of the Eighth Army that the Army Commander would be forced to order a general retreat.

Moving down the Trigh el Abd in a number of columns of all arms, the Germans reached the frontier wire in the neighbourhood of Sheferzen by nightfall. Thanks to the secure air cover provided by the R.A.F. and the skilful way the supply dumps were concealed, the enemy force was ignorant of their locations. The advancing troops only missed them by narrow margins; had their positions been known it is inconceivable that they would have been passed by, for on them depended the survival of the greater part of the Eighth Army. The southernmost Germans actually passed through the water-point of one of the Forward Maintenance Centres.

On the 25th part of Rommel's force drove into Egypt, creating

F

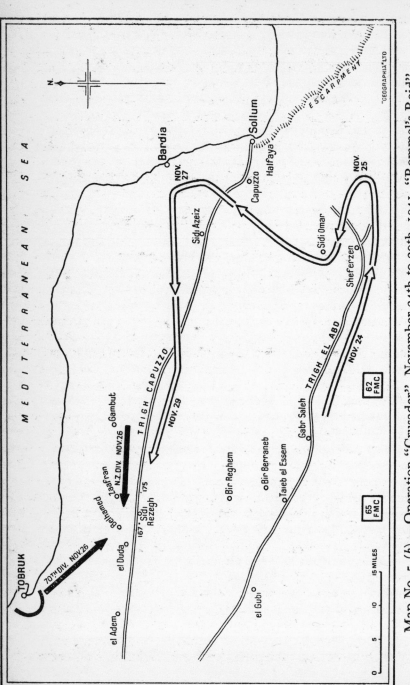

Map No. 5 (b).—Operation "Crusader", November 24th to 29th, 1941. "Rommel's Raid"

*Note:* The movements of 7th Armoured Division are not shown. The Division was operating in most of the area between the Trigh Capuzzo and the Trigh El Abd

consternation and alarm over a wide area; others turned north and south. They were harried on the ground and from the air, and there was little the German air force could do to help them. On the 26th the whole force turned north for Bardia, and on the next day they swung west for Sidi Rezegh where they were badly needed.

*Activities of the Division*                              *November 24th*
The 7th Armoured Division was not deeply involved in this German operation, except that as the enemy columns went along they were shadowed by the 11th Hussars who sent back a continuous stream of information until they ran out of wireless range.

The 4th and 22nd Brigades, now reduced to only thirty-five and twenty-one tanks respectively, were ordered to concentrate in an area about five miles south of the New Zealanders at Point 175. From 10 o'clock in the morning a large number of columns were reported moving south-east, south and south-west. Some of them turned out to be friendly but the whole situation was obscure. Two of the largest columns were composed of about fifty tanks and three hundred lorries each, and these continued to move south-east all day.

The northern column was engaged by the Support Group and the southern by the survivors of the 7th Armoured Brigade under Brigadier Davy whose Headquarters had been attacked during the morning; he had with him the four surviving tanks of the 8th Hussars. These two enemy columns were soon seen to be followed by other columns including many tanks. Brigadier Davy continued to shadow the southern column and a running fight took place which continued until dark by which time the enemy were at Sheferzen. Both the other Armoured Brigades attacked and harried German columns. A column from the Support Group under Colonel Currie was ordered to move during the night to safeguard No. 62 F.M.C. and the rest of the Group closed with Brigadier Davy's small force nearby.

*November 25th*
The orders for the day were for the 22nd Armoured Brigade to come under command of the XIIIth Corps in order to assist the New Zealanders, and they were lightly engaged in the afternoon. The rest of the Division were to concentrate in the neighbourhood of No. 62 F.M.C. while the three Armoured Car Regiments were

to operate on the general line Sheferzen-el Gubi from first light, the 4th South Africans on the right, the K.D.G.s in the centre and the 11th on the left. These Regiments were extremely busy all day and sent back a torrent of valuable information, that from the South Africans earning special mention.

For the rest it was a day of comparative inactivity but only to the extent that there were no major engagements and no heavy casualties. The 4th Armoured Brigade was sent during the morning to support the 1st South African Brigade at Taieb el Essem where the latter had just repulsed an attack by fifty tanks. The arrival of the Armoured Brigade deterred the enemy from renewing his efforts and caused him to retire to the north in the evening, but there could be no question of pursuit, for the fatigue of the tank crews was such that many drivers were continually falling asleep. Columns from the Support Group under Colonels Currie, 4th R.H.A., Wilson, 3rd R.H.A., Mayfield, Scots Guards and Douglas, Rifle Brigade spent the day harassing the enemy and in the evening they caused a good deal of damage to the troops withdrawing from the South African position where they had been repulsed.

Not the least important of the day's activities was the collection of damaged or bogged tanks from various parts of the battlefield. The 11th Hussars record that no less than seventy were recovered in the southern part of the area on this one day, while Major Wainman's squadron, who were operating with the 22nd Brigade south of Sidi Rezegh, were similarly occupied and competing with parties of Germans and Italians engaged on the same task. This valuable work meant that a number of dismounted crews could be sent into action again. Later in the war, the process of recovery became a well-organized and well-equipped feature of all operations. In the Desert where there was always a shortage of tanks and transport, and where the supply of new equipments was never easy, recovery was of vital importance.

Away to the north the New Zealand Division under General Freyberg was still battling forward. They took Zaafran early on the 25th and Belhamed that night. To the east the enemy were being hammered by the R.A.F. round Sheferzen and the determined German attacks on Sidi Omar were firmly held by the 4th Indian Division who reduced the strength of the 21st Panzer Division to ten tanks. The German situation was, in fact, deteriorating, for to the west the XXXth Corps and the South Africans were consolidating their hold on the Trigh el Abd, and to the north-west the troops breaking out from Tobruk constituted a menace that Rommel could not disregard much longer.

## November 26th

On the northern portion of the battlefield matters went well this day. The 6th New Zealand Brigade, although failing in a dawn attack to capture Sidi Rezegh, succeeded with a night assault, following which a battalion of the 4th New Zealand Brigade moved forward to el Duda which the 70th Division had taken in the evening. General Auchinleck was able to report to the Prime Minister that the news, though scanty, was good, and that Rommel's "raid" had "failed signally". The centre of interest now shifted from the Trigh el Abd to the Trigh Capuzzo, for, in order to get his armour back, Rommel now had to fight west and the New Zealanders were menaced by attack from the rear.

The Armoured Car Regiments advanced their line of patrols and when night fell the K.D.G.s had reached the Trigh Capuzzo and made contact with the 22nd Armoured Brigade near Bir Reghem. On the left the 11th Hussars fought a successful action and knocked out three enemy tanks and eighteen lorries from a column near el Gubi.

During the night 25th/26th the 4th Armoured Brigade, now numbering forty tanks, had escorted the 1st South African Brigade to No. 65 F.M.C. After replenishing at midday they moved north to the area of Bir Berraneb and reached there as it was getting dark, having done some damage to the enemy on the way. At the F.M.C. they had been reinforced by thirty Light tanks and nine anti-tank guns. The 22nd Brigade were also strengthened by the addition of ten Cruisers brought forward under Lieutenant-Colonel Shepherd of the 4th Hussars. The Support Group continued its task of harassing and in the evening returned to Gabr Saleh.

## November 27th

The patrol line of the Armoured Cars was advanced further and before the morning was out the K.D.G.s were reporting a very large enemy column five miles long moving west. The 4th Armoured Brigade, now numbering sixty-five tanks, and the 22nd with fifty tanks, were ordered to move forward to the attack. Covered by a screen of tanks, the enemy force was moving in four columns amounting to between 1,500 and 2,000 lorries. During the progress of this huge army along the Trigh they narrowly missed swamping the combined Headquarters of the two British Corps; it was only due to the efforts of some of "B" Squadron of the 11th Hussars, assisted by some tanks from the 22nd Brigade, that this mass of Headquarter vehicles was able to get away unmolested.

About 2 p.m. the 22nd Brigade attacked the head and the 4th Brigade the southern flank of this enemy force. Both Brigades immediately became heavily engaged with tanks, anti-tank guns and artillery. A fierce fight lasted until dark by which time much damage had been done to the enemy and many casualties, both in men and in vehicles, inflicted. The Germans were brought to a halt and parties broke off to the east, north and north-west. Twice during the afternoon the R.A.F. bombers came down and added to the confusion and damage. During the fight Colonel Carr was wounded when his tank was knocked out. The R.H.A. came in for much praise for their excellent shooting, and when the enemy were finally halted about 5 p.m. they had little ammunition left. This action by the two Armoured Brigades seems to have prevented the Germans from attacking the New Zealand Division in the rear. As night fell, the two Brigades pulled back and leagured just to the south of the scene of these successful operations.

The Support Group spent the day harassing enemy columns in the frontier area. The remnants of the 7th Armoured Brigade and the 1st Battalion K.R.R.C. left the Division to return to Cairo for re-organization, taking with them 300 prisoners, and the 11th Hussars were withdrawn to No. 65 F.M.C., their reconnaissance area being taken over temporarily by the 4th South Africans.

In the Sidi Rezegh area things did not go so well, for an enemy counter-attack broke through and separated the 70th Division from the 4th New Zealand Brigade, one of whose battalions had joined the 70th. Ammunition and supplies ran short, but after dark a column led by Colonel G. Clifton, the Chief Engineer of the XXXth Corps, with an escort of the 8th Hussars, got through. The 5th New Zealand Brigade, back at Sidi Azeiz, were cut off from the remainder of their Division and with the bulk of the German armour separating them it seemed unlikely that they could get forward. The New Zealanders had had heavy losses and the only infantry available to reinforce them were the 1st South African Brigade. It was decided to move them forward the next day to Point 175; the 7th Armoured Division were to endeavour to hold off the German armour, and the New Zealanders and the 70th Division were to try to join hands again.

*November 28th*

During the night 27th/28th the survivors of the huge enemy column had leaguered very close to the supply columns of the New Zealanders, but fortunately this was discovered by a patrol of the 11th Hussars who got warning to the latter in time before the German tanks got on the move.

During the forenoon of the 28th the 4th Brigade, now numbering sixty tanks, and the 22nd Brigade, composed of a composite Regiment of thirty tanks under Lieutenant-Colonel Jago, were continuously engaged with enemy columns. In the early afternoon they were covering the northward move of the 1st South African Brigade towards Sidi Rezegh. They were then heavily attacked by at least seventy tanks and fighting went on till sundown. Although they held their ground and cost the enemy dear, they themselves lost many tanks, Colonel Jago was wounded and Major Kidston took command. The skeleton squadron of the 2nd R.G.H. under Major W. A. B. Trevor did a lot of execution among the enemy. Well as they fought, they were consistently out-matched by the armour and guns of the Germans.

The Support Group had a column out again under Colonel Currie, harassing the enemy along the Trigh Capuzzo. On their way out they had an engagement with a mixed force that included about forty tanks thought to be from the Italian Ariete Division; these they dispersed and they then operated on the Trigh with much success. They were told to continue this good work next day and were given the 11th Hussars, less one squadron, to assist.

The rear of the New Zealanders was still exposed and it seemed that the enemy design was to surround them and the 70th Division and so again close the ring round Tobruk. The 7th Armoured Division had at least prevented Rommel from attacking the New Zealanders with the bulk of his armour that day.

*November 29th*

About noon there were signs that the enemy were about to launch an attack on the New Zealanders at el Duda. The 7th Armoured Division was ordered to do all it could to prevent this, so General Gott moved the Armoured Brigades forward, the 4th with sixty tanks for Point 175 and the 22nd with twenty-four tanks to cover the right flank of the 4th. On the way, however, the 4th Brigade were attacked on the left and from the rear by about thirty or forty tanks, and their movement was halted. With its task of

covering the flank of the 4th, the 22nd were not able to remain in
close protection of the South African Brigade, so their move, also,
was forced to cease. By the time this action was over it was clear that
the tank losses of these two Armoured Brigades had been so heavy
that they could no longer fight as separate formations, so they were
amalgamated as the 4th Brigade under Brigadier Gatehouse.

The Support Group was busily engaged all day harassing and
driving north various parties of the enemy along the Trigh Capuzzo.
During the night a squadron of the 8th Hussars under Major
Phillips escorted a large supply column which had been assembled
at Divisional Headquarters up to the New Zealanders whom it
reached at dawn with no loss.

By engaging the enemy all day the Division had again prevented
an attack on the New Zealanders by the main German tank force.
Nevertheless they were hard pressed, but they beat off all attacks and
even gained ground and captured General Ravenstein, the commander of the 21st Panzer Division. The corridor to Tobruk was
open once more and Headquarters XIIIth Corps moved into the
town. Both the 7th and the New Zealand Divisions were, however,
appreciably weaker as a result of the day's fighting.

*November 30th*

The new 4th Armoured Brigade was given the tasks of keeping
open a corridor to the New Zealanders west and south-west of
Point 175 and of covering the 1st South African Brigade. The latter
were unable to reach their objective until dusk owing to enemy
resistance. While the new 4th Armoured Brigade Headquarters was
being organized, the Regiments moved north of Bir Reghem to
engage a portion of the Ariete Division. "This was a very pleasant
day in which nineteen enemy tanks were destroyed and set on fire."
Most of the damage was done by Captain Doyle's squadron of the
5th Royal Tanks who got round the enemy's flank; they had no
casualties.

The Support Group were again at work north and south of the
Trigh Capuzzo and as far afield as Gambut, doing much damage.
During the afternoon the New Zealanders were very heavily attacked
and lost Sidi Rezegh, and other enemy attacks, which went on for
most of the night, were made on el Duda, Belhamed and Zaafran.

A special task was given to the 4th South African Armoured Car
Regiment under Lieutenant-Colonel D. S. Newton-King. This was
to raid the Gazala–Acroma area and to prevent the supply of petrol

to the enemy. They returned from their raid on December 2nd, having destroyed much petrol and many vehicles and having had a widespread effect on the enemy's morale. Unfortunately, however, they had suffered many casualties from heavy and sustained air attacks, but the destruction they caused was to affect Rommel's plans in a few days' time.

*December 1st*

The 4th Armoured Brigade, by now made up to over a hundred tanks, were ordered to move to the New Zealand leaguer south-east of Belhamed. The Brigade crossed the Sidi Rezegh airfield under heavy fire and moved down the escarpment to the leaguer. This was being shelled and many vehicles were on fire. As the New Zealanders withdrew eastwards the tanks formed up to cover them. The shelling intensified and soon the enemy attacked with tanks from the south and south-west. Part of the Brigade took up a position on top of the escarpment and remained there until the infantry were clear and they themselves were nearly surrounded when they pulled out at top speed and got away. Although by then most of the 4th New Zealand Brigade had been over-run, the survivors of General Freyberg's great Division were protected from further attack and enabled to rally without molestation. The 4th Brigade then leaguered near Bir Reghem.

The Support Group, which had three columns out, watched the flanks of the South African Brigade during the day and were engaged with many enemy parties.

As reference has been made once or twice to confusion and difficulties in the identification of friend from foe, it may be of interest to quote the 7th Armoured Brigade's orders on the subject for November. "All armoured vehicles which have wireless masts will wear pennants in the position of the day. Tanks wear a red-and-white sign, but some newly arrived may not have had them painted on. Armoured cars have no colour sign, but they show they are friendly by holding a flag out to their right." But with the immense clouds of dust thrown up by the fighting and the frequent shimmering haze, the problem of identification was almost insoluble.

With the withdrawal of the New Zealand Division on December 1st ended the Second Battle of Sidi Rezegh. They had had severe losses and so had the 7th and 70th Divisions, but the determined resistance of the British (which includes Dominion) infantry had made Rommel's situation impossible and his losses had been such as to force him to the conclusion that he could no longer carry on the investment of Tobruk.

The actions in which the Division had been engaged can be summed up in the words of the Support Group War Diary written on November 30th: "thus the month ended. On more than one occasion it has seemed that the battle was lost; fortune had visited both sides, but not to stay. This constant change of fortune was the chief feature of the whole battle. Indeed, even as the battle on the 30th appeared to be favouring the Support Group, the New Zealand Division was being over-run near the littered, smoky field of Sidi Rezegh where the Support Group had experienced its most savage struggle of the war and had given as good as it got—as witness the German graves at the foot of de Salis Ridge".

## "CRUSADER"—THIRD ROUND

### December 2nd to 10th, 1941

Both contestants were now suffering from the gruelling effects of the fighting of the past fortnight. In the coastal area the British garrison of Tobruk was again cut off, but so were the German and Italian garrisons of Bardia and Halfaya. The British had had heavy losses, but so had the enemy.

In the Desert the area was covered by abandoned vehicles which both sides were striving to collect and repair, while supply columns were feverishly endeavouring to bring forward materials of all sorts to build up again the reserves without which the battle could not be continued. The 7th Armoured Division was woefully weak, but they kept up their activity with Jock Columns who never ceased harassing the enemy over the whole of this wide area. These columns inflicted tremendous damage on the enemy as captured documents later testified. A good many guns that had been lost were also recovered. Identifications, both of men and of vehicles, had become even more difficult. By now all uniforms had assumed a dull Desert colour and vehicles were equally hard to identify, for both sides were using ones taken from their opponents, as well as captured weapons. The task of any small party of armoured cars or from a column in identifying any troops they might meet was rendered very hard.

The phase of the operations that lasted from December 2nd to 10th saw the withdrawal of the enemy from the perimeter of Tobruk, leaving his garrisons in the east isolated. The British attempted to cut him off by a thrust from el Gubi towards Acroma. For this operation the XXXth Corps consisted of the 7th Armoured Division (now only the 4th Armoured Brigade and a much reduced Support Group), the 4th Indian Division, the 1st South African Brigade and five Armoured Car Regiments. The first objective was el Adem.

While the XIIIth Corps attacked with the 70th Division from the positions they had gained in their sortie, the XXXth Corps were to capture el Gubi with the Indians and then to advance north to seize the ridges north and south of the Trigh Capuzzo west of el Adem. The 7th Armoured Division were to be so positioned as to be able to attack Rommel's tanks if they tried to interfere. Armoured cars were to raid his supply dumps.

*December 2nd*

The activities of the day were confined to the armoured cars which kept continuous watch on the enemy and reported the preparation of defensive positions in several places. The 4th Brigade stayed in the area of Bir Berraneb. During the day the 22nd Guards Brigade (Brigadier J. C. O. Marriott) and the 11th Indian Infantry Brigade were put under command. General Gott's intention was to secure the ground south of el Adem in order to bring the enemy armour to battle; to do that, he had first to make good the ground north-west of el Gubi. The launching of these operations had to await orders from Corps. The 2nd R.H.A. recorded that by this date they had fired 900 rounds per gun and travelled 500 miles since November 18th.

*December 3rd and 4th*

The plan was for the 11th Indian Brigade supported by sixteen "I" tanks to capture the el Gubi position, and the 4th Armoured Brigade was to be positioned to the north-east to hold off the enemy armour; later, the 22nd Guards Brigade was to carry the attack on northwards.

On the 4th there was heavy fighting all day, both at el Gubi and at el Duda. In the south the Indians were unable to dislodge the Italian defenders, while in the north Rommel launched a series of attacks on the 70th Division who, however, held on to their positions.

Another armoured car raid was made to the west and a large quantity of petrol, diesel oil, ammunition and food was destroyed in a dump fifteen miles north-west of el Gubi. The 4th Brigade, who now mustered ninety-eight tanks, were engaged all day with enemy columns north of el Gubi and the Support Group harassed along the Trigh Capuzzo.

### December 5th

Rommel's retreat now began, helped by the surprisingly stout defence of el Gubi. It was a well-conducted withdrawal and never became a rout, and the German armour was handled with skill, generally behind a screen of anti-tank guns which our armour could not penetrate.

The Indian attacks on el Gubi continued but did not meet with full success, and by the end of the day the chances of cutting off Rommel's retreat were receding, for so long as the enemy held el Gubi they constituted a menace to the communications that could not be ignored. All day there was a steady westward movement of German tanks and transport along the Trigh Capuzzo and in other areas. The K.D.G.s reported large concentrations of troops south of el Adem.

### December 6th

Soon after daylight a large force of enemy tanks appeared to the north along the route that it had been intended that the 4th Indian Division should take. Whenever the 4th Armoured Brigade advanced to try to engage them, the enemy tanks retired behind a screen of anti-tank guns and the Brigade had not the resources to outflank them nor the technical strength to attack frontally.

Meanwhile, the Support Group columns had been ranging about the Trigh, and by midday they reported that the whole area east of Sidi Rezegh was clear of enemy. Soon afterwards they gained contact with the 70th Division. Colonel Wilson's column had made for the New Zealand hospital which had been in enemy hands, and there they recovered eight hundred wounded British prisoners, two hundred of whom were stretcher cases.

By the end of the day it was clear that the enemy was going to abandon the whole area and pull right back. His frontier troops were lost to him but the British had not the strength to outflank him and cut off his retreat. Not only was there not enough transport to lift the Indian Division forward, but there were not enough tanks to afford them protection on any long move. Besides, the Light tanks which now formed the majority in the 4th Brigade had a limit of only forty miles on one fill of petrol. This meant that they had to stop and re-fuel every twenty miles, for they had to keep a reserve for manœuvre in action. Any wide outflanking movement was therefore impossible, and a frontal attack was always met by a stronger force of anti-tank guns, against which the British tanks could do nothing. The superiority of the German tanks and guns still told.

*December 7th*

At 8 o'clock in the morning the leading Regiment of the 4th Brigade became engaged with a force of about forty tanks with the usual artillery support in which 250 rounds per gun were fired. The engagement went on all day; a good deal of transport was destroyed and a number of enemy tanks disabled. Again, the Support Group operated in the northern part of the area, and they made further contacts with the Tobruk garrison. The 4th R.H.A. record: "We fired hard again all day and captured many more Hun prisoners. We also recaptured about two hundred New Zealanders in the afternoon; also much loot and food."

*December 8th*

The 4th Brigade pushed on in a north-westerly direction, their opponents of the previous day having withdrawn during the night. Before long they ran up against an extensive enemy position along a ridge on the Trigh el Abd about ten miles from el Gubi. Efforts to outflank it from south or north, or to advance frontally were all repulsed; indeed, in the evening the Germans launched a counter-attack, which was halted by artillery fire.

The Support Group were engaged with tanks as well as the usual parties of infantry. Somewhat unwisely, their Headquarters had been congratulating themselves for some days on their freedom from air attack. About 10.15 on the morning of the 8th intensive air attacks were made on them, some aircraft coming as low as twenty feet to machine-gun individual vehicles, and, although its armour kept out the bullets, the Command vehicle had all its tyres punctured and a spare can of petrol that was on the back was set on fire.

*December 9th*

Again the enemy withdrew during the night and the 4th Armoured Brigade followed up in the morning. By noon they were in contact with a defensive position a few miles south and

south-east of Knightsbridge which was a large track junction twenty
miles west of el Adem. In an attack at 2.30 p.m. the Brigade gained
some valuable ground at the north end of this position and by
four o'clock they were on high ground overlooking el Adem. Soon
afterwards, Colonel Wilson's column from the Support Group came
up, and an attack was made on twenty German tanks that appeared
to be on their way to molest the 4th Indian Division's march. There
was much fighting until dark and the enemy were halted.

### December 10th

Columns from the Support Group, as well as the Armoured Car
Regiments, ranged over a wide area, for the enemy had withdrawn
to the Gazala line. By sundown the Indians had reached Acroma,
and patrols were fifteen miles west of there and nine miles west of
Knightsbridge. On the south flank of the Division the Royals had
relieved the K.D.G.s.

### Some Afterthoughts

For such as was left of the Division's armour a brief pause now
ensued. Of the operations of the past three weeks the following
words were written in the *Royal Armoured Corps Journal* seven
years later by an officer who had been present.

"To all who took part in it, and to those who watched it from
near and far, it had been an exhausting battle full of disappoint-
ments. The casualties had been heavy; we had lost a great many
prisoners and much equipment. Even to those few who had been
able to see the battle as a whole, it had been very difficult ever to
get a clear picture of the situation before another blow would fall
and confuse the situation anew. Many of the troops and the commanders had been fighting or moving without a break for three
weeks; most of them were utterly exhausted in body, mind and
nerves. Many mistakes were made, the greatest by Rommel. To
those who watched it anxiously from afar, the changes and chances
of the battle were inexplicable; they only knew the disappointment
of hopes buoyed up, only to be dashed again and again, so that when
victory came at last and Rommel's hold on Cyrenaica collapsed
they failed to appreciate the lion-hearted determination and
persistence that had won through in the end.

"To those who took part a bitter taste remained; those who
fought in tanks cursed those who sent them into battle, inferior in
armour and equipment and in tanks that broke down endlessly. The

infantry, with a sprinkling of useless anti-tank guns, looked to the tanks to protect them against enemy tanks, and were bitter at their failure to do so. The armoured commanders, hurrying from one spot to another to protect infantry from the threat of enemy tanks which did not always materialize, blamed the infantry for wearing out their tanks and crews by such a misuse of the decisive arm in Desert warfare.

"Above all the recrimination stood out the inspiring example of those who had braved all odds and won; Jock Campbell and many others at Sidi Rezegh; General Bernard Freyberg and his intrepid New Zealanders; 'Strafer' Gott, calm, decisive, undaunted, unwearied, ever-cheerful, a rock of strength to all above and below —these and many others, whose refusal to be beaten or to give up the struggle, however hopeless the outlook, must be remembered. That all which had been gained at such cost was lost six months later by many of the same men to whom victory was now due must not be allowed to obscure the remarkable feat of a victory snatched out of the jaws of disaster. More and better tanks and tank anti-guns were what we needed most. Had we had them many lives would have been saved and many would not have spent the next four years in the misery of prison camps."

## "CRUSADER"—LAST ROUND

### December 11th to 27th, 1941

This final phase of the operations saw the clearance of the enemy from Cyrenaica and carried the 7th Armoured Division back to the scene of their triumph in February 1941.

Up to the 16th Rommel held a defensive position stretching roughly south from Gazala. All the British troops who could be maintained forward were placed under command of the XIIIth Corps; they comprised the 4th Indian Division, a New Zealand Brigade, a Polish Brigade, the 22nd Guards Brigade and the 7th Armoured Division, who had only the much reduced Support Group and one Armoured Brigade, commanded first by the Headquarters of the 4th Brigade, then by the Headquarters of the 22nd Brigade.

### December 11th to 14th

Columns of the Support Group under Colonels Currie and Wilson and Major Lord Garmoyle carried out a number of operations, discovering the extent of the German position, putting in probing attacks and harassing generally. On the 16th an attempt was made by thirty tanks of the Royal Gloucestershire Hussars under Major Trevor to outflank the position to the south, but a highly mobile screen of anti-tank guns thwarted them. On the next day thirty Cruisers got round this south flank to attack from the west; they did some damage but lost nine tanks in the action.

On the same day the Guards Brigade drove the enemy from a defended position about six miles south of their main system, but that evening a strong counter-attack was delivered against the Indian Division north-west of Alam Hamza and they were forced back with considerable loss.

All the time, the armoured cars of the K.D.G.s, Royals and 11th Hussars operated far and wide in their usual tasks of collecting information and attacking such enemy as they could find.

The 14th was a quiet day. In the evening the 4th Armoured Brigade moved out to take up a position from which to operate next morning.

### December 15th and 16th

The 4th Brigade, with the Royals under command, started before dawn on the 15th with the intention of threatening the enemy's positions in the Gazala line by working round the south. The going was extremely bad and it was well on into the afternoon before they reached the area from which they intended to operate. It was then clear that the supply lorries would not be able to get up to them till well on into the following morning, so bad was the ground. Accordingly, they moved south to facilitate replenishment later. During the day there were further heavy attacks upon the Indians, on whose south flank the Support Group were operating.

On the 16th Rommel suddenly pulled out and began a retreat right back to Agedabia. The Royals fanned out again and sent a column to Tmimi. It was not until nearly noon that the 4th Brigade completed replenishing; they then advanced to the area Bir Temerad–Sidi Breghisc, but on the way they were bombed and attacked by tanks on the right flank, meeting at the same time a stretch of very rough ground. Until dusk they were in continuous action. One squadron attacked the Headquarters of the 15th Panzer Division and knocked out four tanks for the loss of one of their own.

*December 17th to 27th*

This was a frustrating period. Pursuit was difficult owing to the bad going for there had been heavy rain in places and even some flooding; attempts at cutting off the enemy as he retreated from Benghazi were therefore doomed to failure. By now there were four Armoured Car Regiments in the Division; the 12th Lancers were retained under Divisional control, while the Royals were put under the 4th Brigade, the K.D.G.s under the Support Group and the 11th Hussars with the Guards Brigade, now itself temporarily in the Division.

The administrative situation was an anxious one and its alternative solutions presented a puzzle worthy of the best administrative instructors at the Staff College. Briefly, the whole Division could be maintained up to one hundred miles from any Forward Maintenance Centre that was established, which, of course, took time. Alternatively, the Support Group and two armoured regiments, only, could be maintained as far as the Benghazi–Agedabia road, but only if the 22nd Armoured Brigade Headquarters and the rest of the armour did not move from Mechili (which had fallen on the 18th), and provided that an F.M.C. was set up there by the 21st.

This retreat of the Germans was no rout such as had characterized the Italian *débâcle* of the early months of the year. Throughout their retirement the enemy were never run off their feet, they always managed to retain rearguards strong enough to hit back hard, and as they pulled out of Benghazi they threw out a left flank guard of sufficient force to prevent interference with the main body.

Columns from the Support Group met resistance from flank and rear guards wherever they advanced. They recorded that the night march on the 19th/20th was the worst in anyone's memory, and that on the next night it was pitch dark, bitterly cold and the hills and wadis so steep and numerous as to raise petrol consumption to a dangerously high level. At 1.30 p.m. on the 22nd they were brought to a halt and unable to go on until they received 12,000 gallons of petrol—not far away some of the cars of the Royals had actually run out of petrol while in contact with the enemy. A small force was organized to continue the advance; this consisted of a squadron of the Royals, a company of the Rifle Brigade, a Troop of the 3rd R.H.A. and a detachment of the Royal Engineers all under command of Major A. H. Pepys of the Royals. They reached Benina and found a hundred enemy aircraft abandoned on the airfield. In spite of many difficulties the group covered over a hundred miles on the 22nd.

The Guards Brigade, who had now left Divisional command, reached Antelat on the 22nd, and after some sharp fighting advanced to Agedabia which they attacked on Christmas Day; unfortunately there was no armour available to support them and exploit their success owing to petrol shortage.

Meanwhile, on the 24th, the squadron of the Royals in Major Pepys' force entered Benghazi, and they were followed very shortly by the K.D.G.s who took over the town. On the 26th the 4th Indian Division arrived and assumed control. On the same day arrangements were made for Divisional Headquarters and the Support Group to return to the Delta, starting next day.

By now the latter were a mere skeleton of what they had been. The 1st K.R.R.C. had already been sent back to Egypt; the 2nd Rifle Brigade had only a small proportion of their establishment left, two companies had had to be amalgamated and fifty per cent of the officers had become casualties; the 60th Field Regiment had already left to be re-formed, and the 3rd and 4th R.H.A. had lost many experienced officers, N.C.O.s and men. But an even greater handicap, and one that increased every day, was the heavy loss of vehicles and equipment. Now there were only twelve carriers where there had been forty-four, guns were being towed by lorries and, worst of all, there was a serious shortage of wireless trucks.

The 3rd Royal Tanks were to hand over their tanks at Msus for the use of the 22nd Armoured Brigade, and were then to follow back to Egypt. The 11st Hussars remained under the command of the 22nd Guards Brigade and continued on operations until February.

After an uneventful journey Divisional Headquarters entered Cairo on January 3rd, 1942.

*　　　*　　　*　　　*　　　*

The enemy losses in Operation "Crusader" amounted to 13,000 Germans, 20,000 Italians and 300 tanks. The British and Imperial casualties were 2,908 killed, 7,300 wounded and 7,400 missing, a total of 17,700 and 270 tanks. Nine-tenths of the British casualty list came from the first month of the offensive.

## CHAPTER 4

*April to October, 1942*

# RETREAT AND DEFENCE

*Reference Maps—No. 2, page 34. No. 6, page 102. No 7, page 120*

## General Situation

DURING December 1941 events occurred in two different parts of the world that were to have far-reaching effects on the Desert campaign.

The outbreak of war with Japan caused the diversion to the Far East of substantial reinforcements that were on their way from the United Kingdom to the Middle East, two infantry divisions, anti-aircraft and anti-tank guns and four light bomber squadrons of the R.A.F. From the Middle East itself were transferred ten R.A.F. fighter or bomber squadrons, the 7th Armoured Brigade, and the 6th and 7th Australian Divisions. Those who have been so ready to criticize the Eighth Army for the misfortunes that befell it in the summer of 1942 would do well to bear in mind that while the strength of its opponent was being built up, its own strength was being depleted by the calls from other parts of the world.

Hard blows were struck against the Navy in the Mediterranean. Following the loss of the aircraft-carrier *Ark Royal* and the battleship *Barham* in November 1941, the battleships *Queen Elizabeth* and *Valiant* were seriously disabled by time-bombs in Alexandria harbour. The very next day a cruiser and a destroyer were lost on a new minefield while on their way to intercept an enemy convoy bound for Tripoli. This sudden weakening of naval strength enabled Rommel for the next few months to receive supplies with much more ease than had been the case in the past, and in addition the German and Italian air forces renewed their attacks on Malta with even greater intensity than before, thereby seriously curtailing the activity of the Navy from that important base. The enemy came back to the offensive in Cyrenaica, not only sooner than had been expected but in greater force.

With the departure of Divisional Headquarters for Cairo at the beginning of January, the part played by the Division in the winter operations ended, but several units remained in the forward area, the 2nd Rifle Brigade and others of the Support Group until the middle of the month and the K.D.G.s and 11th Hussars until February; the latter then departed for Iraq and Persia in April, not to return to the Desert until July.

During the early part of January it had been envisaged, both by the Prime Minister and by General Auchinleck, that the Eighth Army, now under command of Lieutenant-General N. M. Ritchie, would resume the offensive in February with a view to advancing to Tripoli. From January 12th to 21st Rommel's army remained in the Agheila position. Facing them were the Guards Brigade and the Support Group of the 1st Armoured Division with the rest of this Division about eighty miles away in the neighbourhood of Antelat. The Division was temporarily commanded by Major-General F. W. Messervy, the original commander, Major-General H. Lumsden, having been wounded almost as soon as he arrived in the forward area. Owing to the administrative situation the troops were widely dispersed, the front itself was weak and reserves could not be held close at hand.

On January 21st the German-Italian Army advanced. Reaching Msus some days later, Rommel struck both north-east to Mechili and north-west to Benghazi, and before the end of the month the port had to be abandoned. By February 4th the XIIIth Corps and the troops that had been sent forward to reinforce them were established on the Gazala line where the situation was stabilized until the end of May.

The enemy had deployed initially about 120 German tanks and 80 Italian against the 150 or so of the 1st Armoured Division whose losses in the fighting had amounted to about a hundred tanks. The British tanks were still inferior in reliability and gun-power to those of the Germans, and it is interesting to note that in one of his cables home General Auchinleck said "there are signs that personnel of the Royal Armoured Corps are in some instances losing confidence in their equipment".

## Changes in the Division

Meanwhile, on February 10th the Support Group held a Memorial and Thanksgiving Service in Cairo Cathedral. Before the Service began, General Auchinleck invested General Campbell with the ribbon of the Victoria Cross. Not long before, General Gott had been promoted to command the XIIIth Corps and General Campbell had succeeded him in command of the Division. The command of the Support Group went to Brigadier Renton, and soon after he took over the name of his command was changed to the 7th Motor Brigade.

A bitter blow befell the Division on February 26th when the Divisional Commander was killed in a motor accident. He had been in the thick of all the fighting from the beginning of the Campaign; wherever there was trouble he was always to be found; times without number he had set an example which inspired those with him to even greater exertions. The Army lost a man whom they could ill spare. He was buried in Cairo on the 28th. Not long after the Battle of Sidi Rezegh he had issued a special Order to his Support Group and he concluded it with what he called their Motto—"First in, last out, and ever ready to go on." For this great leader there could be no better epitaph.

General Messervy took over command. He had long been known to the Division as the commander of the successful 4th Indian Division until the short period when he had acted for General Lumsden.

*Return to the Desert*                                    *April 1942*

At the beginning of April the Division, now much re-organized, returned to the Desert and was concentrated for training south-west of Sidi Azeiz. Soon afterwards General Gatehouse left to take over command of the 10th Armoured Division, and Brigadier G. W. Richards, a former G.S.O.I. of the Division, took his place in command of the 4th Armoured Brigade.

On the 23rd of the month the Division moved up to an area south-west of el Adem, relieving the 1st Armoured Division. The 4th Armoured Brigade was concentrated between el Adem and Bir Hacheim and continued training. They were now equipped with a new American tank, the General Grant, mounting the 75-mm. gun. Each Armoured Regiment had twenty-four Grants and twenty Stuart Light tanks.

The armament of the Motor Battalions had also been greatly improved by the re-introduction of the medium machine-gun and the addition of anti-tank guns. At first the latter were 2-pounders, but in May 6-pounders began to be issued, though in few cases in time for the coming battles. The lack of 6-pounders turned out to be a very important factor and very many opportunities of destroying German tanks were missed on this account; even for those 6-pounders that were issued there was far too little ammunition available. In this forward area the 7th Motor Brigade was employed in the usual Jock Column rôles, keeping in touch with and harassing the enemy.

The Order of Battle in April 1942 is shown in Appendix I.

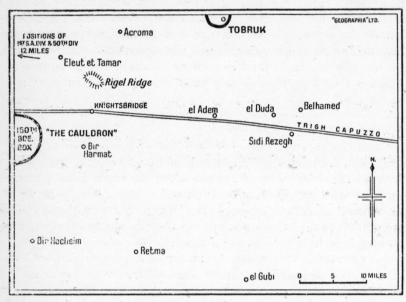

Map No. 6.—The Summer Campaign, May–June, 1942

*The First Phase*                                        *May 26th to June 1st*

The so-called "Gazala Line" consisted of a long and deep belt of wire and minefields interspersed by a number of fortified localities, known as "Boxes", which were generally held by a Brigade with supporting arms. The "Line" stretched from the sea at Gazala to Bir Hacheim forty miles to the south-east. Like all the Desert battles up till then, the first move was one round the southern flank and this took place on the evening of May 26th when Rommel's armour drove forward with the intention of seizing the el Adem–Sidi Rezegh area and moving on to take Tobruk.

Before considering the actions of the Division it is helpful to summarize the first week of the enemy's offensive. This was characterized by hard fighting. The resistance of the British and Allied troops prevented Rommel from achieving his aim and he soon found himself in difficulties over the problem of getting his supplies forward. He therefore cleared two lanes through the mine-belt in the southern portion of the "Line", one on each side of the Box held by the 150th Infantry Brigade of the 50th Division. On May 31st he withdrew all his tanks and transport into this area. Bombing by the R.A.F. and much severe fighting went on here and the area became known as "The Cauldron". Here, Rommel found himself in a serious situation, and the elimination of the 150th Brigade Box became a vital necessity. Savage attacks were launched by the Germans and by June 1st the position had been taken. Rommel described the resistance as "the toughest British resistance imaginable".

## Into Action Again

There are some gaps in the records, for the Divisional War Diary and other documents for the month of May up to the 27th were destroyed in order to avoid capture when Divisional Headquarters were over-run, as will be narrated later.

When Rommel's attack began the Division had under command, in addition to the 4th Armoured and the 7th Motor Brigades, the 1st Free French Brigade (General Koenig), the 29th Indian Infantry Brigade and the 3rd Indian Motor Brigade (Brigadier A. A. E. Filose). Divisional Headquarters were fifteen miles east of Bir Hacheim.

The 7th Motor Brigade had been broken up into columns at the beginning of May so as to support the K.D.G.s and the 4th South African Armoured Car Regiment who were also under Brigadier Renton's command and operated some seventy or a hundred miles to the west in the area of Segnali and west of Tengeder, almost forty miles south-west of Segnali. During the afternoon of the 26th reports came in from the South African Regiment, on the right, of the advance of strong enemy patrols. This movement continued all night south-east from the direction of Segnali, and the 7th Motor Brigade columns and the Armoured Car Regiments retired according to plan. By dawn on the 27th part of the 7th Motor Brigade was in the Retma Box. The 4th Armoured Brigade were about fifteen miles east of Bir Hacheim and seven miles north of Retma.

## THE BATTLE OF GAZALA

*May 27th*

From early in the morning reports had been coming in from the reconnaissance patrols that a large mass of about 400 tanks was on the move south of Bir Hacheim. Both the French Brigade and the Indian Motor Brigade reported large numbers of tanks to the south of them. About 7.30 the 4th Armoured Brigade, who were on the move to the south, ran into the 15th Panzer Division and suffered very heavy loss indeed. The War Diary of the 8th Hussars, who were commanded by Lieutenant-Colonel G. Kilkelly, records that an enemy force in overwhelming strength approached at 7.30. They were engaged first by "C" Squadron commanded by Major J. W. Hackett whose tank was knocked out almost immediately and he himself badly burned. "A" and "B" Squadrons then formed into line on either side of "C" and the brunt of the enemy assault fell upon "A", all but two of whose tanks were quickly put out of action. Soon afterwards all "B" Squadron's tanks became casualties as did all those in Regimental Headquarters. The enemy force was estimated to comprise over a hundred tanks with strong artillery and infantry support, and the Regiment claimed the destruction of thirty German tanks in their gallant fight. There were but two Grants left in the Regiment. In "A" Squadron all the officers were gone, but Captain H. Huth and ten men who had been taken prisoner escaped soon afterwards and re-joined. Regimental Headquarters lost the Adjutant, Captain J. N. A. Baldwin, and many men killed and others taken prisoner, among them Major J. W. Phillips, the second-in-command, who escaped three days later and returned to duty. Next day the survivors obtained some new tanks and formed a composite squadron which joined the 3rd Royal Tanks; this squadron was at first commanded by Major Hackett, but he had to be evacuated suffering from his burns and Captain H. H. Firth took over.

The 4th Brigade fought all day and the 3rd Royal Tanks also suffered heavily, being reduced to five Grants and eight Light tanks by the evening. The Brigade claimed the destruction of sixty enemy tanks. In the morning battle their B Echelon transport was over-run by an enemy force that came round a flank, and much was lost. The Motor Battalion of the Brigade, the 1st K.R.R.C., less "D" Company who were escorting the transport, moved first to the Retma Box.

When they got there, however, they found that the 7th Motor Brigade had withdrawn so they moved north towards el Duda. On the way the Commanding Officer, Lieutenant-Colonel G. de Bruyne, moved away to confer with Brigadier Richards and had the misfortune to fall into the hands of a German column that took him prisoner. Major C. d'A. P. Consett took command.

To return now to the morning. The 3rd Indian Motor Brigade had been put under command of the 7th Armoured Division with the specific task of forming a Box east of Bir Hacheim so as to give depth to the left flank static defence of which Bir Hacheim was the main pillar. Mines, wire and 6-pounder guns were going to be issued to them but the German attack came long before any of these essentials were made available, and despite their fierce defence the Indians were overwhelmed by numbers in a short time. During the next few days a great many escaped and they were rallied and withdrawn under orders from Army, and re-formed in the rear areas and fought again.

After overrunning the Indian Motor Brigade, the enemy moved on to the Box at Retma which was held by the 9th K.R.R.C., the 2nd Rifle Brigade, "C" Battery 4th R.H.A. and a Rhodesian Anti-Tank Battery. Unfortunately the minefield was only half completed when the position had to be taken over, but Brigadier Renton had been given orders that the position was not to be held to the traditional "last man and last round". The first attack was repelled by the Rifle Brigade and then the westernmost battalion, the 9th K.R.R.C., was assaulted by tanks and infantry supported by heavy artillery concentrations. Both forward companies, those of Majors J. N. Hogg and A. R. W. Low, were over-run; all the carriers were lost. With the loss of the western side of the Box, the position of the Rifle Brigade became untenable, so the garrison was ordered to withdraw to el Gubi, the survivors of the K.R.R.C. retiring in good order under their Commanding Officer, Lieutenant-Colonel C. E. Grenville-Grey. The Germans did not follow up. As soon as he could, Brigadier Renton organized columns to engage the enemy columns that were streaming past, but the opposition was far too strong for the Motor Brigade to make any great impression on them. During the course of the next twenty-four hours, almost all the officers and men who had been taken prisoner in the Retma Box escaped or were released by the opportune appearance of some South African armoured cars.

It can be seen, therefore, that the morning had not far advanced before the whole Division became hotly engaged over an area that stretched from Bir Hacheim almost as far as el Gubi. The situation was confused, and control had already become difficult when disaster fell upon Divisional Headquarters itself.

*Divisional Headquarters Over-run*                *May 27th*

This dramatic event is best told in the words of the officer who was then commanding the Divisional Signals, Lieutenant-Colonel (later Brigadier) H. N. Crawford.

"During the evening of the 26th it was obvious that the enemy was well on the move. I was roused at 4 a.m. on the 27th with the information that we were out of touch with the Free French. Shortly after 4.30 the Divisional Commander and the G.3 Ops joined me in Armoured Command Vehicle No. 1 and soon afterwards the French came up on the wireless. A.C.V.1 became very busy. At 8 I was told there were no immediate orders for a move, but as I was not very happy about things I told the Signal Office to pack up as far as possible. Just after this, an order came placing Headquarters at ten minutes' notice.

"About 8.30 the battle which had been taking place in the 4th Armoured Brigade area, just to our west, appeared to be coming our way, and trucks containing crews from knocked-out tanks started to pass through our leaguer. At 8.45 some Grant tanks began to pass us going eastwards and some odd shells were arriving in the neighbourhood, so Divisional Headquarters moved off on a bearing of 79 degrees. I followed in my car, travelling just behind the left of the A.C.V.s.

"When we had gone some two miles firing started at very close range from the east and south-east, and bullets appeared to be going in all directions. There was so much dust and smoke that it was very difficult to see what was happening, but there were evidently a number of enemy armoured cars well mixed up with the front of our column and some of the A.C.V.s were right in the centre of it.

"As things were pretty hot I turned north and saw two of the A.C.V.s heading in the same direction. After half a mile I stopped and we collected together what we could of the vehicles that had escaped from the mêlée. The General was missing, together with the G.1, G.2, G.3 Ops, the G Office and clerks, A.C.V.s 1 and 5 and a number of other vehicles. The driver of A.C.V.1 had been killed and the vehicle immobilized, it was learned later. We collected round us a variety of transport from the 4th Brigade's B Echelon and other units. Of the Command vehicles we still had A.C.V.2 (Intelligence) and the Signal Office. The former were already 'netted' on the command net; with their other set they were trying to get onto Corps. I found that I was the senior officer remaining.

"As we were virtually defenceless against armour, it was obviously useless to go back and rescue the General, and as I considered we might be surrounded at any moment, we moved off north in a formed body. I was navigating in front. The 'I' staff stuck to the wireless, passing on reports, etc., as best they could. The operations map, main wireless logs and up-to-date information had all been lost in A.C.V.1."

The survivors of Divisional Headquarters had to move several times during the day in order to avoid enemy columns, and on the next morning they joined up with the XXXth Corps Headquarters —the Corps had taken over command of the formations in the 7th Armoured Division soon after the disaster occurred. About the middle of the day on the 27th, A.C.V.3 with the cipher staff joined the column; they had had bullets through the door and the Cipher Sergeant had been wounded.

About noon on the 28th General Messervy turned up with Lieutenant-Colonel H. E. Pyman the G.1, Major J. A. Richardson the G.2 and Captain D. G. R. Reid. During the night they had made a daring escape from the Germans who had failed to realize the high rank of their principal prisoner, for he had removed his badges of rank when he saw that capture was imminent and had posed as a private soldier. Major P. Hobbs and Captain C. S. Elliott had been killed, and numerous other ranks had been killed, wounded or taken prisoner, among the last category being Brigadier S. Williams the C.R.A. "The Boche had a couple of things on me, in their G.O.C.'s reserve motor, and they thought they had got something really worth having in me, a Willoughby Norrie (our Corps Commander) at least, but were very sadly disillusioned later." It was fifteen months before Brigadier Williams escaped, not for the first time, from captivity.

In his report Colonel Crawford paid a high tribute to all ranks for their coolness in the emergency, particularly the drivers of the A.C.V.s; to the way Captains Vaux and Viney had stuck to the wireless and kept communications going; to the officer in charge of the Signals personnel, Lieutenant Summerlin, and his men who, through casualties, had to work without rest for many hours; and to all survivors for "keeping their heads, keeping together, and

handing back to the Divisional Commander a Headquarters ready
for work."

By nightfall on this eventful day the 29th Indian Brigade and
a rather battered 7th Motor Brigade were at el Gubi. The 4th
Armoured Brigade, which had lost a very large number of its tanks,
was a few miles south-east of el Adem and had held the 90th Light
Division from its objective. The 3rd Indian Motor Brigade had
almost ceased to exist, but the Free French were still at Bir Hacheim.

### May 28th

This was a comparatively quiet day. The 7th Motor Brigade
remained near el Gubi operating columns against the enemy's flank.
The 29th Indian Brigade was moved up to el Adem. Here, in the
evening, the 4th Armoured Brigade made a number of attacks
against the 90th Light Division who had approached from the south.
The 3rd and 5th Royal Tanks forced the enemy to withdraw, and
they were helped by a column of the 1st K.R.R.C. who were
operating on the top of the escarpment south of the Sidi Rezegh
airfield under Major J. A. Hunter. These drove back an enemy
force who would otherwise have had observation over the Armoured
Brigade on the lower ground.

### May 29th

Rommel had now failed in his attempt to reach Tobruk and
Acroma in his first rush. His administrative situation was becoming
serious and he drew back his forward units to the areas where his
engineers were opening passages through the minefields. Much fighting took place round the Knightsbridge Box, which was garrisoned
by the Guards Brigade, but the 7th Armoured Division was not
involved until the evening when, in a thick dust storm, the 4th
Brigade, reinforced by the "I" tanks of the 4th Royal Tanks,
moved from reserve positions near el Adem to attack the 90th Light
at Bir Harmat. It was not until late that they were able to launch
their attack and fighting was soon stopped by darkness.

During the day both the 29th Indian Brigade and the 7th Motor
Brigade concentrated near el Adem, and the latter operated columns
whose work, however, was impeded by bad visibility.

### May 30th

The 4th Brigade were again in action and knocked out ten
German tanks. In the evening they were heavily bombed and

seventeen men were killed and forty wounded. The 7th Motor Brigade were in action with their columns, and the 13th (D.C.O.) Lancers, Indian Army, who had come temporarily under Divisional command on May 24th, operated south of Bir Hacheim.

*May 31st*

The small number of tanks available gave cause for much anxiety. The 8th Hussars and the 3rd Royal Tanks, who were combined into one Regiment, could muster only nine Grants and twenty-four light tanks, the 5th Royal Tanks had sixteen Grants and twelve lights, and Brigade Headquarters mustered three of each type. Attached were the 4th Royal Tanks who had thirty-six "I" tanks, the speed of which was much below that of the other tanks in the Brigade.

The columns of the 7th Brigade were very active. They attacked an enemy force of twenty-three tanks, and during the night they worked forward as far as Mteifel, twenty miles north-west of Bir Hacheim.

Throughout the day very heavy attacks were made by the enemy on the 150th Brigade's Box, but the defenders held on although running short of artillery ammunition.

*June 1st*

The fall of the 150th Brigade's Box soon after midday, when they were overpowered after a desperate resistance, marked the turning point of the battle. From now on, Rommel had a secure line of communication as far as the salient he had driven into the British positions and he could feel free to resume the offensive. However, to make assurance doubly sure, he decided to eliminate the Free French Box at Bir Hacheim before again attempting to drive forward to Tobruk.

Except for patrols of Light tanks, the 4th Brigade was not engaged this day. A rather glowing report was sent in by one patrol that they had captured 200 lorries—this figure was soon reduced to fifty—then to "rather less". The Brigade War Diary suggests this was due to "wishful thinking and dust".

Again the 7th Motor Brigade were very active. They were on the move soon after midnight and navigated by the stars. Their columns worked forward to positions south of Mteifel where they spent the day enjoying "excellent shooting on enemy defences and transport columns". They were well supplied with information by the South Africans. The K.D.G.s, too, were very enterprising. Major Palmer's squadron operated round the Segnali area without artillery or infantry support for several days, and the rest of the Regiment, now commanded by Lieutenant-Colonel G. Kidston, reconnoitred and skirmished between el Gubi and Bir Hacheim.

## THE CAULDRON BATTLE
### June 2nd to 11th

Events during this period took the form of attacks by the Eighth Army against the enemy troops in the Cauldron area. Very large numbers of British tanks were lost and the effects on the enemy were very much less than had been hoped. The Free French defended their Box at Bir Hacheim with the greatest determination until the night of the 10th/11th when General Koenig had orders to evacuate the position; this was done with a considerable measure of success as told below.

By the end of this phase the situation for Rommel was much improved. The menace from Bir Hacheim had been eliminated and his opponents' losses had been such as to limit considerably their power to resist a further advance.

### June 2nd

The 90th Light Division moved down to Bir Hacheim with a view to attacking on the morrow. The 21st Panzer Division was moved north to Eleut et Tamar in order to cut off the 1st South African and 50th Divisions who were still holding their original positions from Gazala to Alam Hamza with their left flank thrown back for some miles and facing south.

The 4th Armoured Brigade again had a hard day. The visibility was very bad and one of the effects of the storm was to make wireless communication difficult. An attack by between sixty and eighty tanks was made against the 5th Royal Tanks and "B" Battery of the 1st R.H.A. The latter's gun positions were over-run and only two guns were saved, and then only at the last minute when the enemy were within two hundred yards of their position. Lieutenant-Colonel Uniacke, commanding the 5th Tanks, was killed, and the Brigade had now only the 3rd Tanks as an effective fighting force, for the 5th were left with only one Grant and two Lights. Their casualties in personnel had fortunately not been so severe as the heavy loss of tanks might indicate, but three officers and forty-two rank and file were missing. Major E. R. S. Castle took command of the remnants.

General Messervy called back the far-flung columns of the 7th Motor Brigade to assist in the protection of the French at Bir Hacheim. An enemy raiding party destroyed a large part of the transport of the South African Armoured Car Regiment, "a severe blow to a Regiment whose work had been, and continued to be, beyond praise".

*June 3rd to 8th*

Bir Hacheim was proving a harder hut to crack than Rommel had thought and his forces were becoming too dispersed, so, on the 3rd, he called back the 21st Panzers to the Cauldron area. At Eighth Army Headquarters plans were being drawn up for a concerted attack on the enemy in the Cauldron. The 4th Armoured Brigade were to protect the left flank of the 23rd Army Tank Brigade ("I" tanks) and the 22nd Armoured Brigade came under command of the 7th Armoured Division.

The attacks on the Germans in the Cauldron on the 5th were unsuccessful and costly, and in the evening the 15th Panzers themselves attacked. The 3rd and 5th Royal Tanks found themselves faced by sixty-four German tanks which, however, did not press their attack. In the Cauldron the situation of the 10th Indian Infantry Brigade was critical for they were surrounded, and it was decided to place all Armoured Brigades temporarily under the command of the 1st Armoured Division in order to co-ordinate the efforts to relieve the Indians.

To the south Bir Hacheim was by now menaced by several columns, but the 7th Motor Brigade managed to introduce a small supply column in the early hours of the 5th. It seemed probable that this would be the last column that could be brought in.

The 6th was another disappointing day. The 22nd Brigade was involved in heavy fighting and the Royal Gloucestershire Hussars lost their Commanding Officer, Colonel Birley, and their Adjutant, Captain H. M. Muir, who were both killed. The 4th Brigade moved up to the south side of the Knightsbridge Box, where the 3rd Royal Tanks had a successful shoot and knocked out twelve enemy guns. When night came, however, the 10th Indian Brigade had been destroyed.

On the 7th attempts were made to attack Rommel's lines of

communication. The 4th Armoured Brigade, who were reinforced by the 6th Royal Tanks (Lieutenant-Colonel H. M. Liardet), endeavoured to penetrate the enemy anti-tank gun screen but without success, though a German counter-attack was held in the evening. Both the Commanding Officer, Lieutenant-Colonel G. P. B. Roberts, and the Adjutant of the 3rd Royal Tanks were wounded. The 22nd Armoured Brigade reverted to the 1st Armoured Division who relinquished command of the 4th. That night the tank state of the 7th Armoured Division was fifty-eight Grants and thirty-four Light tanks.

*June 9th to 11th*

From June 9th onwards the enemy increased his pressure on the Bir Hacheim Box with air attacks of great intensity, heavy artillery concentrations and assaults by tanks and infantry. On the 10th over a hundred aircraft attacked. The Eighth Army owed a deep debt to the Free French for their heroic resistance which delayed the Germans for so long, but they could not hold out for ever. The Division did what it could with its meagre resources to check the attacks and the 4th Brigade were engaged every day until orders came for the Box to be evacuated. The 7th Motor Brigade were more closely involved.

A party of the Rifle Brigade under Major the Hon. M. G. Edwardes was inside the Box for some days assisting in the distribution of supplies; they were taken out on the last night but one. The evacuation was carried out on the night 10th/11th when "D" Company of the 2nd K.R.R.C. under Major P. G. Chapman brought in sixty-nine 3-ton lorries and thirty-three ambulances. This force was covered by a column under Lieutenant-Colonel J. C. Christopher of the 4th R.H.A. First, the wounded were got out without a hitch, then two lorry convoys brought out all the other men who could be collected. Luckily the morning dawned misty and the Rifle Brigade carriers were able to carry out sweeps for stragglers. In the end, over 3,000 men were evacuated; about 1,000 fell into the enemy's hands. Major Chapman concluded his report of the night's work, "We draw a veil over the rest of the day when my vehicle broke down just as I reached advanced Brigade Headquarters who were already on the move; it proceeded to break down a further twelve times before I caught up with them at the next halting place."

During the past week and longer the 7th Motor Brigade had

operated to the south and west of Bir Hacheim. Many columns were sent out to harass and incommode the enemy's supply trains, and at times they made their way so far north that they were on the west side of the Cauldron battle. One of the most successful columns was that led by Lord Garmoyle, now the Commanding Officer of the 2nd Rifle Brigade. They shelled the main track on which the Germans relied for their supplies from positions fifty miles from the main body of the Motor Brigade. By the 9th they had more or less brought all traffic to a standstill; they captured prisoners, released British prisoners and in the course of three days destroyed more than forty lorries and a number of guns. So far out did these columns travel that a special supply organization had to be set up for the Rifle Brigade only. This was managed by Major J. Fawcett, second-in-command of the Divisional R.A.S.C.

## THE RETREAT BEGINS

### June 11th to 16th

During this period the 7th Armoured Division was to operate in two widely separated portions, the 7th Motor Brigade and the armoured cars far to the south and the 4th Brigade in the centre of the battle.

With the elimination of the Bir Hacheim Box, Rommel was free to resume his original object, the seizure of Acroma, el Adem and Tobruk. On the 11th he advanced with the 90th Light and the reconnaissance elements on the right, the 15th Panzers in the centre and the Italian Trieste Division on the left, while the 21st Panzer and the Ariete Divisions maintained the fight in the Cauldron. By nightfall the enemy were within five miles of the defensive position at el Adem. On the next day the 90th Light and the troops operating with them by-passed this position, reached el Adem and cut the Trigh Capuzzo.

### The Knightsbridge Box

The 4th Armoured Brigade was by now in action between el Adem and Knightsbridge, and on the 12th they were heavily engaged by a group of about a hundred tanks from the 21st Panzer Division who attacked from the rear. The Brigade, who lost about twenty tanks, were forced to pull back, but they still covered the Box. By now the 6th Royal Tanks were reduced to four Grants,

H

and the 3rd and 5th Tanks had to be combined into one Regiment. While on his way to Corps Headquarters General Messervy was cut off by the enemy near el Adem and was forced to remain out of touch for some time. Temporarily General Lumsden took command of the tank forces engaged. At nightfall the situation was that the Knightsbridge Box still held firm, but the 29th Indian Brigade at el Adem was surrounded. The only bright spot in the day's work was that a large enemy tank force in leaguer was soundly bombed by their own Stukas, "an encouraging sight".

On the 13th the fighting was concentrated to the north of the Knightsbridge Box, and in the afternoon a fierce tank attack was hurled against the Rigel Ridge which was held by the 2nd Battalion Scots Guards. The 4th and 22nd Armoured Brigades were rushed up to support, and their counter-attack drove some of the enemy back and destroyed eleven tanks, but at a cost to the British of another twenty-five tanks. Most of the Scots Guards position was, however, over-run.

After a most gallant defence that had inflicted great loss on the Germans, the Knightsbridge Box was evacuated on the night 13th/14th. Brigadier Marriott, who had commanded its garrison of the 3rd Battalion Coldstream, two companies of the Sherwood Foresters and the 2nd R.H.A., has recorded that they could never have got out if it had not been for the magnificent shooting of the R.H.A. and the skill of the 22nd Armoured Brigade in keeping open a corridor. It was now clear that the Gazala position could no longer be held. The problem arose how to extricate the 50th and 1st South African Divisions who were still in their positions north-west of Knightsbridge. Orders were issued for the former to break out to the south and move via Bir Hacheim, and for the South Africans to retire by the coast road through Tobruk. Both Divisions were to re-organize in the frontier area. Rommel ordered the 15th and 21st Panzer Divisions to attack north with a view to covering the coast road and cutting off the South Africans. A good deal of fighting then ensued but the Armoured Brigades held off the German advance until dark when they themselves withdrew. This was described as a bad night march as the drivers were so weary that they kept falling asleep on the move. At the best of times a night march, whether in wheeled or tracked vehicles, is apt to have the attributes of a nightmare; under conditions such as prevailed at this time, there can be few more exhausting experiences, particularly for all the officers and N.C.O.s whose duty it is to guide the column, to keep it organized and to keep it going.

On the 15th, most of the 50th Division succeeded in getting clear by the southern route, and the South African Division retired along the coast road, getting safely away except for the rearguard.

By now the tank strength of the 4th Brigade was twenty-three Grants, twelve Crusaders and twenty-four Light tanks. During the night they moved through Tobruk, being guided by Major Palmer of the K.D.G.s, who was familiar with the minefields and tracks, having been there during the siege. He carried out his difficult task with only one mistake when the whole column, in single file, had to turn round. By dawn on the 16th the Brigade had reached the perimeter wire and they moved south to watch the south-eastern approaches to Tobruk near Sidi Rezegh and Belhamed, while the K.D.G. Squadron patrolled to the south and west. Soon afterwards the Germans attacked the Indian Brigade in their position just north of Sidi Rezegh and the 4th Brigade were moved to their support. However, every attack the latter put in was met by a screen of anti-tank guns of which the enemy seemed to have an unlimited supply.

The 9th Lancers (Lieutenant-Colonel J. R. Macdonnell) now came under command of the 4th Brigade; they had with them half a dozen tanks of the 4th County of London Yeomanry under Major G. Willis. In the evening of the 17th a converging attack in great strength was made by the Germans with the setting sun behind them. The Grants were outnumbered by four to one and the Brigade was almost surrounded. Under a smoke screen laid by the Crusaders they withdrew, the tanks firing backwards at the enemy as they emerged from the smoke. A hundred and seventeen German tanks were counted in this engagement.

The defensive position at el Adem was evacuated and by nightfall there was nothing left between Tobruk and the frontier save the remnants of the 7th Armoured Division in the Desert to the south. Rommel was free to invest Tobruk for the second time.

Throughout this week the 7th Motor Brigade had been operating columns over the southern portion of the battlefield, attacking the enemy wherever they could be found and, as the German records show, making a thorough nuisance of themselves and diverting troops from the main battle. The K.D.G.s had been brought back from the Segnali area and also operated in the south, keeping up a continuous flow of accurate information which was of great value.

## BACK TO ALAMEIN

### *June, 1942*

Hopes expressed in telegrams exchanged with London that Tobruk could be held against another siege and that the area of the frontier defences could be made use of to prevent any further advance by Rommel did not last long.

The losses suffered by the 4th Armoured Brigade, particularly on June 17th, following on the heavy losses of the other Armoured Brigades, had been such that there was no longer an effective armoured force that could keep open communication with the garrison of Tobruk or launch a counter-attack against the enemy forces arrayed before the town; the 3rd/5th Royal Tanks, for example, were now mounted entirely in wheeled vehicles.

The German assault of Tobruk was made on the 20th and met with substantial success from the start, for the fortifications had fallen into neglect since the raising of the siege the previous year and the troops within, newly-arrived as they were from an arduous battle, had had no time to organize a proper defence. On the morning of the 21st the fortress capitulated, yielding many thousand prisoners and the vast quantity of petrol and other stores that had been laboriously accumulated there for many months past. Few escaped—the largest body consisted of some two hundred Coldstreamers, a number of South Africans and some of the Scots Guards; these were led out by Major H. M. Sainthill of the Coldstream, and after a circuitous journey reached the British lines a few days later. Fort Capuzzo was also occupied by the Germans at this time.

The rest of the Army drew back, the sky behind them black with the smoke of burning dumps, reminders to the "old hands" of better days seventeen months before when they had watched the stores of the Italian Army being destroyed.

On June 25th General Ritchie gave up command of the Army and, for the second time, General Auchinleck took personal and direct command in the field at a critical moment. Last time, in Operation "Crusader", he had turned uncertainty into victory; this time he had to revive the fortunes of a shattered Army and bring them to a state in which they could fight back with success. Again he accomplished his task.

Two courses were open to the Eighth Army. One was to stand on the frontier defences, the other to pull back to the Mersa Matruh area while delaying the enemy along the frontier with such mobile forces as could be assembled and kept in the field. The former course entailed the risk of a further defeat of the infantry unless sufficient armour could be made available, and as this was impossible the decision was taken to retire to Mersa Matruh.

The 2nd New Zealand Division was now again on the scene and they were placed in a defensive position twenty-five miles south of Mersa Matruh with the 29th Indian Infantry Brigade further north. On their right, the Matruh position was held by the 50th and the 10th Indian Divisions. What were left of the 1st and 7th Armoured Divisions were positioned on the Desert flank to the south of the New Zealanders.

On the evening of June 26th the enemy broke through the area held by the 29th Indian Brigade, who had not had time to complete their minefield, and on the following morning the New Zealand position was surrounded and attacked from three sides. General Freyberg was badly wounded and command devolved on Brigadier Inglis. It seemed that the Division's fate was sealed, but during the night 27th/28th the 4th New Zealand Brigade deployed on a wide front, fixed bayonets and drove their way out in hand-to-hand fighting. Rommel himself was personally involved in this and was compelled to order his troops to give way. The rest of the Division drove south and also got clear, and they all re-assembled eighty miles back near the Alamein position. Earlier, the XXXth Corps had been withdrawn there and by the last day of the month the whole Army was concentrated in the defensive position of el Alamein. They owed their survival in large measure to the squadrons of the R.A.F. who had operated from their advanced landing grounds often until the enemy were upon them. Their devoted efforts to hold back the advancing Germans should not be forgotten.

### The 7th Armoured Division in the Retreat

Until June 20th the K.D.G.s maintained patrols west of el Gubi, but on the 21st they began to pull back, frequently under attack by the German air force. On the 24th the Regiment crossed the frontier into Egypt, still in contact with the enemy, and by the evening they were due south of Mersa Matruh. By now all squadrons were having difficulty in keeping their cars going and some amalgamation had to take place. So mixed did regiments become that at one stage the Royals were composed of two Royals squadrons, one K.D.G. squadron and one 12th Lancer squadron.

The 7th Motor Brigade acted as rearguard and were continuously involved in difficult fighting. Companies often found themselves moving along at night in rear of enemy columns from whom they occasionally picked up prisoners. Command of the Brigade was taken over by Lord Garmoyle in place of Brigadier Renton who at this time succeeded General Messervy in command of the Division. Major the Hon. M. G. Edwardes took over command of the 2nd Rifle Brigade temporarily.

The 9th Rifle Brigade had operated in June in a variety of detached missions. Major P. A. D. Boden's company had spent some time in the neighbourhood of the Free French both at Bir Hacheim and during their withdrawal. The remainder of the Battalion had been involved in the fighting near Knightsbridge, entered Tobruk and were then fortunately ordered out to the east. They operated columns round Sidi Rezegh for some time and then made for the Alamein Line "in close company", their History records, "with the Afrika Korps".

The 1st K.R.R.C., operating with the survivors of the 4th Armoured Brigade, withdrew steadily. They were never very heavily engaged, but there were frequent small actions and a steady drain of casualties. They reached the Alamein position on July 1st.

## ALAMEIN

### *July and August, 1942*

The Alamein position differed from all other positions occupied during the Desert Campaigns in that both flanks were secured by natural features. At el Alamein itself, which was barely fifty miles from Alexandria, there was the sea. Thirty-five miles to the south was the Qattara Depression, a large area of quicksands which was to all intents and purposes impassable, although some alarm was caused in high places when Major the Hon. R. Plunkett successfully led his squadron of the Guides Cavalry across and cast doubts upon the impregnability of this left flank.

A good deal of work had been done in the past, particularly round el Alamein, in creating permanent fortifications; further south the works were disconnected. Not the least of the advantages of the position lay in the fact that communications with the Base in the Delta were very short and so the administrative situation was, for once, not complicated by long hauls with insufficient transport. For the enemy, on the other hand, there was a very difficult supply problem indeed, and his troubles had not been eased by the postponement of Hitler's projected assault on Malta which had been deferred when the conquest of Egypt seemed to be imminent.

General Auchinleck had no intention of maintaining a passive defence and it was not long before his troops, whom the Prime Minister has described as being "amazed rather than depressed", were again engaged in offensive operations. Reinforcements, too, were in sight; the 8th Armoured Division arrived from England early in July and were at once put to equipping themselves with American tanks, the 44th (Home Counties) Division was expected later in the month and the 51st (Highland) Division in August. But the Army Commander was not waiting for these, and he soon showed that although the Eighth Army had been driven back, it was far indeed from being either a defeated or a demoralized force.

On July 1st Rommel launched an attack designed to capture el Alamein; this was repelled and the next day the XIIIth Corps themselves attacked; there were several days of fighting of which the British had the best, but there were not the reserves to carry the offensive through as far as the Army Commander would have liked. West of el Alamein was the important ridge of Tel el Aisa; this the 9th Australian Division took on July 10th and they held it against counter-attacks. A few days later the New Zealanders and the 5th Indian Brigade gained valuable ground on the important Ruweisat Ridge. Fighting continued for most of the rest of the month but then the situation quietened down, for General Auchinleck realized that, although he had mastered Rommel, he had not yet been able to build up the resources necessary to carry out a full-scale offensive to drive the enemy from Egypt.

For the Division the month of July was not a very active period. The armoured cars patrolled as usual on a wide frontage forward of, and between, the localities held by the infantry and tanks. There was a good deal of soft sand in this part of the Desert which hampered their operations. Lieutenant-Colonel R. A. Hermon took command of the K.D.G.s in place of Colonel Kidston who returned to command his own Regiment, the 12th Lancers, in the 1st Armoured Division.

The area occupied by the 7th Armoured Division was at the southern end of the front and the 1st Armoured were in reserve

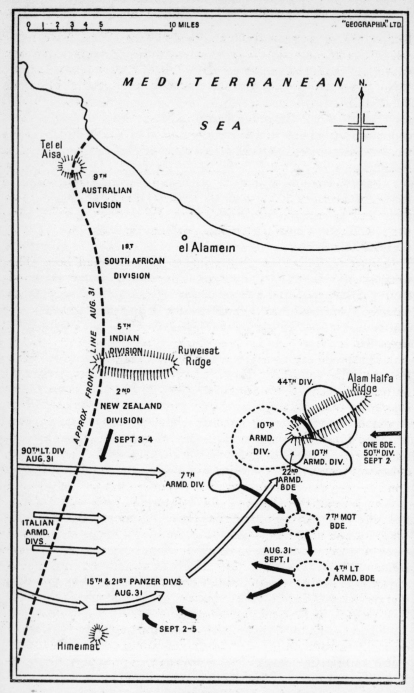

Map No. 7
The Battle of Alam Halfa, August 31st to September 5th, 1942

behind. Under command of the 7th Armoured Division were the 7th Motor Brigade and the 4th Armoured Brigade, now equipped with Light tanks and armoured cars. It had been re-named the 4th Light Armoured Brigade and was under the command of Brigadier W. G. Carr.

The 7th Motor Brigade covered their portion of the front with columns. The entire length of the Line had been fronted with barbed wire, and minefields had been laid before the defended localities.

About the middle of July the 4th South African Armoured Car Regiment returned to the Delta to re-fit and the K.D.G.s took over their area in addition to their own on the extreme south. Later, the 12th Lancers, now part of the 4th Brigade, took over some of the K.D.G.'s front.

Living conditions were as trying as ever they had been. The weather was very hot and the large number of troops attracted hordes of flies, as a result of which there was an unusual amount of sickness. Uncovered food became infested immediately with a coating of flies and throughout the hours of daylight they were a perpetual torment.

A great variety of small actions were fought by the Motor Brigade. The 2nd Rifle Brigade were for the most part on the southern portion of the front, but the 9th Battalion were being constantly moved about from one command to another. Both Battalions were always in contact with the enemy. On July 4th, Brigadier Lord Garmoyle was mortally wounded in action. He was one of the most experienced and most successful of the Desert fighters. Brigadier T. J. B. Bosvile, also of the Rifle Brigade, succeeded him.

On July 21st the Divisional Troops comprised the K.D.G.s and the 4th South African Armoured Car Regiment, and the 69th Infantry and 22nd Armoured Brigades, were temporarily under command of the Division. The 4th Light Armoured Brigade included the 3rd R.H.A., the 11th Hussars, the 12th Lancers, a squadron of the composite 4th/8th Hussars, the 9th Rifle Brigade, the 3rd Field Squadron R.E., Nos. 5 and 58 Companies R.A.S.C. and the 14th Light Field Ambulance.

The 7th Motor Brigade was composed of the 4th R.H.A., a composite squadron of the 1st Royal Tanks, the 2nd K.R.R.C., the 2nd Rifle Brigade, the 4th Field Squadron R.E., No. 550 Company R.A.S.C. and the 15th Light Field Ambulance.

*August*

August was a month of re-organization, re-equipping, perfecting the defensive positions, and training and planning for the future. Important changes took place in the higher command. Early in August the Prime Minister spent some time in Egypt and he records that on his visits to the troops they seemed "very cheerful, confident and proud of themselves, but bewildered at having been deprived of victory on repeated occasions". Nevertheless the situation was one of considerable anxiety, for there was but one single canal to stop Rommel from reaching the Nile, and extreme measures were taken for the defence of Cairo—officers and men of the Staffs were armed, positions were prepared and full plans drawn up for holding the city.

General the Hon. Sir Harold Alexander succeeded General Auchinleck as Commander-in-Chief, and General Gott was appointed to command the Eighth Army. Unhappily, while flying back to Cairo from the forward area a few days later, his aircraft was attacked by a German aircraft and brought down. The General survived the crash but was killed by machine-gun fire while rescuing others from the wreckage. The 11th Hussars record that "his death dealt a stunning blow to all the old-timers of the Desert . . . there was not a man in their ranks but felt his passing as a personal loss. To many it seemed the last of a long series of bitter deals, and it was only too short a step to the feeling that they would never see his like again."

His place was taken by Lieutenant-General B. L. Montgomery, who was flown out from England at very short notice.

On August 5th the Order of Battle included the Queens Bays in the 4th Brigade and the Royal Scots Greys in the Motor Brigade. The 22nd Armoured Brigade joined the Division temporarily and was then composed of the 1st R.H.A., the Royals, composite Regiments of the 1st/6th Royal Tanks and 3rd/4th County of London Yeomanry, the 5th Royal Tanks, the 2nd Royal Gloucestershire Hussars and the 1st Rifle Brigade.

### THE BATTLE OF ALAM HALFA

*August 31st to September 7th*

*See Map No. 7, page 120*

The Alamein position was held by the 9th Australian Division in the north. Next to them were the 1st South African, the 5th Indian and the 2nd New Zealand Divisions in that order. From them to the Qattara Depression the 7th Armoured Division watched the area on a front of about twenty miles. About six miles behind the New Zealand Division was the 10th Armoured Division at the southern end of the Alam Halfa Ridge. During August General Montgomery brought up the 44th Division to hold this ridge in addition to the armour.

Facing the Eighth Army was the Afrika Korps with its two Panzer Divisions and one Light and one infantry Divisions, and the Italian Army which included two armoured divisions.

The Alam Halfa Ridge formed one of the principal keys to the whole defensive system, and when General Gott had reconnoitred this area some time previously he had come to the conclusion that if the enemy penetrated the minefields he would have to swing north and attack the ridge. It dominated a large area and so long as it was held by the British the enemy could have no freedom of action. In the enemy's hands it would menace the Ruweisat Ridge, the key to the central and northern sectors.

In the very early hours of August 31st Rommel commenced his attack, having previously issued an order to his troops proclaiming that the coming attack would result in the final annihilation of their enemy. The advance was in three thrusts. The most northerly was easily held by the Australians. The central one at first achieved some success against the Indians, but a counter-attack later in the day restored the situation.

In the south, which was the main thrust, all four Armoured Divisions and the 90th Light Division were employed between the south flank of the New Zealanders and Himeimat, and the minefields were penetrated. The orders that had been given to the 7th Armoured Division were to impose the maximum delay on the enemy, to harass his advance and to be prepared to exploit westwards.

Both the 2nd and the 7th Battalions of the Rifle Brigade, in the 7th Motor Brigade, were watching the minefields with instructions to prevent any small advance, but in the event of a full attack to withdraw. Accordingly, when the attack came, the Riflemen pulled back after inflicting considerable losses, and carried out the planned withdrawal. On the extreme left were the 1st K.R.R.C. occupying Himeimat hill. They watched the Rifle Brigade's 6-pounder anti-tank guns knock out about a dozen German tanks at once and the supporting armoured regiment account for another twenty or so.

They themselves were in action continuously for the next three days, shelling, machine-gunning and directing air attacks. "B" Squadron of the 12th Lancers (Major N. H. R. Speke) also did very good work.

The 22nd Armoured Brigade, who were no longer under the command of the 7th Armoured Division, were in positions south of Alam Halfa Ridge and the enemy reached them in the evening of the 31st. The German attacks were repelled and as night came on the R.A.F. bombers, who had not been able to act previously on account of the great clouds of dust, began to hammer the enemy. Major H. Woods of the K.R.R.C. described the scene: "At 12.30 a.m. our bombers returning from Tobruk found his whole strength had moved eastwards and located him with flares in the valley below us. It was one of the most awe-inspiring sights I shall ever see, I think —there were seldom less than twenty flares in the air at any one time and the whole valley with its mass of the Afrika Korps stationary was lit up like a huge orange fairyland. All the time, red-orange, white-green tracer was darting hither and thither like little 100-mile-an-hour coloured fairies. The huge flash of the bombs, which included two of 4,000 lbs., also inspired the whole thoroughly warlike scene, with little figures silhouetted against their vehicles as they tried to find cover from our bombs. The bombers were so accurate that they bombed right up to the minefield beyond which, 2,000 yards away, was another of our companies."

On September 1st Rommel made two armoured attacks against the Alam Halfa Ridge and twice he was driven back. On the next day there was no great keenness on the part of the Germans and Italians to resume their assaults, and preparations were made for a counter-stroke from the New Zealand area southwards.

On the 3rd the enemy began to pull back, leaving the battlefield covered with damaged and destroyed vehicles and tanks. When their move began they were harried all the way by the R.A.F. from the air, the 4th Armoured Brigade from the south and the New Zealanders and the 132nd Brigade from the north, while the 7th Motor Brigade followed them up. The harassing attacks were kept up at full pressure, but General Montgomery was insistent that there should be no great surge forward, for he considered that the state of training and equipment of the Army was not sufficiently far advanced for a major offensive. The fighting continued on the 4th, 5th and 6th, and early on the 7th the Army Commander ordered operations to cease. The fact that a small portion of the original forward British minefield remained in enemy hands was off-set by the desirability of the enemy retaining troops in that sector during the operations that were then being planned for the future.

The situation was now stabilized. The importance of this victory lay, not only in the great damage caused to the Germans and Italians, but also in the proof it gave that British tanks and infantry could stand up to the Germans and inflict a crushing defeat; morale rose to great heights and confidence was re-established. The battle marked the limit of the German advance in North Africa.

On September 7th it was decided that the 22nd Armoured Brigade should form a permanent part of the Division and come under command forthwith, but at present there was little for the armour to do. For the armoured cars, also, this was a fairly quiet time. The 11th Hussars were at the extreme south and were molested only by the German air force. One attack destroyed Colonel Leetham's motor-car and possessions a few days before he left on promotion for another appointment. He was succeeded by Lieutenant-Colonel A. T. Smail. The K.D.G.s, also, were not closely engaged.

For the Motor Battalions there was much work, harassing the enemy and interfering with his movements. Many of the troops had had a close view of what the R.A.F. had done and were much encouraged by what they had seen.

Between the end of the Battle of Alam Halfa and the start of the Battle of Alamein many changes took place in the Division. After very long service abroad and seeing much hard fighting, General Renton gave place to Major-General A. F. Harding. The latter had been Chief of Staff to General O'Connor and his successors in the earliest days in the Desert and had then served for a time on the General Staff in Cairo.

Brigadier R. Mews became C.R.A. in place of Brigadier G. B. Vaughan-Hughes. Lieutenant-Colonel H. H. Withers succeeded Lieutenant-Colonel P. A. Clauson as C.R.E. and Lieutenant-Colonel the Hon. S. A. Maxwell took command of the Divisional Signals in place of Colonel Crawford who had been with the Division from the beginning. As the chief administrative Staff Officer, Lieutenant-Colonel C. E. F. Turner replaced Lieutenant-Colonel J. G. Cowley, and Colonel Pyman's successor as G.1 was Lieutenant-Colonel R. M. P. Carver.

Throughout the Army there was much re-organization of units and formations. A great blow was the departure of the 7th Motor Brigade, the old Support Group, with the 4th R.H.A. and the 2nd Rifle Brigade, two of the oldest units in the Division. The 44th Divisional Reconnaissance Regiment, which was a special unit organized as a Regiment of carriers for assault on a minefield, came to the Division temporarily.

The Order of Battle just before the Battle of Alamein is shown in Appendix I.

## CHAPTER 5

*October 23rd, 1942 to May 9th, 1943*

# ALAMEIN TO TUNIS

*Reference Maps—Front Endpaper. No. 2, page 34. No. 8, page 128*

> "The hum of either Army stilly sounds . . .
> The Armourers accomplishing the Knights,
> With busy hammers, closing rivets up."

THE Battle of Alam Halfa in which the 22nd Armoured Brigade had played such a prominent part had not only established confidence in Generals Alexander and Montgomery, but had also confirmed the tactical doctrine of employing armour in the mass and in the closest association with artillery, infantry and the Air Force. Since then, the Eighth Army had been increased by the arrival of the 51st Division, and by the middle of October the armoured force had been built up to a total of seven Armoured Brigades with more than a thousand tanks, some of them the new Shermans from the U.S.A. The R.A.F., under Air Marshal Coningham, totalled about 1,200 aircraft.

The Navy contributed to the forthcoming operations very materially. During September a third of the Axis shipping crossing to North Africa had been sunk, some of it by air action, but most by the Navy, and during October this proportion was greatly increased. Two-thirds of the petrol in transit was destroyed.

Of particular interest to the Armoured Divisions were the considerable advances that had been made in the system of recovery and repair of tanks, and their delivery to units. With the creation, some time previously, of the Corps of Electrical and Mechanical Engineers and the addition of a new Head of Service in the shape of a C.R.E.M.E. to the Divisional Staff, who worked in close co-operation with the D.D.M.E. of the Corps, it was possible for the Division to put into action a greater number of battle-worthy tanks than ever before. The control of C.R.E.M.E. extended to the

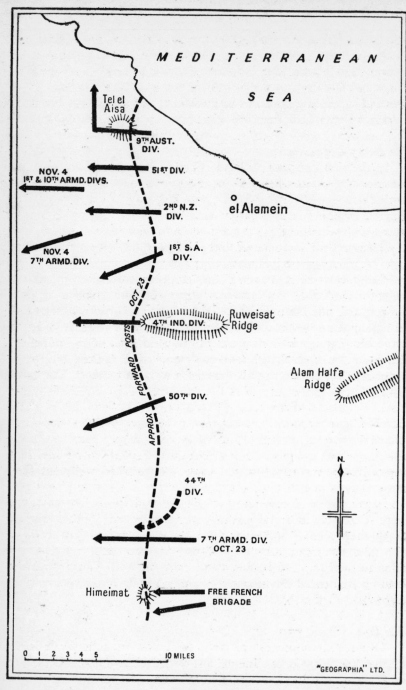

Map No. 8
The Battle of Alamein, October 23rd to November 3rd, 1942

Brigade and unit Workshops, so it was possible to co-ordinate the
efforts of all these technical specialists and thus avoid much wastage
of time and labour. The creation of Tank Delivery Squadrons in
Corps and Divisions meant that there was a quicker flow forward of
new and repaired tanks and other vehicles, and they arrived at their
units in a better state than had often been the case in the past.

*The Enemy Dispositions*

In the past two months Rommel had strengthened his defences
considerably, particularly in the northern sector. Minefields extended to a depth varying from 5,000 to 9,000 yards and they were
covered by the fire of a large mass of artillery. In the southern
sector, with which the 7th Armoured Division was to be concerned,
there was not the same depth to the defences, but they were sited so
as to canalize any penetration made.

The development of minefields had been carried to an extent
never known before. The principal mine was that intended to blow
up vehicles, but large numbers of anti-personnel mines were also
laid along the edges of, and within, the main minefields. In order to
avoid blowing up their own troops, the near limit of the minefield
was generally marked with wire or tape or small notices, but it was
never safe to assume that all minefields were so marked. The principal counter to the mine was the detection device handled by the
Royal Engineers; this will be referred to in more detail later on. By
October, 1942, another device had been made, by which a number of
chains were rotated at the front of a tank; these "flails" were intended to beat the ground hard enough to explode any mines that
might be underneath. On the whole they worked well, but they
moved slowly and their chains soon wore out.

In the southern area the 21st Panzer and the Ariete Divisions
were in reserve and the forward troops were all Italians, mostly
northerners and of higher quality than the average. The Italians
also held the front line in the north, together with one German
infantry division, and behind them were the 15th Panzer and the
Littorio Armoured Divisions; the 90th Light Division was another
eight miles further back.

*The Plan*

General Montgomery's plan was to use the four infantry divisions
of the XXXth Corps (Lieutenant-General Sir Oliver Leese) to
create two corridors through the defended belt towards the north

I

portion of the front, and through these gaps to pass the Xth Corps
(General Lumsden) with the 1st and 10th Armoured Divisions who,
unlike the 7th Armoured, included the new Shermans among their
tanks. The XIIIth Corps (Lieutenant-General B. G. Horrocks) was
to mislead the enemy into thinking that the main attack was to take
place in the south, and it was hoped to detain the 21st Panzer there
for several days.

An essential preliminary to success was that the R.A.F. should
obtain mastery in the air before the battle began; thereafter, they
were to co-operate closely with the ground troops. So as to mislead
any of the German air force who might come over the area, an
elaborate deception plan was prepared which included the use of
dummy lorries in large numbers so as to maintain an even density
over the whole area. Genuine vehicles moving forward took the
place of dummies which were moved back to the areas vacated by
the real articles.

The task of the 7th Armoured Division, who formed part of the
XIIIth Corps, was to contain the 21st Panzer Division in the south,
but if all went well the 7th Armoured were to pass through the mine
belt and swing north towards Daba. The particular difficulty that
faced General Harding was to reconcile two conflicting tasks, to
put in an attack sufficiently strong to deceive the enemy into thinking
this was the main attack, and at the same time to comply with the
Army Commander's implicit instructions to keep the Division in
being as an effective fighting formation for future use elsewhere.

The Divisional Commander planned to penetrate the minefields
immediately north of Himeimat, and to capture Himeimat hill and
the escarpment immediately west of it. This latter task was given to
the Free French Brigade. The breaching of the minefields was to be
done by the 44th Divisional Reconnaissance Regiment (Lieutenant-
Colonel J. L. Corbett-Winder), the specially organized unit trained
for this particular task, and they were to have the support of all the
artillery of the 7th and 44th Divisions. The Armoured Brigades were
to establish bridgeheads, and the 44th Division were to take over
when these had been gained.

Twenty-four hours before the battle was due to begin, lanes
were cleared in the British minefields. The day of the 23rd was
spent making final preparations, cleaning weapons, loading vehicles
and all the hundred-and-one preliminaries to battle. The Army
Commander had himself already briefed all the senior officers in the
Army, and the information he had given had been passed on to the

troops before the battle started. General Harding has recorded that "the atmosphere of well-designed, objective preparations, lively expectancy and quiet confidence that pervaded the Division, and indeed the whole Army, is the outstanding feature of my recollections of this period".

*October 23rd and 24th*

The enemy minefields had been given the code names of "January" and "February", the latter being the more westerly one. Operations began with a barrage opening at 9.40 p.m., the same time as the great barrage on the northern portion of the front.[1] Although there was some delay owing to soft going and the narrow gaps becoming blocked by damaged vehicles, and despite a great deal of artillery, mortar and small-arms fire, the night's operations were not unsuccessful.

The traffic control arrangements were in the hands of Major J. Lawson's Squadron of the 11th Hussars with two Troops of the Derbyshire Yeomanry, and the lanes were marked by lamps partially dimmed. The impression left in the mind of one witness is of a snake-like procession of a mass of tanks and guns and other vehicles in an atmosphere of dust and smoke and noise, all vividly illuminated at one point by a blazing carrier. The distance was lit up by streaks of machine-gun bullets and the occasional ricochet of an armour-piercing shot.

Shortly before dawn "January" had been penetrated by the 44th Divisional Reconnaissance Regiment and the Sappers, and the leading armoured regiments had passed through and established a bridgehead beyond. This was held by the 5th Royal Tanks on the right and the Scots Greys on the left, with two companies each of the K.R.R.C. and the Rifle Brigade. About the same time the Free French reported that they had gained a footing on Himeimat; this was important news, for the hill overlooked the Divisional front and it was most desirable that the enemy should not be in occupation when day dawned.

By the time the bridgehead had been established sunrise was not far off, and it was clear that the penetration of "February" would no longer be possible under cover of darkness—in daylight it would be a most costly operation. A further deterrent to a daylight

---

[1] As a matter of interest it should be recorded that the 7th Medium Regiment R.A. fired on the opening night of the attack for five hours continuously at an average rate of one round per gun per minute. During the battle this Regiment fired a total of 22,000 rounds. There is no reason to suppose that this Regiment was exceptional.

operation was the news that the French had been driven back by a
German counter-attack; they had not been able to bring up their
anti-tank guns owing to soft sand. Accordingly General Harding
decided to hold the ground gained and to renew the attack the next
night. Some of the armour was pulled back, and the 44th Reconnaissance, who had suffered a good many vehicle casualties, were withdrawn at 7.40 to re-form. The remaining tanks held the ground
gained with the support of the Riflemen, and were subjected to
artillery and other fire all day.

Meanwhile, in the north, the 9th Australian, 51st and 2nd New
Zealand Divisions, in that order from north to south, had attacked
westwards, the 1st South African Division attacked south-west, and
the 4th Indian Division launched a series of heavy raids from the
Ruweisat Ridge. By dawn, deep lanes had been cut in the enemy's
minefields, but there was as yet no clear way for the armour to go
through.

### October 24th and 25th

The 131st (Queens) Brigade was put under command of the
Division for the night's operations and two battalions, the 1st/5th
and 1st/6th Queens Royal Regiment, quickly secured a bridgehead
west of the second enemy minefield, "February". Then troubles
began. The infantry were pinned to the ground by the enemy's fire,
and efforts to clear the lanes for the armour proved slow and costly.
At last two gaps were reported clear, and the 4th C.L.Y. and the
1st Royal Tanks moved forward. Both Regiments immediately
began to lose tanks and in view of the instructions that General
Harding had had, there was no alternative but to make no further
attempts to move the armour through, so he decided to hold the
ground gained with the 1st Rifle Brigade and the two Queens
Battalions with an armoured regiment in support.

On the morning of the 25th the Corps was ordered not to press
this attack in the southern sector. In the afternoon, the 4th/8th
Hussars, who were covering the right flank of the Division, were
ordered to advance north-westwards in support of operations by the
50th Division on the right. Almost at once they ran into minefields
covered by anti-tank guns and began to lose tanks, so this operation
also had to be called off.

Throughout the day of the 25th the area between the two minefields was much congested and very exposed, and there was continuous long-range medium and heavy artillery fire on the troops

there. The C.R.A., Brigadier Mews, was wounded, and in the evening while the Divisional Commander was driving back in his Jeep his A.D.C., Captain H. Cosgrave, who was navigating the car, was killed. Although the successes gained during these two days' fighting were limited, they achieved their main object in keeping the 21st Panzer Division in the southern sector for that period.

In the north Rommel had resumed command of his Army; during September he had gone to hospital in Germany but had hurried back when the Eighth Army attack began—his place had been taken by General Stumme who died of a heart attack a few days later. There was much hard fighting on the 25th and 26th, and the 15th Panzer Division attacked repeatedly and lost heavily.

During the next few days the 44th Division took over responsibility for the front, and the units of the 7th Armoured were pulled out and placed in support. On the 31st the Division, comprising the 22nd Armoured Brigade and the 131st (Queens) Brigade, moved north into Army reserve fifteen miles east of el Alamein. Here General Harding was told that the Queens Brigade would form a permanent part of the Division and would be equipped as a lorry-borne Brigade. The 4th Light Armoured Brigade was left behind, but rejoined the Division later. Now, the 7th Armoured were to await the opportunity to exploit the break-through which was expected shortly in the northern sector.

The Australians had struck north and thrust towards the coast where they threatened to cut off the German troops in the forward zone, and the other divisions were taking very heavy toll of the German tanks in their desperate counter-attacks; in this they had invaluable support from the R.A.F. who carried out numerous bombing attacks in close support of the forward troops.

## Break-through and Pursuit

"And nightly pitch my moving tent
A day's march nearer home."

*November 2nd to 5th*

During the 2nd and 3rd, further attacks were launched by the infantry to open a corridor for the Xth Corps, under whom the 7th Armoured now came, and the Division spent these two days slowly making their way through the immensely congested area that lay behind the battlefront. Although the tracks were well marked and

well controlled, the visibility was very bad, for they were knee-deep
in dust and the traffic, mingled with bursting shells, raised dense
clouds.

When night fell on the 3rd, the Division was close behind the
fighting with the 22nd Brigade in the lead and the 11th Hussars
with them. The attack that night disposed of the final resistance of
the enemy, and as dawn broke the Division moved forward into
comparatively open country. For the first five miles, on a rather
southerly course, there was no opposition. Then, in the early afternoon, the 22nd Brigade encountered the remains of the Ariete
Division which they did their best to destroy; after an engagement lasting several hours many of the Italian tanks and guns had
been knocked out. Soon afterwards the Division leaguered for the
night with the Queens Brigade closed up to the 22nd.

On the left, the 10th Armoured Division had also got clear,
but the 1st Armoured Division to the north was still engaged with
German rearguards. Meanwhile, the New Zealand Division, with
the 4th Light Armoured Brigade, had made a big sweep round and
gained the coast at Fuka. By now, Rommel realized that the Battle
of Alamein was over and that his only hope lay in retreat.

*November 5th to 7th*

The Division continued its advance all day on the 5th, at first
towards Daba and then, since both the 1st and the 10th Armoured
Divisions had closed in on the town, in a due westerly direction in the
hopes of cutting off the German forces. There was some delay on a
minefield on the escarpment near Fuka, and when that had been
negotiated (unfortunately it proved to be a dummy laid by the South
Africans in the previous June) darkness was coming on and the
Division had to halt for the night.

On the 6th the advance was resumed at first light. Some confusion
was caused before starting by an enterprising party from a German
reconnaissance unit getting mixed up with the "A" Echelon transport of the 22nd Brigade, capturing and trying to get away with
some petrol lorries; the situation was cleared up after an engagement
in which Divisional Headquarters took part. By 9 a.m. the 22nd
Brigade were in battle positions facing a rearguard of the 15th and
21st Panzer Divisions, and they were in high hopes of cutting off the
retreat of this body and destroying them. Unfortunately their operations during the morning were severely handicapped by petrol
troubles. First the Light tanks of the 1st Royal Tanks attempted to

cut the enemy off but ran out of petrol; then, an attempt by the 4th
C.L.Y. was similarly stopped, and soon after 11 a.m. the 5th Tanks
were also grounded by lack of fuel. All that could be done was to
harass the enemy with fire from the 4th and 97th Field Regiments,
and to follow up and harass them with companies of the Rifle Brigade
who pursued German vehicles that were streaming north onto the
main road.

Replenishment took place at noon, and in the afternoon the 22nd
Brigade put forth every exertion to eliminate the enemy. Gradually
a semi-circle was formed round them, but the visibility became very
bad and the rain poured down. Soon after 6 p.m. the C.L.Y.
reported that the Germans were withdrawing; by now about
twenty-five tanks had been destroyed and two 88s, and some two
hundred prisoners taken—the strenuous exertions of the Brigade
had not been in vain, but still there was disappointment that the
dash and enterprise of the Troop and Squadron-leaders had not
been blessed with better fortune; the shortage of fuel and the closing-
down of the weather had come at a critical time. "The night was
spent in intense discomfort, the rain was incessant and many vehicles
were bogged as the leaguer was formed."

The rain continued all night and had a serious effect on the
pursuit. When morning came the Queens Brigade lorries were
almost all firmly stuck in the mud, and tanks of the 22nd Brigade
had to be used to pull them, and their own wheeled transport, out of
the bogs. Although the supply lorries were in sight of the vehicles
they had come to fill, they were not able to move up to them. It was
not until late in the day that replenishment became possible, and all
that time the Germans were hurrying westwards on the one and
only metalled road while their pursuers, who had been continually
trying to cut them off by moving across the Desert, were fuming
at the delay and praying for the sun to come out and dry the
ground.

"C" Squadron of the 11th Hussars were sent off independently
early in the morning to join the South African armoured cars on the
plateau south of Mersa Matruh where the latter had been creating
havoc in the rear areas and were much embarrassed by the large
numbers of Germans and Italians who were trying to escape across
country. Throughout their journey the squadron kept meeting
parties of the enemy, none of whom had any more heart for the fight
—they were disarmed and told to walk eastwards, and their arms and
vehicles were destroyed.

*November 8th to 10th*

In order to conserve petrol General Harding decided to leave the
Queens Brigade where they were and to advance with the Armoured
Brigade alone. The only limiting factor in the next two days was the
matter of petrol supply. Even with the reduced Division the 11th
Hussars and the Brigade were held up for some hours on the 8th
waiting for the petrol lorries to arrive, and night fell just before the
leading armoured cars reached the frontier.

On the 9th, for the fourth and last time, the 11th Hussars crossed
the line of posts that marked the boundary between Egypt and
Cyrenaica, and by the evening one squadron was at Sidi Omar and
Regimental Headquarters and another squadron were twelve miles
beyond Sheferzen. On the next day they were ordered to hold a line
of observation while the rest of the Division closed up to them; once
again the 7th Armoured Division were the first Division to cross the
frontier. Already there was anxiety over the tank state, not owing to
enemy action this time but just to plain mechanical inability to keep
going. Unlike the other two Armoured Divisions, the 7th had not
been re-equipped with new tanks and their old ones had for the most
part exceeded by far their theoretical mileage.

It had been contemplated that the Xth Corps with its two
recently equipped Armoured Divisions would carry out the pursuit,
and that the 7th Armoured would go no further than, perhaps,
Daba. In consequence many of the tanks in the 22nd Brigade which
had taken part in the Knightsbridge battles had travelled many miles
in the Desert already. The knowledge that the tanks were nearing the
end of their capabilities was an additional anxiety for commanders
at all levels. The fact that the Division led the pursuit and went
further than any other Armoured Division is no mean tribute to the
efficiency of the crews and the spirit of the Division itself.

*November 11th to 13th*

Early in the morning of the 11th the advance was resumed and at
noon the 11th Hussars and the Rifle Brigade entered Bardia. At
Capuzzo the enemy had been in the process of pulling out, and a
German train successfully ran the gauntlet of the fire of some of the
22nd Brigade's tanks, "an amusing incident". Again pursuit beyond
Capuzzo and Bardia was not possible for lack of petrol. As General
Harding recorded, "the Division cursed their fate and blamed the rain
of the 6th and 7th. It was exasperating having to wait in the Bardia
area while the enemy continued his withdrawal unmolested so far as

the land forces were concerned, though the pause was useful for maintenance and the repair of vehicles."

On the 12th, when the advance continued, there was no opposition and the way was littered with tanks and other vehicles abandoned by the enemy, and the airfield at Gambut was covered with destroyed aircraft. The 4th Light Armoured Brigade re-joined the Division on the 13th and all were able to push on to Tobruk. Again there was no opposition, but there were mines and road-blocks that caused some delay. The first troops into Tobruk were Second-Lieutenant R. G. G. Copeland's Troop of the 11th. On the next day the Division was disposed with the 4th Light Armoured Brigade west of Tobruk and patrolling forward, the 22nd Armoured Brigade in the el Adem area and the Queens Brigade in Tobruk helping to clear the port and unload barges.

The last enemy had been driven from Egypt on the 11th. The New Zealand Division remained in the frontier area and the pursuit was continued only by the 7th and 1st Armoured Divisions.

*November 14th to 25th*

By now the majority of the tanks of the 22nd Armoured Brigade were unable to go any further and administrative difficulties prevented more than a small force being maintained beyond Tobruk until that port was again in working order. The advance had been so fast that there was a risk of the ground troops out-running their air support, but it was remarkable how quickly the R.A.F. managed to get the forward landing-ground in working order again.

The 22nd Brigade were left at el Adem and the Queens Brigade at Tobruk, while the Division continued the advance with the Royals, the 11th Hussars and the 4th Light Armoured Brigade on the 15th. The 4th Brigade advanced along the coast road while the armoured car columns, with whom travelled a small Divisional Headquarters, cut across the Desert. The 11th Hussars were directed on Soluch to cut the coast road there, and then to turn northwards towards Benghazi where they would join up with the 4th Brigade. The Royals were directed to Antelat and Agedabia, where the Divisional Commander expected the enemy to make a stand. The 22nd Brigade were ordered to equip the 1st Royal Tanks with all available tanks, and Brigadier Roberts took forward a force of all arms, motor infantry, armoured cars, artillery and tanks, together with a small Tactical Headquarters and, of course, Sappers, R.A.S.C. and R.A.M.C.

On the 16th the Armoured Car Regiments secured the landing-ground at Msus and were near Tengeder. The day of the 17th was marked by heavy rainstorms, but the advance continued over very bad going and against occasional enemy air attacks. The 4th Brigade was more than half-way to Benghazi, but were being much delayed by mines and numerous demolitions. The Royals reported Antelat clear on the 19th.

At 10 a.m. on the 20th Sergeant Trumper led his Troop of the 11th Hussars into Benghazi and was soon followed by the rest of the column. A thousand Indian and South African prisoners were released and a hospital was found with seventy wounded, all being looked after by a Captain of the R.A.M.C. There was much looting by the local natives going on. The Royals, meanwhile, had gained touch with enemy rearguards at Agedabia. They had been much delayed by wet ground through which they had great difficulty in getting the guns of their supporting artillery. The landing-ground at Msus had been cleared on the 19th, and aircraft started to use it at once for bringing forward petrol and ammunition and removing wounded. The 4th Brigade reached Benghazi on the 21st and the Queens Brigade were brought up there two days later.

On the evening of the 20th the 1st Royal Tanks reached Msus, having come across the Desert from el Adem on transporters, and the next day they joined the Royals at Agedabia. On the 22nd the battle was joined, and consisted of a duel by the tanks and artillery with the enemy's anti-tank guns which were well posted and concealed on an arc astride the road covering the enemy's right flank. There were not the resources to attempt a wide outflanking movement but a number of anti-tank guns were destroyed during the day. General Harding had hoped to pin the Germans down in daylight and to move a company of infantry round them during the night, but the latter were observed, as well as held up by mines and booby-traps, and the Germans managed to hold them off while they withdrew under cover of darkness. The Rifle Brigade company entered the little town at 3 a.m., but most of the enemy had gone. Here, Colonel Pepys, the Commanding Officer of the Royals, was badly wounded on a mine; he was succeeded by Lieutenant-Colonel A. M. Barne.

After Agedabia, which the main body of the force entered on the heels of the Rifle Brigade company, the Germans were followed up and found to be holding a defensive position at Mersa Brega. By now the leading troops of the 7th Armoured Division were out of the covering range of the R.A.F. and were subjected to many air attacks,

ne of which, against Divisional Headquarters on the 24th, wounded
Colonel Maxwell so badly that he died later.

The next task was to prepare to attack the enemy in his Mersa
Brega position, but before this could be done it was necessary to
build up supplies. Until the port of Benghazi could be put into
working order for shipping all supplies had to be brought forward by
road from Tobruk where they had been unloaded from ships. The
R.A.F. alone needed 1,400 tons a day, and it was soon apparent
that the Army could not be ready to resume the offensive before the
middle of December.

Mersa Brega had marked the limit of the two previous offensives,
and naturally the thought uppermost in everybody's minds was
whether Rommel would again stage a come-back. Alternatively, he
had the choice of standing and fighting, or continuing his retreat. For
the moment the tasks of the Division were clear—to keep the enemy
under close observation, to test his strength and intentions, to follow
up if he withdrew, and to try to hold any attack he might launch.

## The Division in the Pursuit

More than two years of Desert fighting had taught many lessons,
and perhaps it is worth pausing for a moment to see how these most
experienced troops carried out their task in the long and speedy
advance from el Alamein. The author is indebted to the Divisional
Commander of the time for the information that follows.

The Division moved across the Desert always in fighting formation, covered by armoured car patrols of the 11th Hussars, experts at Desert reconnaissance, deployed on a wide front astride the
Divisional axis. Following the armoured car patrols, with which
were Engineer reconnaissance parties, came the Armoured Brigade
moving deployed for battle in three Regimental groups, each with
its supporting element of motor infantry, artillery, anti-tank guns,
etc., well dispersed against air attack, but ready to fight in any direction. Following the Armoured Brigade came Divisional Tactical
Headquarters, the Commander, A.D.C., one Staff Officer, the
C.R.A., and one R.A. Staff Officer. The Infantry Brigade followed
in similar formation behind, or echeloned to a flank according to
its task. The whole Division was controlled by the Divisional Commander personally by his wireless direct to subordinate commanders or through main Headquarters.

As the light began to fail each evening and the risk of air attack
passed, Regimental groups closed, as they moved, into a single

column in close formation, and then closed upon each other so tha
when darkness fell and the order was given to halt they formed on
compact group, each vehicle and sub-unit in its appointed place. I
the morning they moved on as soon as there was enough light to se
to drive, opening out once more into battle formation as they ad
vanced. This drill stood them in good stead, it saved time and avoide
confusion, they were always ready for battle and everyone knev
where he stood.

When the armoured car patrols encountered the enemy the
probed his dispositions and reported them in detail as the armou
moved forward to contact and the artillery came into action. Th
Armoured Regiments worked their way forward, supported by thei
artillery, to pin down or outflank the enemy under the wireles
control of the Brigade Commander, using ground and fire to cove
movement or to close the range. Infantry and anti-tank guns wer
disposed to cover the flanks, or held in reserve as the situatioi
required.

As the tanks moved forward the fire fight began, a grim struggle fo
supremacy between tank and tank or anti-tank gun, and betweei
the opposing artillery, like a mediaeval battle on a widely extende
front. The Germans were clever at disposing their tanks and gun
and always fought stoutly. The skill of the troop leader and tanl
commander in the use of ground, the accuracy of the tank gunne:
and of the artillery Forward Observation Officers were the decisiv
factors. The evidence of success was the smoke pile from a brewed-u
tank, or the sight of the remnants of a gun crew scuttling from thei
position when it was hit.

The aim was always first to pin down the enemy and discove
the flanks of his position, then to over-lap or outflank him on on
flank or both, always taking the greatest care to keep all thre
Regimental groups within close supporting distance of each othe
so that the enemy had no chance of dealing with them individually
This, combined with the skill and experience of the commander
and crews, and sound team-work on the battlefield between tanks
guns and infantry, were the secrets of success, plus of course the
fact that for the first time since the Campaign against the Italian
in 1940–41 the British tanks compared favourably with those of th
enemy.

The Germans always fought hard to maintain their position:
until dark and generally succeeded. Facing east with their backs to
the sun, the light gave them a valuable advantage in the afternoor

nd evening. When the half-light came, the tanks moved into close
ange and the rattle of Besas replaced the crack of the tank guns as
'soft" targets presented themselves. At this stage the motor infantry
vere launched to complete the work of the tanks by attacking such
nemy gun crews as remained in position, finishing off lame ducks,
learing the battlefield and pushing forward patrols to harass the
nemy as he withdrew into the darkness.

Then the tanks and guns were concentrated, supply echelons
alled forward, fitters brought up to work on damaged tanks, and the
vhole arduous business of re-fuelling and re-arming was put in hand.
n spite of the most careful foresight it was often far into the night
•efore the supply echelons arrived. Replenishment was seldom fully
ompleted before the early hours of the morning and the fitters were
iard at work until their units moved off. These were the main
easons why it was seldom possible to follow up the enemy at night.
\lso, great risks are involved in moving a mass of vehicles at night
•ver unknown ground which may well be mined as well, in the face
•f an enemy who knows precisely where he is. It is one thing to
vithdraw armour at night over known ground and into areas
ilready in your possession, quite another to advance into the un-
<nown with no means of telling when or where you may run into an
:nemy position or minefield, even if you are fortunate enough to
:omplete your replenishment and give your men the minimum of
'est in time to resume your advance before daybreak. There are, of
ourse, exceptional cases when the risk is fully justified, but as a
;eneral rule it was thought that it would not pay a dividend and
:xperienced commanders believed that was right.

*November 25th to December 11th*

Gradually the Division was strengthened. The 4th Light
\rmoured Brigade, now commanded by Brigadier C. B. Harvey in
)lace of Brigadier M. G. Roddick who had been wounded, took over
he left flank. The 22nd Armoured Brigade was relieved by the
{th Armoured Brigade, consisting of the 5th R.H.A., the 3rd Royal
Γanks, the Sherwood Rangers, the Staffordshire Yeomanry and the
tst Buffs under command of Brigadier N. Custance; the Brigade was
it full strength and equipped with Sherman tanks which were a very
atisfactory change from the old Grants and Crusaders which the
:2nd had had. The 153rd Brigade from the 51st Division arrived
ind soon afterwards the Queens Brigade who had been at Benghazi.
Γhe 7th Medium Regiment R.A. had come under command of the

Division and remained more or less continuously until the end o
January to the great benefit of all concerned. They were com
manded by Lieutenant-Colonel H. C. Elton; one of his specialitie
was speed into action and the Regiment was able, while on the move
to halt, deploy and bring down an accurate concentration in eighteen
minutes.

Headquarters XXXth Corps (General Leese) took over the from
from the Xth Corps (General Lumsden), and finally the New
Zealand Division and the 51st arrived and the anxiety about a come
back by Rommel vanished. Throughout this time both the armou
and the infantry under the Division's command were engaged in
vigorous patrolling.

### December 12th to 28th

This was a period of following up the enemy. There were no
major actions but a number of small encounters with his rearguards
During the night of the 12th patrols discovered signs that th
enemy might be about to retire, and by the early morning of th
13th he was again on the move. Plans had already been made fo
taking the earliest advantage of this, and the Germans were immedi
ately followed up by the 8th Armoured Brigade with the 11th
Hussars in the lead. The New Zealand Division, with the 4th Ligh
Armoured Brigade under command, had already started on a wide
outflanking movement to the south in the hopes of cutting the enemy
off.

On the 14th the 8th Brigade caught up with the main body o
the enemy in a strong position south-east of Agheila and attacked
with all three Regiments. Although the Germans managed to hold
them off till dark they lost a dozen tanks and a hundred prisoners
They pulled out after dark and the 8th Brigade followed up at dawn
but they soon ran into the enemy posted in some marshes. An
attempt was made to get round the position to the south but the
going was impossible. The Germans had mined the whole area very
thoroughly and there was intense artillery and anti-tank covering
fire. It was evident that no progress could be made with armour
alone, so plans were made for a night attack and the Queens Brigade
were brought up. However, before the attack could start the enemy
withdrew. Everyone hoped they would fall into the hands of the
New Zealanders, but the latter had to contend with country that wa
interlaced with countless deep wadis, and to cover the journey in the
short time available was impossible.

There were some anxious moments on the 16th when the Division had to pass through the Agheila defile in daylight, for General Harding was determined to save time by moving with vehicles closed up and to take a chance with the German air force. It was a relief when all were through unmolested and again deployed in the open country. By last light on the 16th the forward elements of the Division were fifteen miles west of Marble Arch, but again administrative difficulties were beginning to raise their heads.

The Eighth Army was permanently short of airfields during this phase. Captured airfields, together with their aircraft parking areas, were invariably mined and took a long time to clear. The Divisional Engineers cleared an airfield at Marble Arch and another between Sirte and Buerat. The R.A.F. used a forward airfield reconnaissance party which kept in touch with Headquarters R.E. for information about likely sites for new fighter airfields and the condition of existing fields. Water, though always short, was not too difficult. The Field Park Squadron possessed a very useful pumping and chlorinating set capable of replenishing one Brigade per day from most of the wells found in the Desert.

The Division passed through the New Zealanders near Nofilia on the 17th and picked up the 4th Light Armoured Brigade there, less the Greys who remained under General Freyberg's command. The advance continued, and although the enemy were manoeuvred out of Sirte by a threat to the flanks and rear by the armoured cars, the advance came to a halt for administrative reasons when contact was made with the enemy's main forces hurriedly preparing a defensive position in the Buerat area, with such armour as they still possessed covering their right flank.

By this time a good toll had been taken of the German tanks and guns and they had been much afflicted by the R.A.F. The Divisional Commander was anxious to push on and reckoned that if he had enough petrol he could force the enemy out of the Buerat position, but the Army Commander was determined to assemble enough troops to enable the Army to go right on to Tripoli in one movement, so the Division was ordered to halt and to limit their activity to patrolling and reconnaissance tasks similar to those they had carried out at Mersa Brega. It was a wider front this time and the forward troops were a long way from support by the rest of the Army.

General Leese and his administrative Staff took particular pains to ensure good Christmas dinners, and the whole Division had an issue of fresh pork, rum and extra cigarettes, luxuries that were much appreciated. There was a Carol Service at Divisional Headquarters. Of this last Christmas in North Africa the 11th Hussars have recorded: "Lieutenant R. A. Rapp had brought a lorry a thousand miles from Cairo with extra food, etc., mails, parcels, Christmas pudding, mince pies, chocolate and beer. It was the third Christmas they had spent in the field and with the tang of victory already in the air, it was certainly the most cheerful of them all. No longer was the Eighth Army fighting by itself across the seemingly endless wastes of Libya; straight ahead of them now, though still six hundred miles away, lay the flank division of General Eisenhower's Americans and Rommel had become the sandwich in between. From far-off Cairo the management of Shepheard's Hotel, which six months before had looked like having to surrender its best suite to the German Field Marshal, sent some of their old patrons in the officers' mess a cigarette case marked with the now famous sign of 'V' for Victory."

On November 8th an Anglo-American Army under the command of General Eisenhower had landed at Algiers, Oran and Casablanca and had but narrowly failed to seize northern Tunisia in their first on-rush.

*Casualties*

Though much has been said about the wounded, no mention has yet been made of the work of the R.A.M.C. The Desert imposed special problems of its own owing to the great distances to be covered in the evacuation of casualties, the absence of roads or fair tracks and, in the early days, the comparative immobility of the Casualty Clearing Stations.

In the Armoured Division, each armoured vehicle carried a first-aid kit which included morphia tablets, and all the crews were more or less trained in first-aid. There were the unit Medical Officers and a section of the Cavalry (or Light) Field Ambulance with each column, the main body of the Field Ambulance being with the Brigade Headquarters. In the early times it sometimes took two or three days for a wounded man to be got back to the C.C.S., but in emergency and if expert navigation was available a case could be taken through in one night.

As experience grew changes were made, and by 1942 Surgical Teams with operating vehicles were allotted to forward medical units. The problem of removing a badly wounded man from a tank still remained, and it was decided that the administration of chloro-

form and the injection of morphia in the tank before any attempt was
made to move the man would be of benefit to the patient, so both
these drugs were issued to all tanks and the crews instructed in their
use.

As an example of the difficulties, in the winter of 1941–42, a
soldier who was wounded at Agheila had to travel 125 miles before
he reached a C.C.S. at Tobruk. There were four Light Field Ambulances in the 7th Armoured Division then, and two of these with two
Field Surgical Teams formed a Medical Centre at Msus. When a
wounded man was fit to travel he was evacuated across the Desert
by ambulance car via Mechili to the road at Gazala. Staging posts
were set up every thirty or forty miles by Sections of the Light Field
Ambulance to care for casualties on the journey. Both then and
later, when the aircraft were available and weather conditions permitted, the more seriously wounded were evacuated by air.

By the end of 1942, with a huge Army surging forward, the distances to be covered from the front line to some sort of hospital
establishment were not so great, but it was still a longer journey
than in European warfare and often a much rougher one, despite all
the care and skill of the officers and men of the R.A.M.C. who
served the Division so well.


## On to Tripoli

*December 28th to January 23rd*

Towards the end of the year planning began for the advance on
Tripoli. The 7th Armoured and the New Zealand Division were to
advance across country inland while the 51st Division moved along
the coast road. The New Zealanders were to be on the left, going
via Tarhuna, with the 7th Armoured Division on their right. Until
the advance began, the period was marked by much patrol activity
and there were some raids by the German air force, one of which
"brewed-up" the officers' mess at Divisional Headquarters. The tank
strength of the 8th Armoured Brigade, who were to lead the advance,
amounted to 56 Shermans, 29 Grants, 43 6-pounder Crusaders and
23 other Crusaders.

At 7.15 a.m. on the 15th the 3rd Royal Tanks crossed the start
line and, with the Sherwood Rangers on the left, made good progress
at first. At 10 o'clock, however, they were engaged by German tanks
at extreme range and found the enemy skilfully positioned behind a

K

ridge. A hard day's fighting followed in which a number of enemy tanks and anti-tank guns were destroyed, though not without loss to the 8th Brigade. Ground was gained, but it proved impossible to penetrate the enemy's position, and the New Zealand Division on the left were also not able to make much progress, for the going was bad and the opposition strong. During the night the enemy withdrew and they were followed up all day over country that was much more broken than the Libyan Desert. By the evening the Division had advanced about twenty miles and just before darkness fell the 8th Brigade was again in contact with a rearguard position where they knocked out three tanks and eight guns before nightfall.

*January 17th and 18th*

By this time it had become apparent that there was not room for two Divisions to advance side by side off the coast road on Tarhuna and Tripoli, so the New Zealanders were halted and the 7th Armoured were ordered to continue the advance alone. The Long Range Desert Group had supplied most valuable information about the going and General Harding decided to advance with the 8th Armoured Brigade on the right, the 4th on the left, and the Queens Brigade following the 8th. The Division avoided the track which the Germans had mined thoroughly and kept to the open Desert—even so, the bad going caused much delay, and the descent from the escarpment above the Tarhuna plain presented great difficulty. In the late afternoon contact was made with the enemy, and the 3rd R.H.A. and the 2nd K.R.R.C. caused much damage to enemy vehicles which they found closely packed near a small village; long after dark they continued to fire their 6-pounders and other guns into the mass.

The advance continued on the 18th over very bad going and there was difficulty in finding a way down to the Wadi Tsmama.[1] By last light the Staffordshire Yeomanry were in action against vehicles and guns moving on a road about ten miles south of Tarhuna, and patrols of the 11th Hussars had reached enemy outposts about six miles south of the village. By now the Division was much strung out, and it was generally considered that this was the worst patch of bad going they had ever struck, including the famous bad stretch near Mechili before the battle of Beda Fomm. The 12th Lancers described the going as "perfectly appalling", which was in marked contrast to the day before, which they rightly described as "success-

[1] Not on map.

ul" with an advance by their patrols of between forty and fifty miles. On the coast road the 51st Division captured Misurata.

The ground was far more broken than the Desert in Egypt and Cyrenaica. Not only was there soft sand and mud, but the whole country was seamed with wadis, steep-sided, soft-bottomed and with innumerable minor wadis branching off them. The Germans had, of course, mined the obvious routes and frequently covered them also with anti-tank guns and other artillery. To the armoured car patrols fell the task of finding a passable route, and it says much for their tactical skill that their casualties were not much heavier.

### January 19th to 22nd

On the 19th the Divisional Commander ordered the 8th Brigade to press on as hard as they could in order to prevent the enemy from establishing a strong front on the escarpment at Tarhuna astride the Tripoli road. The 4th Light Armoured Brigade was still involved in heavy going further to the west, and the 8th Brigade soon became engaged with a strong enemy position which they found it impossible to outflank. While General Harding was sitting on top of Brigadier Custance's tank discussing the situation a salvo of shells landed just in front and he was badly wounded. For him it was a bitter disappointment to be put out of action when so near to Tripoli which had been his goal for over two years, and to the Division it was a severe blow to lose their Commander under whom they had achieved so much during the past four months. Brigadier Roberts, whose 22nd Brigade was in Army Reserve some way away, was sent for to take over temporary command, but he could not arrive until the evening of the 20th.

During the night 19th/20th the R.A.F. bombed the road west of Tarhuna, and in the morning it was found that the enemy had withdrawn into the pass through which the road to Tripoli descends into the plain. Some progress was made and K.D.G. patrols discovered a route, but this was reserved for the New Zealand Division, whose advance was about to begin. Little progress was made on the 20th and 21st, but preparations were made for a night attack by the Queens Brigade on the latter day.

This attack coincided with the enemy's withdrawal. They left huge craters behind them but the South African Engineers with a large bulldozer did magnificent work and the road was open at one o'clock in the morning. The 3rd Royal Tanks advanced, followed by the 11th Hussars and the Nottinghamshire Yeomanry. By dawn they were clear of the pass and moving rapidly forward. By noon both the 8th Armoured Brigade and the New Zealanders were in touch with German rearguards near the airport eight miles south of Tripoli. Again the Queens Brigade were brought up to carry out a night attack, but as they went in the enemy, who had nearly been outflanked by the 3rd Royal Tanks, withdrew to the west.

## The Capture of Tripoli

There was much excitement on the evening of the 22nd at the thought that next morning was likely to see the capture of the first city west of Alexandria, and there was much competition between units as to who should get there first. About 9 p.m. Colonel Smail warned his 11th Hussars that they were to be ready to move at mid night, all depending on when the leading troops of the Queens could confirm their suspicions that the enemy were starting to retire. At 3 a.m. the squadrons began to move up through the 3rd Royal Tanks and the Staffordshire Yeomanry to the forward positions of the Queens. "B" Squadron led, Sergeant Lyons commanding the leading car. Behind the 11th the order of march was Divisional Tactical Headquarters, the 3rd Royal Tanks, Brigade Tactical Headquarters and the Staffordshire Yeomanry.

Under the brilliant light of the full moon the leaders drove forward into the unknown—booby-traps, mines, ambushes, they might meet anything—but all was quiet and, as their History says, it seemed incredible that their entry into what had for so long been their goal should be so easy. At 5 a.m. they entered the deserted streets—no enemy, no civilian population to greet them. The road to the harbour was blocked by debris, and as there seemed to be no duty to be done, the troops settled down to breakfast. When day light came the inhabitants emerged from their houses, and the peace of the scene was shattered as the crowds realized that the troops were British, and they gave way to the wildest enthusiasm, and not long after this began the sound of the pipes was heard and the leading troops of the 51st Division arrived on the tanks of the 23rd Armoured Brigade.

Meanwhile, the 12th Lancers were making a wide sweep round the south, and about 9 a.m. the 11th Hussars moved out of the city to regain contact with the enemy whom they encountered about dusk, a covering force before an anti-tank ditch. The 8th and the Queens Brigades were also soon in contact.

One big milestone on the road to complete victory in North Africa had been passed, the place where, ten days later, the Prime Minister was to say "the achievements of the Eighth Army will gleam and glow in the annals of History".

## INTO TUNISIA

The advance for the next sixty-five miles from Tripoli, which took up to the end of January, was not an easy one. Observation was hindered by palm trees, it was hard to make progress off the road, all roads and tracks were thick with mines and booby-traps and every bridge and culvert was blown. The Queens fought their way forward on foot and the Royal Engineers worked day and night, often under fire, to deal with the various obstructions. The 12th Lancers refused to be daunted by the difficulties and often left their cars to go forward on foot or by any other means they could find— the 11th Hussars were withdrawn on the 25th for a month, during which time they were re-equipped with new Daimler armoured cars and the small Daimler scout car, known as the "Dingo". They also received a larger, lightly-armoured vehicle known as the White scout car and a number of Jeeps. All these vehicles proved a great success.

On the 24th Major-General G. W. E. J. Erskine arrived to take command of the Division; he had previously served in the 50th Division and had since been Chief of Staff to the XIIIth Corps. Brigadier Roberts, who had served in or near the Division since the beginning, left to take up a higher appointment in England, but en route he was diverted to take command of the 26th Armoured Brigade who formed part of the First Army fighting in northern Tunisia. Command of the 22nd Armoured Brigade went to Brigadier R. W. N. Hinde, Brigadier Harvey went to command the 8th Armoured Brigade and Brigadier Newton-King, who had commanded the 4th South African Armoured Car Regiment, old friends of the Division, took command of the 4th Light Armoured Brigade.

Much delay was caused on the 25th by sand dunes which made it impossible for the tanks to outflank the enemy positions, and delay-action mines in the Tarhuna Pass held up the supply columns, so it was decided to continue the advance along the coast road with the Queens Brigade. Very thorough demolitions had been done in the port of Tripoli, and until the harbour could be got into working order again it was not possible to maintain more than light forces forward—till that was done, all supplies had to come by road some 500 miles from the port of Benghazi. By February 2nd repairs had progressed far enough for the first large tonnage of stores to be landed, a fine feat by the Engineers and administrative staffs concerned.

On that day the 12th Lancers and the 4th Light Armoured Brigade came up against a strong enemy position in salt marshes along the Tunisia frontier. The narrow crossing between the marshes and the sea, a causeway over the mud, was covered by fire and, with intervals of cultivation, the marshes extended for several miles inland. There were at least thirty tanks in support of the defenders. The marshes themselves are only passable for light vehicles in dry weather, and both they and the causeways then existing cut up rapidly and became impassable when used by many vehicles. Here, there was also a series of craters, and it started to rain and there was no possible way round. The C.R.E., Lieutenant-Colonel A. D. Hunter, was ordered to make a crossing to take the whole of the Division's wheeled transport, and he decided to construct a wooden "corduroy" causeway on top of the mud. The 4th Field Squadron was given the task of building it, while the Field Park Squadron was made responsible for the supply of timber. It was surprising what a large tonnage of wood was collected in a treeless country. Work proceeded day and night, occasionally interrupted by the German dive-bombers, but the task was finished in two days. Then the C.R.E. had the mortification of hearing his causeway described by the B.B.C. observer as "a kind of rustic bridge".

While this work had been going on, the bridgehead had been held by the 1st Buffs, who had crossed on foot, the 5th R.H.A. and the Staffordshire Yeomanry whose tanks had been used to tow the vehicles of the other units and those of the 12th Lancers through the muddy way. As soon as the causeway was completed, the 8th Armoured Brigade and the 69th Medium Regiment crossed, the Queens Brigade followed them that night and by the morning of February 15th the whole Division was over. The Queens and the 8th Brigade then advanced rapidly side by side towards Ben Gardane with the 153rd Brigade of the 51st Division moving along the coast road and the enemy pulling back fast. There was much soft sand, but by sundown the whole of the Ben Gardane area had been occupied.

During the next few days there was a steady forward movement, much depending on the state of the ground and the speed with which the Sappers could clear the mines. By the 17th the 8th Brigade had only twelve fit tanks left and they were relieved by the 22nd Brigade. The Queens Brigade tactics consisted for the most part of enterprising patrols in carriers by day and active patrols on foot by night, coupled with a close understanding with their supporting artillery.

Colonel Hunter has kindly provided some notes on the problem of mine detection and clearance at this stage of the Campaign. Searching for mines along the coast road in Africa was mostly done by eye. In the same way that a Bedouin tracker can follow a camel's tracks over bare rock the more experienced Sappers could "smell" a mine in the sand; actually, their sense of sight got so acute that it registered the minute disturbance of the surface. One saw them strolling along negligently with a bayonet in the hand, then stop, prod, scrape and there would be a Teller mine or the prongs of an S-mine. Uncanny! There were not many of the electric (radio type) mine detectors then, but, for instance, when the party swept up the main road in the Horseshoe battle in March, which was at night, the Sappers used mine detectors, but the enemy then used metal mines and the detectors would re-act—in Germany the mines were made of glass, etc.

But however the mines were discovered, the finder went on after marking the mine, and it was lifted by a man coming along behind at a safe distance. The lifter felt round it for booby-traps and if he found one a wire was attached and it was pulled from a distance (this was easy until the Germans incorporated a "delay" in the circuit). The drill in clearing a minefield was much the same but on a larger scale. This was, however, a slow procedure and when, on one occasion, the C.R.E. was told to clear one of the Medenine airfields in a hurry, the 4th Field Squadron lined up at six-foot intervals and beat it like a field of roots. They got away with it, but then they had some very experienced men—the squadron commander spent a lot of his time telling them not to be so careless.

In the early morning mist on the 19th the 22nd Brigade, with the 5th Royal Tanks leading, moved fast across country to cut the road leading to Mareth and reached high ground overlooking the road about 10 a.m. just as the mist began to lift. The 4th C.L.Y. came up on the right and the 1st Royal Tanks on the left, with the 5th R.H.A. in support, but they then found themselves overlooked by higher ground and were heavily shelled. During the day they gradually closed with the enemy, and the Queens Brigade entered Medenien.

Skilful reconnaissance by the 12th Lancers and the enterprise of the 22nd Brigade enabled this high ground to be captured and during the next few days their positions were gradually improved. A surprise for Divisional Headquarters on the 18th was a demand for forage for the horses of sixty-six mounted Bersaglieri who had been captured, but the demand was met.

The next fortnight was spent improving positions and concentrating more troops forward. The Mareth Line was a sort of minor Maginot Line which had been built by the French to cover the approaches to Southern Tunisia, and it was the most formidable defensive position encountered since el Alamein. The 22nd Armoured Brigade had skilfully captured the ground that it was necessary to occupy before any assault could be delivered, but the Eighth Army had to assemble many more troops before an assault could be launched. The 201st Guards Brigade, which had been re-forming and training in Syria, was brought forward and came temporarily under command, relieving the Queens Brigade in the forward positions they had taken in a night attack. The 51st Division came forward and took over from the sea to the main coast road. Far away to the south, the 4th Light Armoured Brigade were making steady progress despite appalling country, a wide front and slender resources. The New Zealanders, too, came up on the left, closely followed by a re-equipped 8th Armoured Brigade who joined the Division again, the 4th Brigade and the Royals going to the New Zealand command.

## THE BATTLE OF MEDENINE

Early in March there were indications that the enemy were going to launch a counter-offensive. The Sappers assisted the artillery and infantry in making defensive positions, which in some cases were blasted out of rock with explosives. Mechanical earth-moving equipment, which had proved its value in dealing with the demolitions which the enemy made in his retreat, again proved its value as a permanent part of the Divisional R.E. equipment. Bulldozers were used to make hull-down positions for tanks, as well as other fortifications. Mines were not available, but a dummy minefield was laid on the left flank and proved successful in diverting enemy tanks into areas where they came under concentrated fire. The positions occupied lay on rocky hills, the Djebel Tadjera, some six or seven miles north-west of Medenine on the main road to

Mareth. The Guards Brigade lay astride the road, the Queens Brigade on their right and behind them all the armour of the Division spaced out and ready to intervene if needed.

On the evening of March 5th the troops were warned that the attack was imminent, and early the next morning "A" Squadron of the 12th Lancers gave warning of the approach of enemy tanks along the track that ran between the positions of the 6th and 7th Queens, and of others towards the Guards Brigade. The latter were deceived by the dummy minefield, sheered away and drove up to the top of a ridge which was covered by the anti-tank guns of the 2nd Scots Guards; here, they lost over a dozen tanks to that Battalion and many more to the supporting artillery. About forty or fifty tanks were in the first attack on the Queens who, for a time, were hard-pressed. The first anti-tank gun into action was that of Sergeant Andrews of the 7th Queens; he allowed the first four tanks to pass, knowing they would be engaged by other guns, and opened fire on the fifth tank at a range of 1,000 yards, scoring a direct hit with his first shot. He also knocked out the next tank at once and soon these two were blazing fiercely, a stimulating sight for the defenders who had never been attacked by tanks before.

There were some anxious moments when the tanks began to infilter into a wadi between the two Queens Battalions and a number of the anti-tank guns were knocked out. For some time the wadi was dominated by the gun of Sergeant Crangles whose Bren gunner shot down the crews as they baled out. This anti-tank gun's crew were under continuous fire from the enemy and eventually their gun was knocked out by a direct hit; they had fired forty rounds and the shield of the gun was pierced by nearly fifty bullet holes and three armour-piercing shot holes, but they had held their ground and stopped a break-through. Throughout this time there was intense defensive fire by the artillery and the 65th Anti-Tank Regiment, and the German infantry were engaged in addition by the well-sited smaller weapons of the Queens. Further support came when two Troops of the 1st Royal Tanks moved forward to engage the enemy tanks in the wadi.

In the afternoon the enemy re-organized. By this time the 8th Armoured Brigade had been moved across in readiness to support the 3rd Coldstream, and at about 4 p.m. the Germans attacked with tanks and infantry in this sector. They were met by devastating fire from the artillery, with whom the New Zealand artillery joined, and then by the Coldstream machine-guns. The attack petered out after a few tanks had reached the New Zealand position on the left. Enemy movements during the night were met with very heavy artillery fire on defensive tasks, and the Germans then withdrew into their original positions. Forty-five enemy tanks were left on the front of the Division, twenty-seven of them in front of the Queens Brigade. Our own casualties were very light. The Divisional Artillery, reinforced by the 58th Field and the 7th and 69th Medium Regiments, had fired ceaselessly with great speed and accuracy all day— one 25-pounder regiment fired 12,000 rounds.

## THE BATTLE OF THE HORSESHOE

Before General Montgomery could carry out his attack on the Mareth Line, a preliminary operation was necessary to clear the approaches. About three miles to the south of the main position lay a group of low hills of approximately horseshoe shape and this appeared to be held as an outpost position. It was not anticipated that the operation would be either difficult or costly; there did not seem to be many troops holding the position or any great extent of minefields. Events were to belie these prognostications.

A large wadi lay across the front-line about four hundred yards in front of the proposed start-line. For the infantry it was an awkward barrier but by no means impassable; for vehicles special measures would have to be taken after the infantry had crossed and eliminated the enemy's close-range fire. As there was a considerable extent of open ground to be covered in full view of the enemy, a daylight attack was obviously out of the question; besides, there was a good moon which would assist the attackers to a greater extent than the defenders.

At 8.40 p.m. on the 16th the attack began, the 6th Grenadiers, under Lieutenant-Colonel A. F. L. Clive, on the right and the 3rd Coldstream, under Lieutenant-Colonel Sir Terence Falkiner, on the left, supported by three Medium and five Field Artillery Regiments. Only a few shots were fired as they crossed the wadi, but then both Battalions found themselves in a large and dense minefield which took heavy toll of them. Those who survived pressed on with great gallantry and the Grenadiers, by now sadly reduced in numbers, reached their objectives, as did one of the two Coldstream companies; they, too, had had heavy losses. The prospect of holding the positions gained now depended entirely on whether the supporting weapons could be brought forward in the carriers, but these fared even worse

# The
# Plates

Crusaders going into Action

Light Tanks of the 1st Royal Tank Regiment

German PZ KW III's knocked out at Sidi Rezegh

25-pounders of the 4th R.H.A.

H.Q. 4th Armoured Brigade; Brigadier Richards on his Giant Tank

Another Prisoner for a Jock Column

In Action near Acroma

Forward from Alamein

1st/6th Queens
in Tobruk

The 11th Hussars
enter Tunis

In Action near Vesuvius

Cromwells of the 4th
County of London
Yeomanry leaving the
Normandy beaches

A Cromwell AA Tank of
the 4th County of London
Yeomanry landing in
Normandy

Forming up for Operation "Goodwood"

The road into Aunay

Welcome for the 1st/6th Queens at Ste Margueritte de Viette near Lisieux

Liberation of Gournay en Bray

Entry into Holland

An 8th Hussar "Dingo" competing with an icy road

The 1st Battalion Rifle Brigade at the German village of Masendorf

on the minefield than had the infantry, and almost every carrier and anti-tank gun foundered among the mines, many of the crews being killed. The Brigade Commander had no alternative but to order a withdrawal shortly before dawn, and this was no easier to carry out than the attack had been.

In the Grenadiers, four officers had been killed, five, including the Commanding Officer, wounded, and eighteen officers were missing; 265 rank and file were casualties. The Coldstream lost eleven officers and 148 men. Later, it was found that very heavy losses were inflicted on the enemy.

*March 18th to 30th*

The Division was not closely engaged during this period. The main Battle of Mareth opened on the 21st with the 50th Division attacking the northern portion of the Line, and the 7th Armoured passed to the command of the Xth Corps with the tasks either of supporting the 51st Division if they were counter-attacked or of exploiting a break-through. On the next day the Division came under the XXXth Corps again and for a time held part of the front line, when the Rifle Brigade and the K.R.R.C. were involved in local attacks. On the 30th the Division moved through the Mareth Line and concentrated out of contact with the enemy for the first time since the Battle of Alamein.

During this time the New Zealand Corps, made up of the 2nd New Zealand Division, the 8th Armoured Brigade, General Leclerc's Free French, the K.D.G.s and a medium artillery regiment, were moved round the German right flank, followed by the 1st Armoured Division, in a wide sweep directed on Gabes. The 1st Armoured carried out an attack at el Hamma, which nearly succeeded in cutting off all the enemy in the Mareth Line.

## APRIL

The month of April was one of steady advances. The Division had no part to play in the Battle of Wadi Akarit on the 6th, though the Divisional Artillery supported the attack and the 4th C.L.Y. were placed in support of the 50th and 51st Divisions in a counter-attack rôle; this they carried out successfully but lost a number of tanks in the action. The enemy withdrew that night and the Division followed up, being on the left of the 51st who moved along the coast road. The advance was not a swift one on account of minefields and

the rough country which was laced with deep wadis, making movement by night impossible. The 8th was a notable day for the first
encounter with the new German "Tiger" tank, one of which was
captured intact by an enterprising patrol of the 11th Hussars.

On the 10th the 11th Hussars entered Sfax, just ahead of the 51st
Division and the 23rd Armoured Brigade, and the 22nd Brigade
moved across country ten miles beyond Sfax, meeting no opposition.
On the 12th the Division were ordered to join the Xth Corps at Kair-
ouan, and here they found Brigadier Roberts with his new Brigade
and the 1st Derbyshire Yeomanry, who were commanded by
Colonel Payne Gallwey, a familiar figure from the early days in the
Desert when he had commanded a squadron of the 11th. The 4th
Light Armoured Brigade with two squadrons of the 12th Lancers,
who were in contact with the enemy, came under command again.
For the next week the Division were engaged in pushing the enemy
back, while the New Zealanders took Enfidaville. On the 28th the
Division was withdrawn and moved round to an area south-west
of Enfidaville in preparation for an attack that was to exploit to
Hamamet, twenty miles further up the coast.

## On to Tunis

On April 30th a sudden and unexpected change of plan occurred
and as a result of a conference between General Alexander and
General Montgomery, the 7th Armoured Division with the 4th
Indian, the 201st Guards Brigade and some medium artillery were
transferred to the First Army. The move of the 7th Armoured
started on the night 30th/1st, and for the 22nd Armoured Brigade
this entailed a journey of nearly 300 miles, the tanks being lifted on
transporters. By May 2nd the Division was concentrated at el Krib,
a small village thirty-five miles south-west of Medjez el Bab, which
was forty miles west of Tunis. Here they came under the command
of the IXth Corps; this had been commanded by Lieutenant-
General J. C. Crocker, but he had been wounded a few days previously and General Horrocks came to take temporary command.

For this account of the final operations of the African Campaign
the author has had the privilege of making use of the account
written at the time by General Erskine.

In the drive on Tunis the plan was for the IXth Corps to breach
the enemy's main position near Medjez el Bab with the 4th British
Division on the right and the 4th Indian Division on the left on a

front of about 3,000 yards and to a depth of about the same distance. In support there would be about 350 field guns, forty-eight medium guns and a couple of dozen heavy guns, while the whole resources of the R.A.F. were to be made available on the day of the attack. The tank strength of the 7th Armoured was made up to a total of 72 Shermans, 21 Grants and 47 Crusaders. The two Armoured Divisions, the 6th and the 7th, were to be used side by side behind the infantry divisions, the 6th being on the right. The tasks given them were to secure certain dominating ground south-west of Tunis, to breach the perimeter defences of that city and to help each other if need be.

The 7th Armoured were to move forward in daylight on the 5th, and at dawn on the 6th they were to move again ready to pass through the infantry who, it was estimated, would have taken their first and second objectives by then. Two routes were available for the thirty-five-mile march up to the infantry start-line, but they were not sufficiently broad all the way to make it possible to alter the order of march once they had started, so particular care had to be taken to form up the two columns, each over thirty miles long, in the order in which they would be required to deploy at the other end. General Erskine decided to lead with the Royal Engineers, with infantry escorts from the Queens, so that mines could be dealt with quickly and any obstacles on the routes could be cleared with the least delay. The 22nd Armoured Brigade was to follow with the 5th R.H.A. and a squadron of the 11th Hussars, the rest of that Regiment following the 22nd Brigade; behind them the Queens Brigade came. There was an old minefield area on the way and the tracks were about six inches deep in dust before the operation began, so special care had to be taken with route-marking and there was a strong contingent of the Military Police with the leading troops.

The Divisional Commander's tactical plan was to seize his objectives, which had been selected off the map, with the 22nd Brigade, bring forward the artillery and then take over the ground won with the Queens Brigade, releasing the armour for the next move forward.

On the evening of the 5th, the Vth Corps on the left carried out a most successful attack on some high ground which, if left in enemy hands, would dominate the advance of the 7th Armoured Division, and at 3 a.m. on the 6th a tremendous artillery fire opened on the front of the 4th British and 4th Indian Divisions to cover their advance. Both Divisions met with full success and as daylight came the R.A.F. added their contributions with immense numbers of light bombers and fighter-bombers. The German air force made no appearance.

For the 7th Armoured, all went as planned, and at 7 a.m. on the 6th they were starting to deploy behind the 4th Indian. At 9 a.m. the armour began to move forward and, although the 22nd Brigade met resistance, the advance was steady and relentless. The armour's first objective was taken, but time did not permit of the Queens Brigade being moved up and taking over the position thoroughly, and General Erskine considered that it would be wiser to keep each Brigade in the firm positions they both held rather than to loosen the hold of both and complicate the long task of replenishment; it would also enable the troops to gain some rest, an important point in view of what looked like being an energetic day on the morrow. Long before the day was ended, therefore, both Brigades were fully set for the morning advance.

At dawn on May 7th the 22nd Brigade moved off to its second objective, meeting and overcoming some resistance on the way. This resistance was overcome by good minor tactics in which the Light Squadrons played an important part; much boldness and dash were shown and everyone was determined not to be stopped. While this was going on, the Queens Brigade and the artillery were moving forward quickly to the area left empty by the 22nd and were soon established there, and as soon as the 22nd Brigade had made their second objective the Queens Brigade again moved up. By now it was time for the armour to begin its task of dominating all roads leading into Tunis from the west and the armoured cars began to carry out close reconnaissance of the city itself. At a quarter past three in the afternoon General Erskine gave the order for the 22nd Brigade to go into Tunis.

As the armoured cars of the 11th Hussars had indicated that street fighting was to be expected, the 7th Queens were hurried forward to join the Armoured Brigade and they played a most important part in cutting all roads through Tunis before it was dark. The use of this Battalion was most effective—with their 6-pounder guns they demolished houses where there was resistance, and by bold and resolute leadership they were able to capture all important points and bridges before any demolitions were undertaken.

The Signal Log of the 22nd Brigade records tersely the scene when the first cars of the 11th entered the city—" 'B' Squadron 11th Hussars report right patrol now seems to be right in town itself. Can 1st Royal Tanks send something forward to help? It is raining steadily, the Troop is surrounded by surprised Germans firing at the cars, hundreds of others surrendering, wildly excited civilians blocking way, showering flowers and pressing with wine and other offerings." Colonel Carver, now commanding the 1st Tanks, obliged with part of his Light Squadron.

The enemy in Tunis were completely surprised. German soldiers were walking in the streets with their girls and German officers were strolling casually about. The arrival of the 11th caused a panic on the part of the Germans and a sensation on the part of the French population. The armoured cars were pelted with flowers and received by the civil population with hysterical enthusiasm—at the same time, the bolder Germans threw hand grenades and fired tommy-guns. The cars withdrew embarrassed by this scene, but their work had been done and all Germans in Tunis were in a state of complete confusion and panic.

Early in the afternoon the 5th Royal Tanks (Lieutenant-Colonel W. M. Hutton) sent in a composite force under Major Ward and they were involved in street fighting and sniping from the upper windows of houses. By six in the evening they had two thousand prisoners on their hands and the force reported—"street fighting not facilitated by cheering local populace trying to mount tanks and throwing flowers". Lieutenant-Colonel H. B. Scott's 4th C.L.Y. were denied these pleasures.

By the morning of the 8th all resistance in Tunis had ceased and enormous numbers of prisoners started to come in. The drive on Tunis had split the German armies—some made for the Cap Bon peninsula, others for the Bizerta area or the small harbour of Porto Farina. The last-named were bound for the arms of the Americans coming from Bizerta, and those going to the peninsula were moving into the forces of the First and Eighth Armies directed to Cap Bon for that purpose. The Division pursued vigorously as far as the Medjerda River and some sharp fighting occurred in this area on the 8th. The 11th Hussars followed up to Porto Farina where the enemy was found to have given up fighting and to be busy making rafts— many thousands surrendered. The countryside was strewn with Germans and Italians who had given up the contest and many of them made for the Medjerda where all bridges had been blown. The enterprising local Arabs had kindly organized a ferry service on horseback across the river so that those who paid fifty francs could reach captivity with dry feet. Two rather fat Panzer Ordnance Warrant Officers took a half share each on a horse, but the weight proved too much and the horse collapsed in mid-stream to the intense delight of the onlookers. Altogether, this was an excellent day, and the Armoured Regiments had very good hunting as the number of burned-out vehicles showed.

*     *     *     *     *

Thus ended a Campaign in which the Division had been continuously engaged. Exactly six months before, it had passed through the el Alamein battlefield to take up the pursuit. For six months the Division had chased the German Army across Africa—from Mersa Matruh to Tobruk and then by way of Benghazi and Msus to el Agheila. From there in company with the New Zealanders and the 51st Division to Buerat. With the New Zealanders again to Tripoli, then on its own to Medenine where, with the same two companion Divisions, it held so successfully the vigorous German counter-attack of March 6th. Then the Battle of Mareth and so to the Wadi Akarit, and after that, once more in open country, for Sfax and then the Enfidaville hills, whence to the First Army for the final offensive.

Two thousand miles in 180 days and at the end a victory complete and spectacular. All the way, hardly ever out of first-line contact with the enemy. Several units and formations that served with the Division were not there at the final count; the 8th Armoured Brigade was in the Division for long, the 12th Lancers from Tripoli to Mareth, the 4th Light Armoured Brigade was constantly with it. For every mile of the way there was the 131st (Queens) Brigade, with the 3rd Royal Horse Artillery, the Royal Engineers, the Royal Corps of Signals and all the administrative Services. Like the 11th Hussars, the 22nd Armoured Brigade were only out of the hunt for a short time while they were being re-equipped. It was most fitting that the latter, who included the 1st Royal Tanks, the oldest remaining Armoured Regiment in the Desert, should be in at the kill with the 11th, as usual, in the van.

Finally a special word of praise was reserved in the Divisional Commander's Report on Operations for the Royal Corps of Signals: "The passing of orders and information in the Division by wireless has been brought to such a degree of perfection that not a moment is lost, and not a scrap of information is missed. The credit is due to our Signals and the Staff Officers and Commanders who appreciate how to use them." Those who had the good fortune to serve in the

Division in later Campaigns would heartily endorse those words. "The Wireless Always Works" may not have been the motto of the Divisional Signals Regiment, but it was their pride to see that it always did. Until the end of the war no Division set a higher standard of technical skill or practical use than the 7th Armoured— what this contributed to the fighting of battles and the avoidance of needless casualties can only be appreciated by those who gained the benefit.

## CHAPTER 6

*September 15th to December 20th, 1943*

# ITALY

*Reference Maps—No. 9, page 164. No. 10, page 172*

### Rest, Re-organization and Re-equipment

AFTER the capitulation of all the German and Italian forces in North Africa the Division was withdrawn to an arid spot in the Desert, Bou Arada, fifty miles south-west of Tunis. This caused much disappointment, for it had been hoped that the end of the Campaign would see the Division stationed within close distance of civilization. There was, however, only a short stay there and then they moved to Homs on the coast about sixty miles east of Tripoli, a great improvement on the previous location.

Here, the Division had three months in which to prepare for the next Campaign, and a great deal of work to do. All units had to be completely re-equipped; as shipping was at a premium for the invasion of Sicily all the new equipment had to come by road from the Delta, 1,500 miles. Every wireless set was stripped, serviced and checked. Every vehicle that could possibly be repaired was repaired, and every Workshop and Light Aid Detachment worked as hard as they could. Spares, new *matériel* and new assemblies came very slowly, but by the strenuous personal efforts of the Corps Commander it all arrived just in time.

There were no great changes in the equipment of units except in the case of the 11th Hussars; here, the Squadrons, in addition to the ordinary Troop of two Daimlers and two Dingos, were given a Troop mounted in White Scout Cars who combined the tasks of infantry with those of Sappers, and in place of the Jeep Troop there was a Gun Troop with two 75-mms. mounted in White half-track Scout Cars.

There was need for much individual training, especially weapon

162

training, and grading of technical specialists. In view of the probability that the Division would have to land on a hostile shore against opposition, there was also training in Combined Operations, for which purpose a Landing Ship Infantry was moored in Homs harbour. Much time was spent in rapid disembarkation and in practising driving onto and off ships, and study was made of the lay-out and functions of a Beach Group. Finally, all units and formations had to be trained for fighting in a very different type of country to that to which they had long been accustomed.

At Homs General Erskine took much trouble to provide amenities for off-duty hours. The Jerboa Club was set up with facilities for reading, writing and recreation; there was a cinema and a theatre for E.N.S.A. and other concert parties, a steeplechase meeting was held and there were organized leave parties to Tripoli and other places. A lot of football was played and everyone spent many hours bathing.

Among the highlights of the Eighth Army's sojourn on the coast was a visit by the King. Most troops had an opportunity of seeing His Majesty, and the 11th Hussars, whose Colonel-in-Chief he was, had an informal visit all to themselves. Not long before *The Times* had described them as "those incomparable paladins".

For some of Divisional Headquarters there was a break in July when, on the 12th, General Erskine took his Tactical Headquarters to Sicily. The invasion had been launched on the 10th and it was felt that it might be necessary to weld together the Armoured Brigades operating there—if that happened a controlling Divisional Headquarters would be needed. The necessity, however, did not arise and the party returned to Homs a fortnight later.

A small planning staff was set up under Lieutenant-Colonel P. R. C. Hobart, the G.1. As the Division was a "follow-up" Division and not engaged in the assault, it was chiefly a matter of keeping in touch and studying the theatre of future operations. A number of exercises were held on models, with the principal geographical features hopefully disguised in the expectation that those attending would not be able to recognize the place of landing. One of the chief tasks of the planning staff was to work out the mass of detail required by the Movements Staff for the loading of men and vehicles. The order of embarkation had to be decided early and, once settled, it could not be changed without causing great difficulty and confusion.

The plan decided upon was based on the assumption that the Division might be required to assist in the battle on the beaches

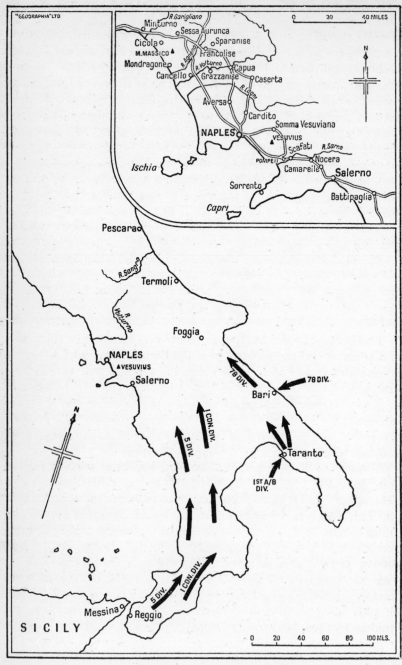

Map No. 9.—Southern Italy

immediately on landing, but that it would not be needed to function as a complete formation in operations far from the beachhead until all component parts were ashore. Accordingly, the order of landing aimed at producing first the 131st (Queens) Brigade Group composed of two Battalions, one Armoured Regiment, one Battery R.H.A. and one Troop R.E. The next stage was to complete this Group, then to land M in Divisional Headquarters, then the Armoured Brigade and more artillery, and finally Rear Headquarters and the rest of the Services. In the event, this worked out exactly right.

A month before sailing the Divisional Commander briefed all senior officers, but without disclosing the exact area. Immediately before embarkation, he addressed all officers and senior N.C.O.s, and before landing all the men were fully informed of the coming operation.

The Order of Battle on the day of landing in Europe is shown in Appendix I.

## ATTACK ON ITALY

The occupation of Sicily was completed on August 16th, and on September 3rd the first troops of the Eighth Army set foot on the mainland of Italy opposite Messina. They progressed rapidly forward although the Germans had made the fullest use of demolitions on roads that lent themselves particularly well to this form of delaying action. On the 9th the Navy carried the 1st Airborne Division to Taranto where they landed unopposed and they soon had their patrols forty miles into the hinterland.

The Bay of Salerno, south of Naples, had been selected for the main Allied thrust, and there the American Fifth Army under Lieutenant-General M. W. Clark delivered the assault on September 9th. This Army was composed of the British Xth Corps and the United States VIth Corps, the latter being on the right. General Horrocks had been the commander of the Xth Corps, but he had recently been badly wounded in an air raid on Bizerta and his place was taken by Lieutenant-General R. L. McCreery, hitherto Chief of Staff to General Alexander. Under his command he had the 46th and 56th (London) Divisions for the assault and the 7th Armoured as the follow-up Division. On the north side of the Bay Commandos and their American equivalents, Rangers, were to be landed.

As the assault forces sailed for their objective on the evening of the 8th they heard General Eisenhower's broadcast announcing the surrender of Italy. This announcement, though unavoidable under the circumstances, had a disturbing effect on troops keyed up for battle and many expected an unopposed landing. The Germans, however, were remarkably quick in disarming the Italian troops and taking over their defensive positions, and the assault was met with well-controlled fire and much opposition, which was the more disconcerting as the convoys, under strong Naval escort, had met with nothing more than slight air attacks on their long voyage.

The least resistance was on the right where the Americans advanced nearly eight miles before dark. New German defensive weapons made their appearance, glider bombs and radio-controlled bombs, and one of these hit and disabled the battleship *Warspite*.

A small advance party of the Division landed with the assault troops; this was composed of the Commander of the Queens Brigade, Brigadier L. H. Whistler, and a representative of each unit due to land with his Brigade, together with a strong contingent of the Military Police with the D.A.A.G. and the Staff Captain Q, the last-named officers being required to lay out the Divisional concentration area. On the evening of the 15th the first main parties of the Division began to land and with them came Divisional Tactical Headquarters. Just before midnight most of the 5th Royal Tanks were ashore, and the first guns to land were those of the 3rd R.H.A. early on the 16th.

A complication arose owing to many of the infantry being left out of the ships carrying their transport; this curious last-minute change by the Movements Staff might have had serious consequences, for the vehicles were there on the beach but not the men to go in them—it was three days before they arrived.

At this stage the whole beachhead was under fire, the situation an anxious one and the area none too strongly held. The 46th and 56th Divisions had fought magnificently, but they had a large area to cover and were thin on the ground. The arrival of the Queens Brigade provided a reserve for the Corps and at first they were positioned for counter-attack, later for reliefs and adjustments of the line.

After some anxious days the assaulting troops gained the upper hand. The Eighth Army had been making strenuous efforts to come to the relief of the Salerno force and covered 300 miles in seventeen days against much opposition and innumerable demolitions. By September 16th it was apparent to Kesselring, the German commander, that he could no longer hope to stop the landings, still less to drive off those who were already ashore, so he ceased his counter-attacks and made ready to meet the threat of the combined Fifth and Eighth Armies whose junction took place on the 16th.

The build-up of the Division was a slow process, for there was no great abundance of shipping, and the turn-round to Tripoli was seven days. The results of the training in Africa were seen in the speed with which the troops and all their equipment were cleared from their ships, and it was reported that their loading in Africa had also been exceptionally speedy. The Tank Landing Ship proved to be the ideal vessel for the transport of an Armoured Division so long as all personnel were in the same ship as their vehicles, while the early phasing-in of the Military Police paid a very good dividend in clearing the beaches and sending the troops quickly forward to their concentration areas.

New problems faced everybody when they got to Italy, not least the Royal Engineers. The emphasis in their work had shifted, and the maintenance of the roads through the Divisional area now be-came of the first importance. It was not enough to ensure that the enemy demolitions were made good; much more had to be done. In a country where very often progress for wheeled vehicles was im-possible off the roads, much labour had to be diverted to the repair and upkeep of these roads. Many of them, too, had originally been constructed for ass-carts, and the effect upon them of the passage of an Armoured Brigade in wet weather was disastrous. This was a new and particularly onerous task for the ever-busy Field Squadrons and one more worry for commanders and staffs.

The bulk of the Division was concentrated four or five miles from the coast in an area that had been reclaimed from the marshes. Here the troops were brought up against the danger of malaria and had to adopt stringent precautions—they slept under nets at night, took mepochrine tablets twice a day and had to smear special grease on the exposed parts of the body. These measures were tiresome, both to carry out and to enforce, but they were most effective and malaria never became a problem in the Division.

The village of Battipaglia, round which the Division concen-trated, gave everyone a first glimpse of what the R.A.F. could do to a European town—hitherto the evidence of the Air Force's superi-ority had been seen in burned-out vehicles alongside North African roads—most houses were destroyed completely, and roads and lanes were blocked with rubble.

## INTO BATTLE AGAIN

By September 27th the concentration of the Division was nearly completed and the time had come for them to take up the running once more. The plan was for the 46th Division to clear the pass through the mountains as far as Camarelle; there, the American Rangers would form a bridgehead and through that would pass the 7th Armoured Division with the 23rd Armoured Brigade under command. At that time, this Brigade, under command of Brigadier H. Arkwright, consisted only of the Royal Scots Greys in Sherman tanks, the armoured cars of the King's Dragoon Guards, the 24th Field Regiment less one battery and a Field Company of the R.E. They had no infantry of their own but had the support of American troops when required.

The first objective was to be Scafati on the River Sarno. From there, the 23rd Armoured Brigade were to advance straight to Naples, moving along the coast road between Vesuvius and the sea, while the main part of the Division were to pass north of the volcano and make for Capua on the River Volturno. Owing to the close nature of the country, the narrowness of the roads and the impossibility of moving off them, the Division was not able to concentrate forward and had to form up in line-ahead behind the 46th. A certain degree of dispersion was forced on them on account of the possible activities of the German air force and, at a density of forty vehicles to the mile, the Division covered no less than fifty-five miles of road, the distance from London to Brighton.

The 23rd Armoured Brigade began their advance on the night of September 27th/28th. The leading group of the main part of the Division was the Queens Brigade with the 5th Royal Tanks (Lieutenant-Colonel R. N. Wilson), the 5th R.H.A. and a Troop of the R.E. under command; they were followed by the rest of the artillery under the C.R.A., the Mediums in the lead. At dawn on the 28th the 7th Queens advanced and quickly seized some dominating high ground just forward of the 46th Division's positions. The remainder of the Brigade then passed through, with the 6th Queens under Lieutenant-Colonel M. Forester in the van.

A Troop of the K.D.G.s under Lieutenant P. W. G. Phillips had got into Scafati and reached the bridge there before the enemy could blow it; they kept it covered by fire until the 6th Queens, who had made a rapid advance, could come up, drive the Germans away and secure it—it was an important gain. Much fighting followed in the streets, for the enemy made strenuous efforts to re-gain the bridge, but by the next day the 6th Queens were firmly in possession of the whole area. This was a fine day's work by the Battalion.

In order to relieve the congestion on the bridge at Scafati the Sappers built a Bailey Bridge a short distance away. This equipment, on which they had trained at Homs, was one of the outstanding inventions of the war. Its characteristics were speed and simplicity in erection, adaptability, and ease of carriage and manufacture. A Bailey Bridge Troop had been formed in the Field Park Squadron (Major B. G. Bloomer); this could carry, in fifteen 3-ton lorries, enough material to construct one 80-foot bridge able to carry up to forty tons, sufficient for the tanks with which the Army was then provided. Another new bridging device also made available at this stage was the Scissors Bridge, a prefabricated construction spanning 30 feet which was carried on the chassis of a tank; it could be lowered into position by the crew without their having to expose themselves. The Scissors Bridge proved its value time and again during the next eighteen months.

Like all the other towns and villages through which the Allies passed, Scafati gave a wildly enthusiastic welcome to the troops. "Cheering all the way," says the Divisional Headquarters War Diary, Fruit of all sorts was hurled into the vehicles, and cheers and kisses marked the strong contrast with the sullen Arabs to whom the troops had grown accustomed, who cared nothing for either side unless there was tea to be exchanged for eggs. A great deal of help was given by the people in the way of information and in helping any of our men who were wounded or temporarily cut off. On the Cathedral steps at Scafati stood a priest robed in scarlet surrounded by acolytes and nuns chanting and swinging incense burners, and as the armoured cars passed he sprinkled them with holy water. All this was a pleasant and encouraging experience.

The 29th and 30th were marked by a slow but steady advance across country that was waterlogged by the recent heavy rain, much cut up by irrigation ditches, with bad roads, against determined rearguards, mines, felled trees and booby-traps.

On October 1st Major Palmer's "A" Squadron of the K.D.G.s entered Naples, setting the seal on the first stage of the Italian Campaign. On September 25th the Germans had evacuated the large and important group of airfields at Foggia, and very shortly after the capture of Naples, airfields there were available for the

R.A.F. to use in close support of the Army. The port had been severely damaged by the enemy before they left, but the American experts, by immense efforts, had it working again in a surprisingly short time—a fortnight after its capture the port was dealing with more than 5,000 tons of supplies per day.

## ARMOUR TO THE FRONT

The country now began to open up, but only in the sense that the tight clusters of villages got fewer and the roads slightly more numerous, so General Erskine sent the 22nd Armoured Brigade into the lead on October 2nd. The 1st Royal Tanks under Colonel Carver were in the van and their progress on the first day was so good that the 4th County of London Yeomanry (Lieutenant-Colonel Viscount Cranley) were able to come up on their left in the evening. The 1st Tanks found Somma Vesuviana a mass of rubble, the roads blocked by fallen houses and the place in flames, but they worked their way round and in the course of the next two days reached Aversa; the opposition had been determined, but there had been much help from local patriots.

It was only with difficulty that the 11th Hussars were able to get forward and deploy. "Gone for ever were the days of free manœuvre in the Desert, of fast movement from one flank to another", says their History. Now, they had to drive down narrow roads with ditches on both sides until a burst of fire at the leading car revealed the enemy's position. Infantry and tanks were generally needed to remove the opposition, and the armoured cars would work along some by-road if one could be found, in the hopes of locating the enemy's flanks. Deep mud from the autumn rains that had now begun in earnest made going difficult and nights unpleasant.

The 4th C.L.Y. met similar opposition to the 1st Tanks and also had to fight their way forward. The country consisted of tall and luxuriant vines up to twenty feet above the ground, festooned between the poplar trees that supported them, and in between were flourishing market gardens or crops of tall maize. The tank commander looking out of his turret could see nothing, so a heavy burden fell upon the Scout Platoons of the Rifle Brigade who were in close support of the armour. The German positions were always skilfully sighted and hard to pin-point with accuracy. Much good work was done by the R.H.A. in putting down fire quickly and accurately. This type of country, too, gave much scope for blocking roads by felling trees or using country carts and booby-trapping the obstructions. The Division's bulldozers were in constant use for clearing away rubble and filling in craters.

On October 3rd the advance was held up by stiff resistance at Cardito, where the Rifle Brigade under Lieutenant-Colonel V. Paley fought a very sharp action. The enemy were driven out by Major W. J. Apsey's "I" Company supported by the guns of Major F. B. Wyldbore-Smith's Battery of the 5th R.H.A. after Major the Hon. H. D. G. Prittie's Company had been stopped by casualties to most of their key personnel. Altogether the two companies lost ten killed and thirty-nine wounded.

On the 5th the 1st Royal Tanks made a causeway crossing over the Regi Lagni, a large drainage ditch, and the Brigade pushed on rapidly for the Volturno, where it was soon found that all bridges had been blown and that Capua was held in strength. The country up to the Volturno was soon cleared of enemy and then a pause ensued while the Army brought up supplies, for both the Fifth and the Eighth Armies had run to the limit of their administrative resources. At Capua the 56th Division came up on the right, and the 46th Division took over the Cancello area from the 23rd Armoured Brigade. The Queens Brigade came forward to the Santa Maria La Fossa sector.

## THE CROSSING OF THE VOLTURNO

### October 7th to 16th

*Preliminary Moves*

The assault crossing of a river is a particularly difficult task for an Armoured Division on account of the small number of infantry available, and the Commander cannot afford to launch a heavy attack with his infantry against a strongly defended position since he has no reserves other than his armour, and they cannot be made effective until a firm bridgehead is established. Here, the task was inevitably allotted to Brigadier Whistler and his Brigade, who were given the 4th C.L.Y. under command and the entire artillery and engineer resources in support.

The plan adopted was, first, to gain all possible information by means of careful patrolling; then, to deceive and harass the enemy with small infantry forces with a great weight of artillery behind them; and, finally, to take advantage of any opportunity that might

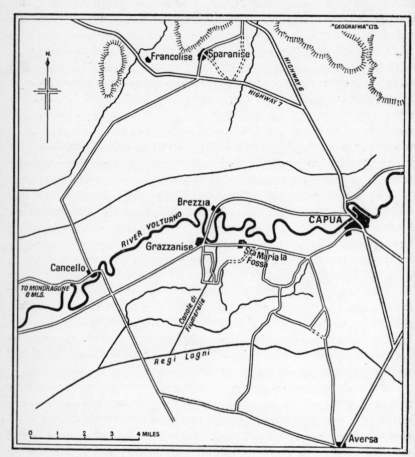

Map No. 10.—The crossing of the Volturno

occur in order to obtain a firm footing on the opposite bank.
Whether or not the operation would prove a success depended
almost entirely on the amount of information that could be gained
about the German dispositions and defensive fire plan. The standard
of patrolling in the Queens Brigade was an extremely high one and
during the period up to the 12th a very complete picture was built
up of the extent of the opposition.

The whole length of the river was defended by machine-gun fire,
with artillery defensive fire on all likely crossing places. The defences
were in depth and it would be no easy task to establish a bridgehead.
High flood-banks concealed enemy mortars and a mile beyond the
river was a triple canal in the banks of which were more enemy
weapons. There was not the material to construct a bridge that
would carry tanks and there was no obvious tank fording place, but
it seemed that there might be a chance to get tanks across if careful
work was done on the banks and the tanks were waterproofed.

Two routes ran up to the river, one parallel with the bank for
what seemed to be a very long mile; the other ran for part of its
length through the area of the 56th Division and, also, was under
enemy observation, so it could not be heavily used. A good deal of
hard work had to be done on all roads, and bridges had to be made
over the Canale di Fiumerelle.

The only possible crossing place over the Volturno in the Divisional sector was by the village of Grazzanise where the river makes
a big loop to the south. Here there was a wooden bridge. This had
been partially destroyed by the Germans; the centre span, which
looked rather shaky, was intact and about eighty feet long, but there
were gaps of similar length at the two ends.

On both sides of the river the banks were very steep and about
fifteen or more feet high, covered with trees and shrubs. The width
of the river was about eighty yards and the depth varied from rather
more than six feet on the far side to little over one foot on the near;
during the operations the river level dropped about two feet and
then later rose sharply. There was a brisk current of about eight or
nine miles an hour which made the handling of assault boats difficult.

Throughout the Xth Corps there was a general shortage of
bridging equipment and the amount allotted to the 7th Armoured
Division was only enough to make one raft, capable of carrying up
to five tons, and one Bailey for nine tons which could be used to
span the two gaps in the wooden bridge. There were enough
assault boats, 72 in all. Tanks would have to find a ford. The task

facing the Sappers was a difficult one, for they had to construct a nine-ton bridge over a long gap with a swift current below, the nature of the river bed being unknown and the opposite bank held by the enemy who often brought down heavy artillery and mortar fire onto the construction site. The courage and determination shown by the Divisional Engineers was of a high order.

Skilful and enterprising patrolling by all arms concerned, and the close co-operation between infantry, tanks, gunners and sappers eventually gained a crossing for the Division at a low cost in casualties.

*Patrolling and Preparation*

Grazzanise had first been occupied by the 5th Queens under Lieutenant-Colonel M. Elrington, and on the night of October 7th/8th two men had swum the river in order to investigate the far bank. On the next night Lieutenant Peaseley and one man also swam across to find out the depths and the strength of the current. On the same night "A" Company of the 7th Queens (Lieutenant-Colonel D. S. Gordon) took over the village and sent out patrols to investigate the defences the next day. On the night of the 9th/10th more of the 7th Queens came in with "C" Company of the 1st Cheshire Regiment, the heavy mortar and machine-gun Company of the Brigade, who had been put under their command.

During the next two nights detailed reconnaissances were made for launching sites for the assault boats, and fighting patrols were sent out to discover the exact positions of the enemy posts and to draw down their artillery fire. There was much action by the 3rd R.H.A., the mortars and machine-guns, and by a squadron of the C.L.Y. who came forward to add their quota of fire to the Germans' discomfiture.

The most valuable patrol was that under Lieutenant R. J. Ashworth on the evening of the 10th. They crossed in an assault boat, but the current was so strong that their paddles were ineffective and they had to pull themselves along by the supports of the wooden bridge. No sooner had they reached the far side than they came under fire from a post only twenty yards from the bank; as they charged this, two other posts nearby opened up and Lieutenant Ashworth was killed. A torrent of enemy small-arms fire now broke out and this was followed by intense artillery and mortar fire all along the south bank and into the Battalion's area behind. This continued until nearly midnight. Evidently the

enemy thought that a serious attempt was being made and he
disclosed his defensive fire plan and the location of his posts. It was
with difficulty and only through the skill and bravery of the Patrol
Sergeant and his men that the rest of the patrol got back, two of them
being wounded, one seriously. "The patrol's fine action", says the
Battalion War Diary, "in which their gallant commander was
killed, will not be forgotten by the Battalion; it was due to them that
the whole Battalion was saved many casualties which would have
been the case if we had tried to cross before knowing the enemy's
strength."

## THE CROSSING

*October 12th and 13th*

The evening of the 12th was selected for the assaults by the 46th
and 56th Divisions. The orders to the 7th Armoured were to carry
out diversionary attacks, mainly with artillery and patrols, but to
lose no opportunity of making a crossing if it were possible.

At Zero Hour the artillery opened up. As some of their concentrations were to be very close to the forward troops these were
temporarily withdrawn, and this saved casualties from the enemy's
defensive fire which came down at once.

The first boat that "C" Company of the 7th Queens launched
was carried downstream by the current and holed by shrapnel, but
the Sapper on board managed to secure a rope to the far bank. The
Queen's tried again at 2.30 in the morning but were again met by
heavy fire, so the attempt was called off. An hour later they tried
again and this time were successful, and by 6 o'clock in the morning
a small bridgehead had been established with two platoons and a
machine-gun platoon of the Cheshires. During the day "B" Company
and the remainder of "C" crossed, and a patrol under Lieutenant
J. B. L. Ainsworth brought back valuable information. It is worth
recording that by this time all the men had become skilled water-men
and showed no fear of the river or its fast current. This was attributed
to the fact that during the stay at Homs nearly every man had
learned to swim.

*October 14th, 15th and 16th*

It was decided to start building the bridge on the night 14th/15th,
Lieutenant Thompson having carried out a detailed reconnaissance
of the standing portions of the old structure. The raft also was put

in hand and soon completed. As the first Jeep was being loaded, a shell cut the cables, but they were mended again by 1.30 a.m. on the 15th and ferrying began. Each trip took twenty-five minutes, and before dawn six Jeeps and four anti-tank guns had been taken over.

The responsibility for moving all the anti-tank guns across, including those of the 7th Queens, lay with Lieutenant-Colonel W. S. Stewart's 65th Anti-Tank Regiment, and Major M. E. Parker's 260th Battery were in charge. Each gun had two sets of drag-ropes and it took thirty men to haul each one up the bank on the north side. A wireless code for reporting progress was used—the four guns were given the names of Matthew, Mark, Luke and John, and the guns' towing Jeeps were their children.

So much fire came down on the bridge site that it was decided to discontinue night work and to confine construction to the hours of daylight when our artillery could more easily dominate the opposition and work could continue more or less unhindered. The officer commanding the 4th Field Squadron, Major D. J. O. FitzGerald, had been badly wounded on the first night. At 4 p.m. on the 16th the bridge was completed.

Meanwhile the C.L.Y. had discovered a fordable site just up-stream of the bridge, suitable for waterproofed Shermans. The Regiment were determined to get their tanks across the river, so the entire personnel of the Squadron set to and dug a large bank away, and the tanks were waterproofed by men from the Workshops who even followed the tanks when in action with a welding plant and attended to the back portions while they were firing at the enemy. The work was made no easier by downpours of rain. On the evening of the 16th two Troops passed through the river. Next day, owing to the rain, the river had risen and the ford was much deeper—the banks, too, had become much more difficult to negotiate—but the rest of the Squadron followed and soon the whole Regiment were across. Colonel Hunter had sent his small bulldozer over the bridge as soon as it was completed, and this did good work improving the bank on the far side. A larger bulldozer, which had been water-proofed in Africa in anticipation of some such job as this, waded over and then helped by towing tanks up the steep bank. Only one tank failed to make the trip and that was rescued by the large bulldozer.

While the 7th Queens were working their way forward, patrols of the 5th Queens were engaged in clearing the banks of all the enemy posts. On the night 15th/16th patrols found Brezzia clear and the 7th Queens occupied it early in the morning. While they paused there, the 5th Queens opened up the bridgehead as far as the next canal, moving north and east, and the 6th Queens likewise moved forward, north and west. The 7th Queens subsequently recorded that during the past few days and nights their mortars had fired more bombs than in the whole of the North African Campaign.

The attacks of the 46th and 56th Divisions were also successful, and by October 22nd both the British Xth Corps and the American VIth Corps were established across the Volturno and ready to engage the enemy's next delaying position, the River Garigliano.

## FURTHER ADVANCES

The 56th Division advanced along the high ground to the north of the Volturno valley with the 7th Armoured on their flank on the lower ground by Highway 7. The enemy withdrew slowly, demolishing every bridge and culvert as he went. For a time he maintained an outpost line round Francolise and Sparanise and in the hills above them, but on October 22nd these areas were cleared by the 5th Royal Tanks, the Rifle Brigade capturing the commanding features. Misfortune befell the 11th Hussars on the 25th when Colonel Smail, with Major Roberts, Captain R. R. Lockett the Adjutant and a trooper, was involved in a bad Jeep accident, as a result of which both the Colonel and Major Roberts had to be invalided home. Major W. Wainman took over temporary command.

A few days later the Division was moved to take over the line on the Agnena river by the coast. The move was a slow one as they had to travel via Capua where the bridge could take only one tank at a time. The Rifle Brigade took over the line and at once developed a small bridgehead. In front was an expanse of marshy plain with, behind it, the bulk of Monte Massico rising abruptly. The enemy's main position was on the mountain, but he also held the coast road, leaving, between the two areas, a few self-propelled (S.P.) guns and parties engaged on mining and demolitions.

"From the mountains he had excellent observation and 'swanning' tank officers doing reconnaissances of the forward defended localities of the Rifle Brigade, with immaculate white belts and large map-cases, were not popular, however much they might have considered that their presence instilled confidence into the infantryman

M

in his slit trench. Their visits were invariably followed by an unpleasant half-hour from mortars and S.P. guns."

Reconnaissance revealed that there was a possible crossing place
for tanks and vehicles, albeit heavily mined, near the beach, and it
was decided to send a squadron of the 5th Tanks across this while the
6th Queens attacked Mondragone and the high ground beyond the
village.

This attack went in at dawn on November 1st and was a complete success. Mondragone was taken and the ridge on Monte Massico
beyond was occupied, all at small cost. The forward companies
spent a miserable night of intense cold with occasional mortar
shelling until relieved by the Rifle Brigade next day. The 1st Royal
Tanks, who had lost four tanks on mines and fifteen others temporarily
in bogs a day or two before, passed through on the 2nd and continued the advance, taking Cicola after a sharp fight. Thence, the
22nd Brigade moved on to Sessa Aurunca where they joined up with
the 46th Division who had come by the mountains. The 7th
Armoured were then pulled back to areas behind Massico, leaving
the Rifle Brigade to hold a scattered line about two miles short of the
River Garigliano, with a squadron of the 11th Hussars and one of
the 5th Tanks in their support.

### HOMEWARD BOUND

On November 7th the Rifle Brigade and the two squadrons were
relieved and went back to join the rest of the 22nd Brigade at
Aversa. By now, news had come that the whole Division were to go
home in the near future. All vehicles were handed over, the majority
to the 5th Canadian Armoured Division, "somewhat to the surprise
of the latter, for some of the wheeled vehicles had been with the
Division since the previous February when they had been obtained,
second-hand, from the 4th Indian Division".

With few weapons and no vehicles at all, the Division was
concentrated on the Sorrento Peninsula, an area that was untouched
by war. There were few amenities or opportunities for recreation.
Some local leave was possible—Capri, Pompeii, Vesuvius, Naples
and other places—but the weather was far from what was expected
from "Sunny Italy" and the prices in the towns were extortionate.
One experienced and well-known figure remained behind to take up
another appointment, Major W. Raper, who had commanded No. 5
Company R.A.S.C. for three years.

Much kindness had been received from the Nuns at Casaluce, where Divisional Headquarters had been situated for some time; although Roman Catholics, they provided the Senior Chaplain, Mr. Wingfield Digby, with a Chapel and were very helpful in a variety of ways. When the Division left, the Workshops made a pair of Altar Candlesticks which were presented to the Nuns and gave much pleasure.

On November 19th the Advance Party sailed for the United Kingdom, but it was another month before the main body of the Division drove slowly through the crowded streets of Naples to embark for home. The voyage was uneventful, but brightened by the celebration of Christmas at sea, and in the first week of January 1944 all arrived at Glasgow, whence they travelled by train to areas in the Eastern and Home Counties, and then dispersed on leave.

The Division's Campaign in Italy had been a short one. There had been much arduous and difficult fighting in bad weather, but no spectacular advances. The greatest contrast with Africa, however, was in the terrain, which was so difficult for armoured forces, close country, limited views, narrow roads, dykes and ditches, deep mud, and demolitions every few hundred yards. All this served as a foretaste of what was to come in North-West Europe, and as a transition stage between the Desert and the well-populated, highly civilized countries where the Division was yet to see fighting as hard as any that it had experienced during the past three and a half years.

## CHAPTER 7

*June and July, 1944*

# NORMANDY

*Reference Maps—No. 11, page 182. No. 12, page 190. No. 13, page 202*

*Preparation*                                                    *January to May, 1944*

THE concentration area of the Division was in Norfolk. The Queens Brigade were in the King's Lynn district and the 22nd Armoured Brigade round Brandon. This latter area was not an attractive one, "a low-lying, sandy waste with groups of decaying Nissen huts clustered beneath tall pines". There were many administrative matters to be dealt with such as the home system of documentation, less generous rations, small fuel allowances, centralized cooking, exact accounting for stores and barrack damages, leave problems and travelling, matters long forgotten by the old soldiers and never heard of by the young ones.

There were new War Establishments, new and sometimes unfamiliar vehicles and weapons to be mastered, more training in Combined Operations as well as ordinary training both for individuals and for the Brigades and the Division. Once again the tricky business of waterproofing vehicles for a landing on a hostile coast had to be undertaken, this time for wading in a depth of at least four feet. There was more than enough work for all. Ranges on which to fire weapons were few and hard to come by and training areas were restricted, a very different state of affairs to the old Desert days and the "wide open spaces". One of the training proposals that came from higher authority was that the Chaplains should attend a course at an Army Battle School. This was successfully resisted by General Erskine who contended that they had already seen enough of the real thing.

The 11th Hussars had gone to Berkhampstead where they became Corps Troops for the XXXth Corps (Lieutenant-General G. C. Bucknall), but happily the coming Campaign was not far advanced before they were back again with the Desert Rat on their shoulders once more. The 8th Hussars returned to their old Division in Norfolk, organized now as an Armoured Reconnaissance Regiment, their equipment being much the same as that of an ordinary Armoured Regiment but with a higher proportion of light reconnaissance vehicles. Lieutenant-Colonel C. Goulburn was now their Commanding Officer. The 1st Battalion the Royal Northumberland Fusiliers provided the Heavy Support Company for the Queens Brigade, 4-inch mortars and Vickers machine-guns, and they were to do fine service for the Brigade in the days to come.

On February 24th the Division was honoured by a visit from the King, part of an arduous programme that he was undertaking to all formations before they went overseas. Many Colonels and Colonels-in-Chief visited their regiments, and the Division also had a visit from General Montgomery, the Commander-in-Chief of the 21st Army Group.

A number of the more senior "key" officers, such as Brigadier Whistler and Lieutenant-Colonel P. R. C. Hobart the G.1, were taken from the Division and posted to other Divisions so as to strengthen them with their wide and up-to-date war experience. These many transfers, though inconvenient to the 7th Armoured, were of very great value to the other formations, and there is no doubt that this was a wise policy.

In armament, much the most important change was the equipment of the Armoured Regiments with the Cromwell tank. This was the latest product and a very different article indeed from its predecessors. Its virtues were its great reliability (for it had a Rolls-Royce engine and needed little maintenance) and its speed on good going—during the advance into Belgium it easily kept up with columns of other vehicles even when the latter were driving their fastest. Its cross-country ability was good, but it was not the tank for the high banks of the Norman Bocage where the Churchill, alone of all tanks on both sides, could go almost anywhere.

Neither the armour nor the gun of the Cromwell could bear comparison with the heavy German Panther and Tiger tanks, but they, on the other hand, were neither fast nor mechanically reliable. Since it is impossible to combine reliability, speed, cross-country performance, thick armour and a big gun in one machine, some people reckoned that they had as good a tank as could be obtained at the time and this opinion was borne out when it came to the "cavalry rôle" of pursuit from Normandy. Others, however,

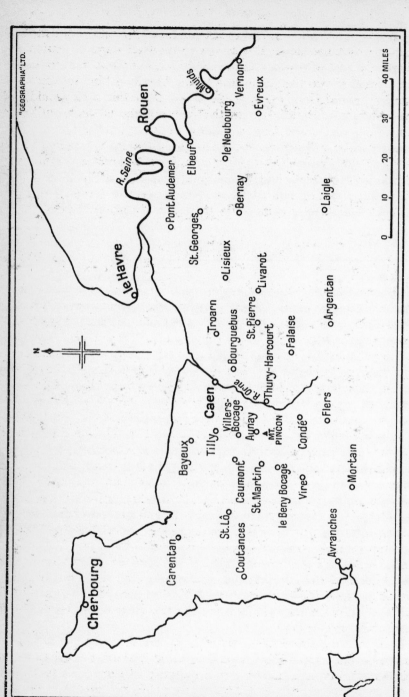

Map No. 11.—Normandy

considered that it was a pity to change to a new tank from the
Sherman which had done good service in the later stages in Africa
and in Italy, and with which all were familiar, but views were to be
altered when it was seen how readily the Sherman "brewed up"
when hit by the German anti-tank shot—often this tank would
burst into flames instantly, giving the crew no time to "bale out".
Each Troop had three Cromwells and one Firefly, the latter a
Sherman with a British 17-pounder gun intended particularly
to combat the Panthers and Tigers which carried 88-mm. guns.
The Cromwells generally had 75-mm. guns, but some had 6-pounders.

The other two Armoured Divisions that were to serve in the
21st Army Group were equipped with Sherman tanks.

## OPERATION "OVERLORD"

### The Plan

The Assault Force was to consist of the United States First Army
under Lieutenant-General Bradley on the right, and the British
Second Army of two Corps under Lieutenant-General M. C.
Dempsey on the left.

The left-hand British Corps was the 1st (Lieutenant-General
J. T. Crocker) and the 3rd British and 3rd Canadian Divisions
were the assaulting divisions. On their right was to be the XXXth
Corps; here, the 50th Division were to assault, the 7th Armoured
to follow up and the 49th Division to come in behind the 7th. On
the British left the 6th Airborne Division were to fly in and seize
the crossings over the River Orne between Caen and the sea. On
both flanks there were to be landings by Commando troops and two
airborne divisions were to land on the Americans' right.

The immediate task of the invading force was to gain a bridgehead that would include Caen and Bayeux and ground further to
the west. On the first two days of the Invasion it was planned to put
ashore over 170,000 men with 3,000 guns, 1,500 tanks and 15,000
other vehicles, many of them armoured. Within the Division the
22nd Armoured Brigade, less the 1st Battalion the Rifle Brigade,
were to land on D-Day and on the day after from assault craft,
while the rest of the Division were to sail in ordinary ships and then
transfer into smaller craft.

Until such time as a port could be captured, the troops on shore
were to be maintained from a pre-fabricated harbour known as a
"Mulberry", but in addition a vast quantity of stores was to be

landed over the open beaches. Over 6,000 landing vessels were made available for the operation, and rather more than half of these were supplied and manned by the Royal Navy. About 190 warships were to support the assault by their fire, 150 of them belonging to the British Navies. There were four British and four American Battle-ships.

The long-term air preparation was designed to sever all land communications with the intended battle area by the destruction of bridges, marshalling yards and railway workshops. The lay-out of the French railways was such that this could be done without disclosing that the point of attack was to be in Normandy rather than the Pas de Calais where the enemy expected it. This interdiction programme, combined with the bomber attacks on the German oil industry, effectively prevented the speedy arrival of enemy rein-forcements on the battlefield.

The Division set up a small Tactical Headquarters in London near the Second Army Headquarters, and there a planning staff under Lieutenant-Colonel N. M. H. Wall, the G.1, worked out the complicated tables for loading and landing the large number and variety of the Division's vehicles.

Very elaborate security precautions were imposed for some months before the Invasion was launched. A wide belt was thrown round the coasts of Britain, and all mail from individuals living within the belt, whether civil or military, was subjected to censor-ship. An unprecedented step was taken when immunity was removed from diplomatic "bags" and the representatives of foreign countries found themselves also subjected to censorship, much to their in-dignation.

*The Country*

For a few hundred yards inland from the beaches there is a strip of fairly open ground, marshy in places. Then comes the "Bocage", many square miles of small fields, farms and villages extending for about thirty miles south of Bayeux. It is heavily wooded and for the most part observation is hard to obtain, especially during the summer months. The fields, many of which are no more than an acre in extent, are divided by high banks on the tops of which grow thick strong hedges with many tall trees. The roads, except for the few metalled ones, are narrow, and the whole country is interlaced by deep, winding lanes barely the width of a cart. In wet weather the mud is glutinous. Fine weather brings clouds of dust of a thickness and impenetrability that compares well with the Desert—"Go slow, Dust brings Shells" was a common road-side sign.

At the time the Invasion took place the crops were high and where fields were not down to corn they carried a heavy head of the famous Norman cattle. There were also many orchards, mature and close-planted. For the tank commander the country was not attractive, for his field of view was very limited and many of the banks and lanes could not be crossed by the Cromwell or Sherman tank. Furthermore, the dense nature of the vegetation lent itself admirably to close-quarter attack by infantry armed with the German equivalent of the American "Bazooka" or British "Piat", tank-destroying short-range weapons, and to the activities of snipers who, hidden in trees, took a heavy toll of tank commanders and other leaders.

To the south and south-east of Caen the terrain was very different. It was open, with few banks or hedges, and it constituted an ideal "tank run" for many miles, leading into the Falaise plain and the heart of France. It was plain that a tank break-through in this area would have disastrous consequences to the whole German defensive position south of the Seine, and so the defence of this portion of the front was a matter of prime importance to the German High Command. It was, however, the Allied plan to effect the break-out from the American sector on the right while attracting to the sector of the British Second Army as much enemy strength, especially in armour, as possible.

The third area of country that requires notice is the stretch of high ground in the Bocage which extends from Point 309, five miles south of Caumont, to Mont Pincon, ten miles to the south-east. The highest points of this range are a thousand feet above sea level and, although thickly wooded in most parts, occupation of the massif afforded observation over a wide expanse. From the planning stage onwards, it was clear that these Norman Alps would form a pivot of the enemy defences.

*The Enemy*

The German forces across the Channel were under the command of Field-Marshal Rommel and comprised the 88th Corps in Holland, the Fifteenth Army covering the coast from Antwerp to the River Orne and the Seventh Army from there to the River Loire. An immense amount of work had been done on the coast defences; all ports were, of course, so strongly protected that sea-borne attack was out of the question. On all beaches and cliffs, wire, mines, emplacements and concrete obstacles abounded. In addition there were many obstacles below high-water mark, poles with mines on the top and similar devices, and their presence required careful calculations as to the best state of the tide for the first wave of the assault to reach the beaches.

Much valuable work had been done by General Hobart, the first commander of the 7th Armoured Division, in devising suitable types of tanks for overcoming the various obstructions and defences of the enemy. The 79th Armoured Division had been formed under his command to experiment with, and handle in action, these special armoured vehicles which varied from "D.D." tanks that could swim ashore and "Flail" tanks to beat up the mines to flame-throwers and pill-box destroyers.

The coast-line itself was held by second-grade divisions; behind them were the infantry divisions for immediate counter-attack, and behind them again were the Panzer, Parachute and infantry divisions for the counter-offensive. It was the German hope that the forward troops could hold up the Invasion long enough to enable the counter-offensive forces to be assembled and launched in an attack that would drive the Allies into the sea.

On D-Day the front which the Second Army was to assault was held by one infantry division in static positions along the coast. Near Bayeux was the 352nd Division, the 12th S.S. Panzer Division was at Falaise, the 21st Panzer Division at Bernay, and further away at Amiens was the 2nd Panzer Division; south of the Loire was the 17th S.S. Division. The Panzer Divisions were equipped with Panther and Tiger tanks, heavily armoured and carrying heavy guns, and they were eminently suited to the defensive fighting that they had to do in Normandy; later, when the battle became more mobile, their mechanical unreliability and lack of mobility told against them.

*The Weather*

In each month there were only three days when the state of the tides and the moon were suitable for an assault. During June these days were the 5th, 6th and 7th. The first of these was originally fixed as D-Day, but so bad was the weather and so unfavourable the forecast that the operation was postponed for twenty-four hours. This was a serious matter, for not only had all the troops been briefed but many convoys had already sailed. General Eisenhower, the Supreme Commander, was then faced by as weighty a decision as has ever confronted any man, since the weather reports continued to be unfavourable. The complications involved in a postponement of the operation for another month were immense, and it seemed impossible that secrecy could still be maintained over the intended place of assault. But if the operation went forward there was a risk that bad weather would prevent the supply or reinforcement of those troops who had got ashore. The forecast for the early hours of the 6th gave a slight hope of some lessening in the bad wind and sea conditions and the decision was taken to seize this opportunity.

The Order of Battle of the Division on D-Day is shown in Appendix I.

### Into Battle

"On the eve of this great adventure I send my best wishes to every soldier in the Allied team. To us is given the honour to strike a blow for Freedom which will live in history, and in the better days that lie ahead men will speak with pride of our doings.

"Let us go forward to Victory, and as we enter the battle let us recall the words of a famous soldier spoken many years ago:

> 'He either fears his fate too much,
> Or his deserts are small,
> Who dare not put it to the touch
> To win or lose it all.'

"Good luck to each one of you.

"Good hunting on the Mainland of Europe."

Such was General Montgomery's D-Day message to the 21st Army Group.

Early in May the greater part of the Division moved from Norfolk to new concentration areas where the waterproofing of vehicles was completed. The 22nd Armoured Brigade went to join the fleet of landing craft at Ipswich and the Queens Brigade, the Services, the 1st Rifle Brigade and other units went to areas near the London and the Tilbury Docks. Accommodation was poor, the waterproofing work arduous and the last-minute shipping problems trying, but by May 28th all was ready and General Erskine briefed all officers in the cinema at Brentwood. After that the camps were "sealed" and there was nothing to do but to await the word to set out.

On June 4th the Armoured Brigade embarked at Felixstowe and the rest of the Division embarked from their areas shortly afterwards. No one who saw it will ever forget the vast array of ships lying waiting in the strong south-west wind with sharp rainsqualls and a falling barometer, everybody wondering anxiously whether the operation was to go forward or was to be postponed for another month. After a day's delay they sailed. The voyage was uneventful and the armada passed down the Channel under the guns of the enemy's coast defences in broad daylight, screened from time to time by smoke-floats which, however, the fresh wind soon dispersed. A few salvoes were fired from the batteries on the French coast and one ship in the convoy was hit and set alight, but the remainder passed steadily on until they joined the huge concourse of shipping, stretching up and down Channel as far as the eye could reach, off the Norman coast.

The whole area of the German defences had been subjected to intense air attack alternated with bombardment by the Navies, and the enemy's ordeal had been concluded by rockets and other supporting weapons fired from the landing craft as they approached the beaches and by the weapons of the infantry themselves. More than 6,000 aircraft were in support of the assault.

The 50th Division had landed at 7.25 a.m. on June 6th. In addition to its normal complement of three infantry brigades and other arms, the Division had been reinforced by the 56th Brigade under Brigadier E. C. Pepper, the 8th Armoured Brigade, an American battalion of large-calibre S.P. guns, two British S.P. field artillery regiments, a medium regiment, two S.P. anti-tank batteries and various special armoured vehicles.

When night fell on D-Day most of the infantry were half a dozen miles inland and patrols were approaching the outskirts of Bayeux. The 1st Corps on the left had also secured a substantial beach-head and the 6th Airborne Division had gained the bridges over the River Orne and had thrown forward a small bridgehead. On the right, the U.S. Vth and VIIth Corps, who had not made use of any special armour and had not had the early support of tanks, had secured small beach-heads on either side of the River Vire after sustaining heavy casualties, but they were not in contact with each other or with the British Second Army.

Two officers of the 22nd Armoured Brigade landed with the

50th Division's Headquarters on D-Day behind the assault, and they reconnoitred an assembly area for their Brigade and marked the route to it. Brigadier Hinde and a staff officer landed the same evening. The next day, June 7th, the Brigade began to come ashore, somewhat behind time on account of the bad weather, and by nightfall all three Armoured Regiments were landed, one without transport as yet, and with them were the 5th R.H.A. also temporarily short of transport. Despite the high waves only one or two vehicles failed to make the trip and they were quickly recovered from the holes into which they had plunged under the water by the extremely efficient recovery teams of the Beach Groups. Waterproofing had been a conspicuous success.

The scene on the beaches was one of great activity. There was a constant stream of DUKWs (amphibious lorries) and landing craft of all sorts bringing ashore more men, stores and ammunition, and taking off wounded and prisoners. Above floated captive balloons to deter enemy low-flying aircraft, and a steady flow of Allied 'planes roared in to engage their targets or were returning home. An occasional enemy shell fell on or near the beaches from posts that were still holding out, and when darkness came a few German aircraft dropped random bombs, a form of attention that continued for many weeks but seldom did any damage.

It was not until the 12th that the Queens Brigade was complete on shore. That things should have gone so slowly was no fault of the Division's—that was the programme and the bad weather had caused delays in its operation. Unloading the ships was a hazardous performance; as the smaller craft came alongside to take their loads they rose six feet on every wave and yawed away from the ship's side. The vehicles sustained no more than sharp jolts to their springs, but the troops had to jump from rope ladders or netting, "involving a considerable degree of physical and nervous agility, particularly in those whose occupation was normally sedentary".

During June 7th the XXXth Corps made a lot of progress, and on their right flank the Commandos made a substantial advance and captured some coastal batteries. Bayeux was occupied and on the next day the 8th Armoured Brigade with some of the infantry of the 50th Division pushed forward to the high ground south of the town. However, resistance was gradually being built up and there was heavy fighting on the right flank, while on the left progress was held up short of the village of Tilly.

So far no German tank formations had been encountered on

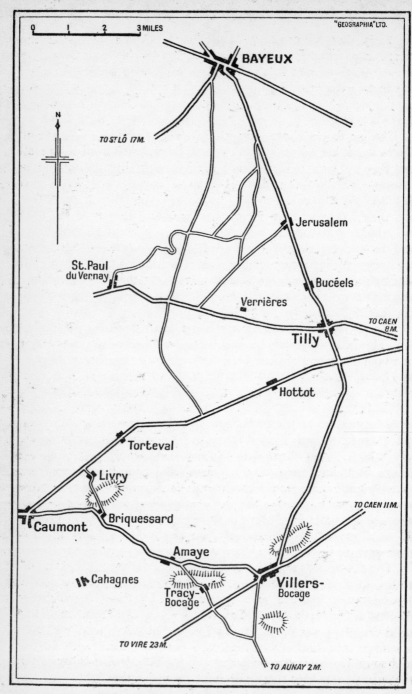

0 1 2 3 MILES

N

TO ST LÔ 17 M.

BAYEUX

Jerusalem

St. Paul du Vernay

Bucéels

Verrières

Tilly

TO CAEN 8 M.

Hottot

Torteval

Livry

TO CAEN 11 M.

Briquessard

Caumont

Amaye

Cahagnes

Tracy-Bocage

Villers-Bocage

TO VIRE 23 M.

TO AUNAY 2 M.

Map No. 12.—The Battle of Villers-Bocage, June 13th to 15th, 1944

the Corps front and no unexpected enemy units or formations except two battalions of cyclists with a few S.P. guns who had arrived north-west of Bayeux after an exhausting pedal; they had no effect on the operations.

### *June 7th to 12th*

The 5th Royal Tanks were the first Regiment to go into action. There was a fast tide racing in as they disembarked from their craft and they lost two tanks, but they hurried on to their assembly area stripping off the waterproofing material as they went. The next day "A" Squadron were sent to assist the 56th Brigade and they had their first experience of serious sniping and close-quarter attack by infantry—Lieutenant Garnett's tank was actually "boarded" and he and his operator had to drive the enemy off with their revolvers. "B" Squadron were engaged in supporting the Commandos. During the day the Regiment took six guns for the loss of two tanks and half a dozen casualties which included Captain Noble of the 5th R.H.A.

The 1st Royal Tanks supported the 69th Brigade, also on the 8th. The Rifle Brigade were much handicapped owing to the ship in which the crews of their Carriers were travelling being diverted to Cowes Roads where it spent five days. The absence of these platoons was a serious disadvantage to the Motor Companies.

On the 10th such of the 7th Armoured Division as were ashore were ordered to advance through the 50th Division on Tilly. At that time there were only the three Armoured Regiments, the 5th R.H.A., part of the 8th Hussars and two companies of the Motor Battalion; there was a general shortage of transport. The 56th Brigade came under command. During the next three days some progress was made, but the enemy were determined to fight strongly for this village and had enough tanks and infantry to do so. The 7th Armoured early felt the need for more infantry than were available.

The 4th County of London Yeomanry led off at 5.45 a.m. on the 10th and they were soon involved in fighting. In the hamlet of Jerusalem they knocked out a German tank but they were unable to disperse small parties of infantry who kept up a continuous sniping until the place was swept by the South Wales Borderers who took a strange collection of prisoners, two Japs, one Turk, one Russian and some Germans. By dusk the C.L.Y. had cleared Bucéels, but the enemy came back there with infantry during the night.

The 5th Royal Tanks had come up on the right of the C.L.Y.
and they, too, were soon in contact with the enemy at a number
of road blocks. In the close country fast movement was impossible,
but eventually outflanking manœuvres by the squadrons in turn
got them as far as some more open country and Major Macdonald's
"A" Squadron made fair progress to Verrières. When they leaguered
for the night they were joined by the 2nd Essex, while the 2nd
Gloucesters held Jerusalem. The two companies of the Rifle Brigade
were deployed with these two leading Armoured Regiments, but
there were far too few infantry for the tasks in hand. The 5th Tanks
had lost five tanks and an officer and fifteen men killed during the
day.

On the 11th the Essex and Gloucesters carried out successful
attacks and they were supported by the Armoured Regiments until
the advance was stopped by a line of thick woods. On the 12th
the Queens Brigade appeared, supported by the 1st Royal Tanks,
and they made a limited advance in very thick country. There was
no opportunity anywhere for a break-through by tanks.

## The Battle of Villers Bocage

### June 13th to 15th

On account of the opposition at Tilly the Corps Commander
decided to move the 7th Armoured Division round the right flank,
for the American 1st Division had reported only slight opposition
in their advance on Caumont. About noon on the 12th General
Erskine received his orders and was directed to advance on Villers
Bocage. The route was by St Paul du Vernay, Livry and Briquessard. The 22nd Brigade were to lead, without the 1st Tanks but
with the 7th Queens, and they also had the 5th R.H.A. and the
8th Hussars (less one squadron) for reconnaissance to their front
and flanks. The rest of the Queens Brigade with the 1st Tanks were
to follow as soon as they could disengage.

The move began at 4 p.m. and all went well as far as Livry
where the advance guard bumped into an enemy force. The tank
of the leading Troop leader of the 8th Hussars was knocked out,
and the motor company of the Rifle Brigade that was moving
with the C.L.Y. had to be called up to clear the village. There
was no alternative route except through the American area and
that was not possible, so there was some delay while this operation

was taking place. By the time the village was cleared it was 8 o'clock
o orders were given for the column to leaguer; it was not till nearly
midnight that the tail reached the leaguer area. The Queens Brigade
were not able to disengage and get on the move until after dark,
but they then moved throughout the night and when daylight came
he head of their column was just past St Paul du Vernay.

By dusk the Americans were on the outskirts of Caumont and
hey occupied the town early next morning.

The orders for the 13th were for the 22nd Brigade to continue
he advance and for the Queens Brigade group to occupy an area
round Livry; one squadron of the 8th Hussars which was already
out on the left flank was put under their command. At 5.30 a.m.
he Armoured Brigade group began to advance. The intention was
hat the C.L.Y. should occupy the high ground a mile or so north-
east of Villers Bocage, the 7th Queens should hold the town and the
5th Tanks the high ground a mile to the south. A battery of the
Norfolk Yeomanry, the Divisional Anti-tank Regiment, was to
cover the area between the two Armoured Regiments.

Up to 9 o'clock there had been no contact with the enemy
except by patrols of the 8th and 11th Hussars who had met nothing
more than small parties, and as "A" Squadron of the C.L.Y. with
"A" Company of the 1st Rifle Brigade drove into the little town
they were greeted by a cheering populace. They had been moving
fast along the good Caumont road and they galloped through and
on to the high ground beyond, followed closely by the Riflemen.
When the tanks turned off the road the latter halted and their
officers went forward as usual to receive their orders from the tank
squadron leader. The Commanding Officer of the 4th C.L.Y.,
Viscount Cranley, also went up to the front in his scout car. Suddenly several Tigers appeared just to the south of the Caen road
and immediately opened fire. In a matter of moments the Company's vehicles and the two nearest tanks were blazing. Sergeant
Bray of the Rifle Brigade got one 6-pounder gun into action and
claimed three German vehicles before a direct hit destroyed his
gun. Thus, in a few minutes, the leading Squadron and Company
of the Brigade were cut off, the Riflemen dismounted and separated
from their officers, and a very nasty situation looked like developing.

Then all hell seemed to break out in the east side of the little
town—German spandaus opened fire from the upper windows of
the houses, the streets became filled with smoke and there was the
crash of breaking glass and falling slates. A Tiger that appeared

N

through the smoke was impervious to the 75-mm. shot that Major Carr, the second-in-command of the C.L.Y., pumped into it, and a few seconds later he himself was badly wounded and most of his crew killed when his tank was set afire. This Tiger went on to destroy various Regimental Headquarter vehicles and two of the three remaining Headquarter tanks—the fourth one, under Captain Dyas, followed it in the hope of getting in a shot from behind, but unfortunately the Tiger rounded on him and destroyed his tank too. Captain Dyas himself baled out and, finding that the wireless of the Regimental Sergeant-Major's blazing tank was still working, managed to get onto Major I. B. Aird and told him what had been happening. Major Aird took command of what was left of the Regiment and disposed the squadrons in defensive positions in co-operation with the 7th Queens who arrived as the battle began.

Colonel Gordon's leading company of the 7th Queens, as they reached the town, encountered a German staff car and two motor-cycle combinations which appeared suddenly from a side road. These they dispersed, but the crews ran into the fields and began sniping from the hedges. Then a Tiger came down the main street and blew down a house at the corner of the main square where some of the C.L.Y. tanks and the infantry companies were gathered. The infantry took to the houses and worked their way through them, stalking another half-dozen tanks that appeared suddenly from the south. Particularly good work was by Major French and his men of "C" Company, and by Captain Beard and some of the Carrier Platoon. In the course of the next two hours they destroyed several tanks and damaged others. For a time the German advance was halted.

Meanwhile the Squadron and Company to the north-east remained firmly cut off, and early in the afternoon a fierce German attack was launched on them. Tigers attacked from behind, destroying the few remaining Cromwells, and large numbers of infantry attacked from the east. The wireless suddenly ceased and it was realized that the position was over-run.

Heartened by their success, the enemy again turned his attention to the town, infantry coming in from the east and tanks from the west and south. Confused fighting went on until nearly dark. Lieutenant Cotton and Sergeant Brammall of the C.L.Y. conducted some successful actions against the tanks, being greatly assisted by the anti-tank guns of the 7th Queens. Between them they claimed a bag of six Tigers. They also had to face an unexpected enemy in the shape of the Pompiers, the local fire brigade, who did their best to put out the flames of the burning enemy tanks.

Identification from prisoners showed that two Panzer Divisions were involved, the Panzer Lehr who had been expected, and the 2nd Panzer who had not. Early in the afternoon it appeared that there was no hope of holding on to Villers Bocage and the ground east and south of it as well as the lengthy lines of communication (the Division was a very long way from support by any other British troops), so it was decided to hold the town until dark and then to pull out to the area of Amaye, a couple of miles to the west. Here the Brigade could be concentrated and reasonably strong with two Armoured Regiments, the 5th R.H.A., the 7th Queens and the 5th Queens who had been sent up during the day. Even so, the centre line was a very insecure one, for it ran for the three miles back to Briquessard parallel to the front and it was also extremely narrow in parts. Fortunately the enemy made only slight efforts to cut it during the 13th, and these were held off.

Very considerable artillery support was available to the forward troops. In addition to the 5th R.H.A. Colonel G. P. Gregson, their Commanding Officer, could call on the 3rd R.H.A., an A.G.R.A. (Army Group Royal Artillery) which included the 53rd Heavy Regiment and the 7th and 64th Medium Regiments, and the artillery of the 1st United States Division. With the latter, Brigadier R. Mews, the C.R.A., had established very close liaison, sending a team to them from the Division and receiving one of their teams. "During the next thirty-six hours many calls were made on all artillery and were answered promptly and accurately." A warm tribute was paid by the troops to the artillery support they received, and in particular to the American artillery whose extra weight and magnificent accuracy was of the greatest assistance during a critical period.

The 5th Royal Tanks, with whom were "I" Company of the Rifle Brigade under Major W. J. Apsey, had taken up a position during the morning near Tracy Bocage where the 5th R.H.A. were also in position. About 5.30 p.m. the 5th Queens began to arrive in the forward area and this coincided with a determined attack by the Germans. "CC" Battery were closely involved and at one time were firing at a range of no more than 600 yards. Soon after this the retirement from Villers Bocage began and it was carried through without difficulty, the 5th Queens holding the west half of the perimeter in the new position and the 7th Queens the east.

"CC" Battery themselves had to pull back and did so under cover of their own smoke-screen.

Back at Livry, Colonel Carver was in charge of the operations as Brigadier M. S. Ekins, who commanded the Queens Brigade, was temporarily cut off with the forward troops. A firm base was formed in the area between Livry and Torteval with Colonel Carver's 1st Tanks, the 6th Queens, two batteries of the Norfolk Yeomanry, a squadron of the 8th Hussars, the 3rd R.H.A. and most of the Northumberland Fusiliers Support Company. Like the C.R.A., Colonel Carver was quick to establish close contact with the Americans on the right. During the day "B" Squadron of the 8th Hussars had worked their way as far as Cahagnes where they were attacked by infantry and Tigers and lost three tanks. The 11th Hussars, now commanded by Lieutenant-Colonel W. Wainman, had only two squadrons ashore, "C" under Major W. V. Burdon and "D" under Major J. A. N. Crankshaw. They were operating under Corps but in close contact with the Division. Their tasks had been to cover the flanks of the 22nd Brigade and they had sent in much useful information.

The evening and night passed with only slight shelling and little activity by enemy patrols. The losses of the 22nd Brigade had been heavy. In the C.L.Y. the whole of Regimental Headquarters and "A" Squadron were gone—Lord Cranley missing, Major Carr wounded, Major Scott the Squadron Leader killed, the Adjutant and eight other officers missing, three officers and many Other Ranks wounded, seventy-six N.C.O.s and men missing. Twenty-seven tanks had been lost and numerous other vehicles. The Rifle Brigade had lost the whole of their "A" Company and Major J. P. Wright, its commander, three officers had been killed and eighty men were casualties. Captain C. F. Milner and a few men had got back.

*June 14th*

When daylight came the 5th Tanks moved out again to their previous day's positions on the Tracy Bocage ridge while the rest of Brigadier Hinde's force held the Box just east of Amaye. The infantry patrolled outwards and found the enemy in Tracy Bocage itself and two other small villages, but Amaye was clear and was taken over.

It did not seem advisable to try to hold the Tracy Bocage feature unless there was some prospect of the 50th Division being able to come forward; this they were trying to do, but they were up against stiff opposition from the Panzer Lehr Division. The Corps Commander accordingly directed that the 7th Armoured were to adjust their dispositions so as to keep their right flank in the closest possible touch with the Americans, and this necessitated pulling back Brigadier Hinde's force—it was decided to do this during the coming night. It was a sad disappointment that the brilliant thrust conceived by General Bucknall which had carried the Division to Villers Bocage, far behind the enemy's lines to a deeper penetration than was to be made for many weeks to come, could not be supported. It was a remarkable gain at a time when expansion of the beach-head was badly needed, but there just were not the additional infantry available to give the Division the backing required in close country of this type—nor was there that element of good fortune which might have made just the difference.

During the morning of the 14th a good deal of shelling was directed on to the 22nd Brigade's areas and many vehicles were brewed up. Hull-down positions for the tanks were hard to find, for the woods and orchards were thick and the slope of the ground unfavourable; further, the enemy were able to overlook much of the position from north, south and west of Villers Bocage. In the afternoon enemy patrolling became more active and about 2 p.m. an attack was put in against the 7th Queens by infantry supported by tanks. The left-hand platoon of the forward company, "C", was over-run, but a counter attack by the rest of the Company put this right. The mortars and the 5th R.H.A. put down heavy concentrations of fire and the enemy were driven back. " 'C' Company fought a fine action this day despite their weariness." There was plenty of artillery and a large reserve of armour, but the anxiety was the shortage of infantry for counter-attacks. Another worry was the cutting of the centre-line, but this was finally secured by the 1st Tanks and a company of the 6th Queens.

The most difficult part of the withdrawal plan was the question of the composition of the rearguard. It was finally decided to make it up of tanks carrying one company of the Rifle Brigade and one company of the 7th Queens with a detachment of the 5th Queens, the infantry being carried on the tanks of the 5th Royal Tanks and the 8th Hussars. Lieutenant-Colonel C. H. Holliman, of the former Regiment, was to command the rearguard, and the rear party was to be composed of "B" Squadron of the 8th Hussars who had been in position about Amaye, with the men of the 5th Queens who had been with them for local protection. This Squadron had been engaged during the day and had lost their Squadron Leader, Major N. G. F. Dunne, wounded, and an officer and some men killed—they had knocked out two Tigers.

About 7 p.m. the Germans put in a fierce attack from the south on the rear portion of the Box with two battalions supported by about thirty tanks. The country was so thick that it was possible to see only to the next hedge. Colonel Gregson brought down his full artillery resources with devastating effect, both on to the attacking troops and on to their probable forming-up places. The attack was completely shattered and the perimeter was ringed with burning German tanks "brewing up merrily"—the anti-tank gunners claimed eight. It was thought that the enemy losses amounted to a thousand infantry and a dozen tanks—there was no doubt that they had been struck a heavy blow, for there was no more trouble from them for the rest of the night. By 9 p.m. all was quiet.

The Brigade had about six miles to go and the move began, as planned, half an hour after midnight. Arrangements had been made for the R.A.F. to carry out a heavy raid on Villers Bocage, both to distract the enemy's attention and to cover the noise of the move. This was done and was of great assistance; "we felt very naked when the air attack ended," said one who was there. "C" and "D" Companies of the 7th Queens remained in their positions until 2 a.m. and then pulled out on the tanks of the 5th Royal Tanks. This Battalion had had a gruelling two days and had distinguished themselves, and it was appropriate that they should be the last to leave the main positions. They had lost eight officers and 120 rank and file in the past thirty-six hours.

Finally, the rear party of the 8th Hussars and 5th Queens formed up, mounted and moved slowly back in pitch dark and clouds of dust to the steady clanking of the tracks and the dull roar of the Rolls-Royce engines. It seemed too much to hope that the Germans would let them go unmolested, but the enemy had been hit too hard—he had had enough.

The tail of the rearguard passed through Briquessard at 5.50 a.m. Further north a traffic block developed, so Brigadier Hinde diverted the latter part of his column through Caumont. The move had been no easy one, officers and men were dead tired, the way was hard to find and the dust appalling. It is recorded that the dust created by the S.P. anti-tank guns was incomparably worse than that from any other armoured vehicles; the Norfolk Yeomanry were enveloped in a blinding dust-cloud, and it is a tribute to their driving and to the driving of those following them that there was no serious accident and that the road was never blocked. By contrast the small amount of dust kicked up by the Cromwells was a welcome feature.

## June 15th to 30th

After the successful withdrawal from Tracy Bocage and Amaye, new positions were taken up, the right being in touch with the Americans a mile or two east of Caumont and the line running through Briquessard and Torteval. There was a gap of about three miles between the Rifle Brigade on the Division's left and the nearest troops of the 50th Division. This was covered by the tanks of the 8th Hussars who, despite the difficulties of patrolling in a noisy machine like a tank, did very good work until an advance by the 56th Brigade improved the situation. On the 17th there was a sharp fight in Briquessard and "C" Squadron of the 8th, who were supporting the 6th Queens, lost five tanks and had an officer and seven men killed. The advantages of holding Briquessard, which was forward of a fairly high ridge, were outweighed by the casualties which were bound to be incurred, so General Erskine withdrew the line in this area to behind the Briquessard ridge.

Here the Division remained for the rest of the month and it was a trying period. The frontage was wide, infantry were scarce and the hard work fell on all of them all the time. They lived in slit trenches and there was a steady drain of casualties from shelling and mortaring. The nights were short, with morning Stand-to at 4.15 and evening Stand-to at 10.15, so there was little sleep even for those who did not have to go out on patrol. Large numbers of men were required for this and the work was made more difficult by the enemy's posts constantly changing their positions. Gaps through the almost impenetrable hedges were generally mined, trip-wires and booby traps abounded, and altogether it was nervy and anxious work with little to show for it. On the 26th Colonel Forester was wounded and command of the 6th Queens went to Lieutenant-Colonel J. H. Mason. The armour had to be held back, for there was no real task for them. The Rifle Brigade re-formed their "A" Company in the transport area. Major F. A. Dorrien-Smith went to command, but he, Lieutenant J. V. Caesar and Captain G. S. W. Talbot were all killed by some random shelling one day.

With the 1st American Division a close liaison was established and the neighbouring troops shared emplacements, and artillery

and mortar support with the happiest results. At the end of the
month the 7th Armoured handed over their area to the United
States 2nd Armoured Division and went back to an area near
Jerusalem for a period of badly-needed rest and refitting. During
their three weeks in Normandy they had lost 1,149 officers and men

On June 22nd Lieutenant-Colonel W. Rankin took over command of the 4th C.L.Y. On July 2nd Brigadier E. C. Pepper succeeded Brigadier Ekins in command of the Queens Brigade, and
on the 5th Lieutenant-Colonel J. B. Ashworth took Command of
the 5th Queens.

*July*

By the beginning of the month the Allies had a firm beach-head
from which to launch more extended operations. The most important
territorial capture to date had been the port of Cherbourg which
had fallen to the Americans on June 26th. The whole Cherbourg
Peninsula was now in their hands and their front line ran as far as
Caumont where the inter-Army boundary lay.

On the Second Army front Caen had not yet fallen and there
had been bitter fighting almost everywhere. Twelve British Divisions
were now ashore and a number of independent Armoured Brigades.
Altogether, over a million Allied troops had been landed, together
with thousands of tons of stores—the whole area of the beach-head
was packed with dumps or men or vehicles, and there was hardly
a vacant piece of ground.

By July 1st the infantry reserves of the German army were
very seriously depleted. Four Divisions had been cut off and destroyed
in the Cherbourg Peninsula and four others had been reduced to
little more than battle-groups. The seven Panzer Divisions that
had been engaged had all suffered severely, and never-ending Allied
air attacks were making supply and reinforcement almost impossible
—it took Divisions as long to travel from east France to Normandy
as from Poland to east France.

The German High Command still feared an attack in the Pas de
Calais and kept there Divisions that would have been invaluable
in Normandy. Elaborate deception plans in south-east England
were continuing to keep up the illusion that the main attack was to
come in that area.

Early in July the 1st Corps attacked Caen and by the 10th the
city had fallen. During the following week the XIIth and XXXth
Corps gained valuable ground between Tilly and Caen after much

evere fighting. At the same time the United States Army was
moving steadily forward against stiff opposition and over difficult
country; by the 18th they had taken St Lô.

## OPERATION "GOODWOOD"

### *July 18th to 20th*

The next operations were to consist of an attack south-east
from Caen by three Armoured Divisions, the 7th, the 11th (which
was commanded by Major-General G. P. B. Roberts) and the
newly-arrived Guards. The objects were to retain on the front of the
British Second Army as much enemy armoured strength as possible
so as to facilitate the break-out by the Americans which was due to
start shortly, to gain ground from which the Second Army could
advance to the Seine when the American operations were well under
way, and to destroy as many Germans and as much German equipment as possible.

At the time, many people thought that this operation, "Goodwood", was the main Allied attempt to break out of the beach-
head, and of course it was not possible for reasons of secrecy to dis-
close the over-all plan. It is quite clear from the instructions issued
by Generals Montgomery and Dempsey before the battle that there
was neither intention nor expectation of a "gallop" to Falaise—
the limits of the advance were plainly defined, but naturally if
matters went unexpectedly well the situation would be exploited
to the full.

The operation was to be carried out by the VIIIth Corps,
the commander of which was that old friend of the earliest days in
the Desert, General Sir Richard O'Connor who, only a few months
before, had escaped from his prison camp in Italy. Unfortunately
this was the only occasion on which the 7th Armoured were to be
under his command in North-West Europe.

### *The Country*

The country over which the Division was to operate was very
different from the Bocage where the previous six weeks had been
spent. It was mostly open agricultural land broken by few hedges
or fences and interspersed with villages surrounded by tall trees
and orchards. The ground rises steadily up to the Bourguebus ridge
behind which are villages and woods. Across the line of advance

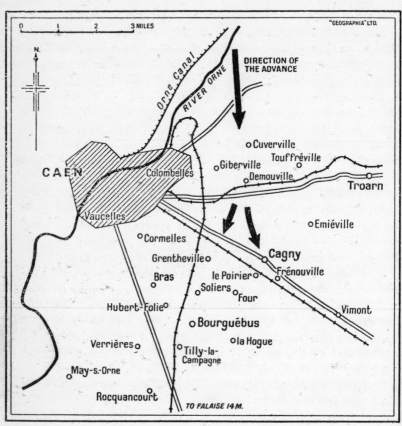

Map No. 13.—Operation "Goodwood", July 18th to 20th, 1944

lay two railways, one from Caen to Troarn and one from Caen to
Vimont. The first had embankments six feet high which were
impassable to wheeled vehicles, and the other ran alternately through
cuttings or along embankments, in both cases comprising ten-foot
obstacles over which for most of the way tanks could not pass.

The defender had a good view over the plain to the north, the
woods and villages behind him gave good cover for the movement
of his troops, and the villages, too, were well situated to form a
series of mutually-supporting strong-points. General O'Connor had
been very anxious that the bombing attacks should neutralize all
these natural defensive positions, but unfortunately they did not
in all cases do so.

On the right flank of the advance lay the Caen factory area
which included a number of tall chimneys, and much of this area
remained in enemy hands for a couple of days after the operation
began. Away to the left flank, for several miles north-west and
south-east of Troarn, was high ground, much of it wooded, and
from here also the enemy had good observation over the Caen plain.

It was known that the enemy defences between the Orne and
the Dives, the river on which Troarn is situated, were very strong,
and what the task amounted to was that the Corps had to break
through a series of defensive lines which were supported by a great
deal of artillery with, behind them, a mobile reserve of more than
two hundred tanks. Even before the Invasion, Rommel had appreciated the importance of the Bourguebus ridge and about the end of
June he had authorized the local Corps commander to withdraw
from Caen if necessary in order to be certain of establishing sufficient
strength along this ridge.

The deployment of three Armoured Divisions over the Orne,
and the Canal which adjoined it, was an extremely complicated
task, and it was quite impossible to provide enough bridges of
the correct weight to enable more than one Armoured Brigade
to go forward at a time. Even if it had been possible in the con-
stricted bridgehead east of the Orne to assemble two Armoured
Brigades side by side, as it was highly desirable to do, a further
complication arose in that the forward area was thickly mined.
It must be remembered that this bridgehead had been one of the
most valuable D-Day gains and every possible step had had to be
taken to ensure that the Germans did not recover it. Dense minefields
had been laid, charts had been lost in the subsequent fighting, more
mines had been laid, and to clear gaps for more than one Armoured

Regiment to pass through at a time would have taken many days
and nights of work, all in view of the enemy. Accordingly the Corps
had to advance in line-ahead of Divisions and to pass through the
front line in line-ahead of Regiments, not the formation that
anyone would have chosen if it could have been avoided.

The routes forward on both sides of the river needed an immense
amount of engineer work, both in their improvement and in their
maintenance, and there was, of course, a traffic control problem
that was enough to daunt even the Military Police. The total
strength of the VIIIth Corps, including the Corps Troops and the
8th A.G.R.A., amounted to 3,000 officers and 58,000 men, and
practically the whole of these had to be passed over less than half a
dozen bridges and through a few gaps in a wide minebelt in a very
congested area and in view of the enemy, both ahead and on
both flanks.

## The Plan

The 11th Armoured Division were to lead, directed first on
Cuverville and Demouville; then they were to make for Bras
and Roquancourt. The Guards Armoured Division were to follow;
they were to go for Cagny and form a firm base at Vimont. The
action of the 7th Armoured Division was to depend on the progress of the other two Divisions; the 7th would probably have to
support the 11th and position itself in the La Hogue area, sending
out patrols to the south and south-east.

On the right of the VIIIth Corps, the Canadians were to
advance through the outskirts of Caen, and take in succession the
factory and suburban areas of Colombelles, Cormelles and Vaucelles, while on the left the British 3rd Division were to establish
themselves in the areas round Troarn, Emiéville and Touffréville.

The attack was to be preceded by a stupendous air assault
starting at 5.45 a.m.; first, forty-five minutes from a thousand
R.A.F. heavy bombers, then forty-five minutes by five hundred
United States medium bombers and finally half an hour by the
big American day bombers, the whole attack from the air to finish
by 9 o'clock. Weight of 7,700 tons of bombs was to be dropped.
The Corps Commander was most anxious that there should also be
an air assault about 3 o'clock in the afternoon, but, most unfortunately,
this was not possible to arrange. It is interesting to record that in
the next operation in which his Corps was involved, Operation
"Bluecoat", General O'Connor's similar request was met, and the

heavy bombardment that was put down on Point 309 during the afternoon of July 30th had, almost certainly, a decisive effect in enabling the attacking troops concerned to break right through the German positions that day.

The massed artillery amounted to 760 guns and included thirteen Medium and three Heavy Regiments. In addition, there was Naval support for dealing with any coast batteries that might be able to bear on the Caen plain.

*July 18th*

On the 17th the Division had moved up from the Jerusalem area to concentrate north and north-west of Caen, and the 11th Hussars came under command.

The advance began to time and by 8.30 all three Armoured Regiments of the 11th Armoured Division were clear of the mine-belt and soon after eleven the leading squadron was fighting at Bourguebus. During the early stages of the advance the enemy troops were still stunned by the weight of the bombardment to which they had been subjected and it was some hours before the survivors in the forward area were sufficiently recovered to offer serious resistance. The leading armour of the Guards followed the 11th and were soon held up at Cagny which held out all day. This had serious consequences further back and greatly delayed the deployment of the 7th Armoured.

The Division moved slowly forward over the bridges and through the minefield gaps amid clouds of choking dust and in dense traffic congestion with a good deal of hostile shell-fire as well. Major A. Reid-Scott's "B" Squadron of the 11th were the first troops of the Division to become engaged—they were among the German dug-outs before the occupants had fully recovered from the air and artillery attacks. The 22nd Armoured Brigade were led by the 5th Royal Tanks, and when they reached Cuverville they were held up by the troops ahead. It was not until 4 p.m. that the Brigade were able to deploy. At 5 p.m. they reached Grentheville where the 5th Tanks had an engagement with infantry and were then counter-attacked by tanks; these they drove off at a cost to each side of two tanks. Altogether, during the day's fighting the Regiment lost an officer and eleven men and six tanks.

When night fell, the 1st Royal Tanks were just west of Demou-ville and the 5th Tanks a couple of miles south of them. The Corps was held up by the line of villages, Cagny, le Poirier, Four, Soliers,

Bras, Hubert-Folie, la Hogue and Bourguebus, the garrisons of most of which were reinforced during the night with comparatively fresh S.S. troops and more tanks.

The day's tank losses of the VIIIth Corps amounted to 150, of which 120 were those of the 11th Armoured Division whose Regiments had pressed home their attacks regardless of losses and with the greatest gallantry against the stiffest opposition that the Germans had yet put up during the Campaign. Many of these tanks that had been put out of action were, of course, recovered and repaired during the night, and came back into action next day. A more serious loss was incurred when the surviving tank crews and the replacement crews of the 11th Armoured were caught in a severe air attack during the night 18th/19th in the rear areas of the Division, and there suffered heavier casualties than they had in the battle itself.

On the right the Canadians had made good progress in the areas on the east side of Caen, and had cleared Colombelles. On the left the 3rd Division secured Touffréville.

*July 19th*
During the night there was a great deal of shelling of the Orne bridges and their neighbourhood and the Division was fortunate to escape casualties. The battlefield was aglow with the fires of burning tanks and other vehicles and lit up from time to time by occasional explosions of ammunition, but there was no fighting activity on either side—both were busy replenishing and preparing for the morrow.

When the advance was resumed in the morning, progress was very slow and opposition much stronger. On the flanks the Canadians cleared Cormelles and Vaucelles, and the Guards Armoured Division occupied Cagny. The forward move of the Queens Brigade was much hampered by traffic congestion. Further forward, "I" Company of the Rifle Brigade supported by the 5th Tanks captured Soliers; here, Major Apsey, the company commander, was badly wounded. After destroying two Tigers and a Panther the 5th Tanks then went on to Bourguebus which their leading squadron reached about 6 p.m. Resistance here was very strong and a direct assault was out of the question; the squadrons worked round both flanks and by nightfall the village was almost surrounded. By 9 p.m. the 1st Royal Tanks, now commanded by Lieutenant-Colonel E. H. Gibbon in place of Colonel Carver who had been promoted to command the 4th Armoured Brigade, had taken Four supported by "C" Company of the Rifle Brigade. Among the casualties of the 1st Tanks was their Medical Officer, Captain Wells, who received wounds from which he died later.

In the evening the 11th Armoured Division, now so greatly reduced in strength, took the important commanding position at Bras and later they went on to take Hubert-Folie, so by last light all the objectives ordered by the Corps for the day had been taken with the exception of Bourguebus. To date, over 2,000 prisoners had been captured and sixty enemy tanks knocked out. Identifications showed that the enemy were bringing reinforcements from other parts of the front, some from as far away as Caumont.

### July 20th to 24th

On the 20th the 5th Tanks occupied Bourguebus, and the C.L.Y. cut the Caen–Falaise road near Bras. They took a hundred prisoners and several guns and destroyed a Tiger and some other tanks. A party of eight German tanks were caught by the artillery as they withdrew and all eight were accounted for. The Canadian attacks on Verrières were repelled but the Guards took Frénouville.

In the afternoon a torrential downpour of rain began and in a short time slit trenches were flooded and the tracks became so bad that no wheeled vehicles could move at all; indeed, in the Divisional area several tanks were so badly bogged as to become immobilized. The weather thus put a full stop to further armoured fighting, and in the evening the Armoured Brigades were pulled out, the Queens Brigade taking over from the 22nd and having the 8th Hussars under command. The Canadian Corps began to take over the right portion of the VIIIth Corps sector and the 1st Corps the areas that the Guards Division had occupied. The 22nd Brigade moved back out of contact with the enemy but by no means away from their attentions, and as the 5th Tanks came into their leaguer at Demouville they were heavily shelled.

The whole Division was concentrated into a very small area all of which was well within enemy artillery range, and the next eight days were as unpleasant a time as the troops were to have throughout the whole North-West Europe Campaign. Shelling was incessant, all movement could be observed by the Germans, there was a steadily mounting toll of casualties and much damage was caused to vehicles. "The remains of the villages had to be

held," says the Short History, "and there were no covered localties
for reserves and artillery emplacements. Thus harassing fire on the
villages and along and behind the crest of the ridge, where lay the
slit trenches of the forward defended localities and the crowded
reserve companies and squadrons, was certain to be effective. The
tank crews were often confined inside their tanks during daytime,
while the infantry could only sit in their trenches, watching the
first rounds throwing up their mushrooms on the ridge, the range
increasing after every few salvoes. At last light, moreover, the
enemy sent over considerable numbers of reconnaissance aircraft,
of which quite a few were shot down or damaged by the concentrated fire of the Bofors guns. These were followed afterwards by
one or two visits to the gun areas by a small number of medium
bombers who made up in accuracy for what they lacked in numbers.
Divisional Headquarters were particularly unfortunate in this
respect, being sited on a bare ridge immediately outside Vaucelles
in the midst of a large and completely uncamouflaged ammunition
dump and a battery of medium guns."

Close and most effective support was given to the forward
troops by the rocket-firing Typhoons of the R.A.F. who were
directed on to the enemy's positions by a contact car which operated
from Brigade Headquarters. It was always an inspiring sight to
watch them go diving into action, to listen to the roar of the rockets
and the crashes as they struck their targets. This form of close support
soon became a regular and most welcome feature of the Campaign,
and the skill of the pilots in identifying their targets was only
matched by the speed with which the aircraft were called down
upon them. Apart from their devastating effect on the enemy
troops, the rockets were a match for the largest German tanks and
there was many a successful "brew" to cheer the watching infantry.

## OPERATION "SPRING"

### July 25th to 29th

On the 25th a further attack was launched by the 2nd Canadian
Corps (Lieutenant-General G. G. Simonds) with the object of
gaining ground on the east side of the Orne and down the main
road from Caen to Falaise. The 7th Armoured Division were
placed in support of the 2nd and 3rd Canadian Divisions, the
2nd attacking May-sur-Orne and the 3rd Tilly-la-Campagne.

During the early part of the day all went well; the preliminary air bombardment and the artillery support were effective and there was always plenty of close air support available. The C.L.Y., in support of the 2nd Division, were involved in heavy fighting as the infantry approached May and Verrières where the armour knocked out four enemy tanks. In the evening here there was a fierce counter-attack and fighting went on for some hours. The 1st Royal Tanks were brought up to help the hard-pressed infantry and shortly before dark the counter-attack was beaten off, but the British positions were made unpleasant by the presence of enemy tanks hull-down on the ridge to the north-east and Verrières was almost isolated. East of the main road the attack towards Tilly had been almost as strongly resisted. Here, the 5th Royal Tanks supported the 3rd Division and despite Typhoon attacks the defenders of the village held on to most of it until dark, after which a night attack cleared the area.

Once again, after an advance of only a few thousand yards and in spite of the very great gallantry shown by the Canadian battalions, the attack had reached stalemate. By now the Germans had the elements of six Panzer Divisions in this small area east of the Orne and their forces were estimated to include 350 tanks, 150 S.P. guns and 300 anti-tank guns. Consolation for all this hard fighting and all these sacrifices may be found in the words of the Official History of the Canadian Army: "The real fruits of Operation 'Spring' must be sought in its contribution to the development of the plans of the Supreme Commander. It served the purpose of concealing from the enemy, on this all-essential day, the direction of the main Allied thrust and of delaying the movement of German reserves to the American front."

From the 26th to the 28th the Division remained in defensive positions in support of the Canadians with the 5th Tanks near Verrières, the C.L.Y. astride the main road, the 1st Tanks in reserve and the Queens Brigade in the area Tilly, Soliers and Hubert-Folie. Here they were never free from shelling and mortaring, and the unpleasant conditions were much the same as they had been for the previous ten days. On the 28th the Division was ordered to join the XXXth Corps in the Caumont sector and gladly handed over the area to the 4th Canadian Armoured Division. The losses sustained since the middle of the month amounted to over four hundred; there had been much damage to vehicles of all types, the battalions were considerably below strength in infantry and the armour had

o

had no opportunity for rest or refit. The losses in men and material were not as severe as those of the 11th Armoured Division whose casualties in Operation "Goodwood" had exceeded 950, but the 7th Armoured had spent a further period in close contact with an aggressive enemy who had an ample supply of guns and mortars and who overlooked the whole Divisional area all the time. A few days' rest were very badly needed but, alas, not forthcoming.

By now the Americans had broken out of the Cherbourg Peninsula and the entire German line was in danger of being turned. In the British XXXth and XIIth Corps sectors continuous offensive operations had not only gained some valuable ground but had helped to keep away from the Americans at this critical time substantial armoured forces which were badly needed at the western end of the battle front.

On the 29th the 4th C.L.Y. were transferred to the 4th Armoured Brigade in order to amalgamate with their sister regiment, the 3rd C.L.Y.—there were no longer sufficient reinforcements to keep both Regiments up to strength. This was a sad parting. The 4th had formed part of the 22nd Brigade from the first days of the reconstituted 1st Armoured Division, went with them through much fighting in the Desert and first came to the 7th Armoured in 1942. For most of the time since then they had shared good times and bad with the 7th Armoured Division, and no regiment had played their part better. It was with sad hearts that the old-timers saw their friends depart.

CHAPTER 8

*July 30th to September 5th, 1944*

# FROM NORMANDY TO BELGIUM

*Reference Maps—No. 11, page 182. No. 14, page 212. No. 15, page 222.*
*No. 16, page 230*

### BACK TO THE BOCAGE

*Operation "Bluecoat"*                              *July 30th to August 10th*

B AD weather delayed the start of the American break-out
offensive until July 25th, but on that day two Corps, after a
very heavy air bombardment, began the attack and made
steady progress, particularly on their right. On the 27th the
Germans started to retreat on the American front and the operations
moved more swiftly. In order to assist the American advance which
was meeting stiffer opposition in the St Lô–Caumont sector than
further west, General Montgomery decided to launch an attack
southwards from Caumont directed on Le Beny Bocage, Vire and
Condé. Much of this area is the thickest and roughest part of the
Bocage. Further, the Germans had been left unmolested there for
the past six weeks and had ample time to build strong defensive
positions and to lay plentiful minefields. This operation, "Bluecoat",
was to be carried out by the VIIIth and XXXth Corps.

Under the former were the 15th (Scottish) Division who had
recently taken over the Caumont area from the Americans, the
Guards and 11th Armoured Divisions and the 6th Guards Tank
Brigade who were equipped with Churchill tanks. The two
Armoured Divisions, the Tank Brigade, the 8th A.G.R.A., the
Corps Troops and Corps Headquarters itself all had to be moved at
short notice from areas between Bayeux and Caen across the supply
lines of the XIIth and XXXth Corps in the course of one day and
two nights, over distances up to fifty miles. In addition to that, all
the planning for this battle had to be done during the forty hours
between the time when the Corps received the order and Zero Hour,

which was 7 a.m. on Sunday, July 30th. It was a remarkable achievement on the part of General O'Connor and his staff under Brigadier
Sir Henry Floyd that both the moves and the battle itself were
completely successful.

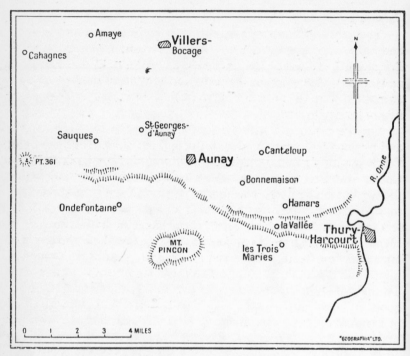

Map No. 14.—Mont Pincon

The XXXth Corps was composed of the 43rd and 50th Divisions
who were already in position, and the 7th Armoured who had not
far to go and were not required in the opening stage. The 43rd
Division on the right was to secure Pt. 361, and the 50th on the
left were to take the high ground north-west and west of Villers
Bocage. Then the Corps was to take Mont Pincon and clear the
whole area down to Condé and Flers. On the left of the XXXth
Corps, the XIIth Corps was to secure a bridgehead over the Orne
at Thury-Harcourt, and the Canadians were to resume their drive
southwards from Caen.

    Shortly before the operations were due to start the 5th Royal
Inniskilling Dragoon Guards joined the Division in place of the

4th C.L.Y. The former had fought in the 1939–40 Campaign in the Low Countries but had not been overseas since; they came from the 9th Armoured Division in England. Their Commanding Officer was Lieutenant-Colonel J. E. Swetenham.

### July 30th and 31st

The 43rd Division met much opposition when their attack began and they were greatly delayed by the stream that runs through Briquessard. However, by the evening the Corps line had been advanced to Cahagnes on the right and Hottot on the left. The 7th Armoured were then ordered forward to a concentration area about five miles north-east of Caumont.

On the right, the 15th Division had broken the German line and by noon had penetrated with the tanks to a depth of three miles. Following an air bombardment on Pt. 309, the 4th Tank Battalion Coldstream Guards had advanced another two miles and gained the summit before dark. Throughout the attack the ground had been so bad that the infantry had been unable to keep up with the leading Churchills, which alone of all vehicles had been able to surmount the great banks and crash through the thick hedges. Soon after dark, the Scottish infantry had begun to reach the dominating high ground where the Coldstream tanks were firmly in possession. To the right of the 15th Scottish the 11th Armoured had also made good progress despite the profusion of mines, and the right-hand of their two columns had had hard fighting. During the night the 11th Armoured pushed on and by dawn they had reached St Martin des Besaces on the important Caen–Avranches main road. From here a Troop of armoured cars of the Household Cavalry continued another five miles and seized a bridge intact over the River Soulêvre north-west of Le Beny Bocage. These important gains interrupted the German reinforcement of their troops facing the Americans.

On the 31st the 11th Hussars returned to the Division permanently. As their History says: "The Black Boar of the XXXth Corps had long been a proud sign in Africa, but the Eleventh felt still more at home in the close family party of the 7th Armoured." The Division was delighted to see them back again.

### August 1st and 2nd

It was not until the 1st that the Division was able to come into action, but movement was very slow to begin with. There was a thick morning mist, the whole area was covered with mines and there were many enemy infantry posts who were determined to stay and fight. In addition, there was a terrible congestion of traffic on all the roads round Caumont—the 11th Hussars, who deployed two squadrons early in the morning, had taken three hours to cover twelve miles on the main road. The 1st Tanks and a squadron of the 8th Hussars led the advance, directed on Aunay, and their first difficulty was to get clear of the 50th Division. By half-past eight in the evening they had made good the ground for three miles south-east of Cahagnes, but then they were firmly held by mines and infantry. The Inniskillings and the 6th Queens were close behind them, and the 5th Queens, who had suffered a couple of dozen casualties in various mopping-up operations, were also in support.

The next morning the advance started at 6 a.m., the 8th Hussars and Inniskillings operating to the left of the 1st Tanks. There was steady opposition all day, but in the evening "C" Squadron of the 1st Tanks gained the high ground north-west of Sauques at a cost of six tanks and twenty-four casualties. It had become clear by then that Aunay would not be reached, so the 6th Queens were ordered to prepare a night attack onto the high ground further east while the 5th and 7th Queens took over the areas which the armour had gained during the day.

In the morning the 50th Division had reached Amaye and the 8th Hussars had got within three miles of Aunay to the north-west.

*August 3rd*

The 6th Queens' night attack went in just after midnight and was completely successful. By 4 o'clock in the morning the new position had been cleared of enemy and consolidated. Three companies were established astride the main road on the important ridge east of Sauques and two miles from Aunay. At dawn the 5th Tanks came up to them and, under the cover of a thick mist, continued the advance with "A" Squadron for another mile and a half. Then, however, when the mist lifted about 8.30 a.m., the leading Troop was attacked and forced to pull back. "B" Squadron then went forward and was soon sharply engaged in the hamlet of La Lande (not shown on map) near where the Troop had been involved. Two enemy tanks were knocked out at a cost of two of their tanks; soon afterwards "B" lost two more.

At 2.20 p.m. a counter-attack was launched by the Germans on the 6th Queens' positions, but this was beaten off with the loss to the enemy of one tank. An hour later it was resumed in greater force by a battalion supported by a dozen or more tanks under heavy mortar and artillery fire and clouds of smoke. The two squadrons of the 5th Tanks were cut off and "B" Company, most of "D" and part of "C" were over-run together with several of the Norfolk Yeomanry's anti-tank guns. For some time the Germans pressed this attack, but when "A" Squadron of the 8th Hussars came up they withdrew, having lost one Panther and eleven other tanks and a great many men.

The two squadrons of the 5th Tanks were, however, still cut off and it was decided to order them to break out after it got dark. This they did at a cost of three tanks. They had lost an officer and six men killed, Major Thomson, four other officers and twenty men wounded, and eight men missing; seven Cromwells had been destroyed, but forty prisoners had been taken. In the 6th Queens there were 135 casualties, of whom seven were officers; "B" Company had lost forty-two of all ranks, and "D" sixty-nine. The Norfolk Yeomanry's losses amounted to thirty-four in all and three guns had been destroyed.

While this battle had been in progress the Inniskillings had reached Tracy Bocage which they reported to be strongly held.

During the first week of August it was decided to make a number of changes in the Division. Numerous officers and men had fought for many months in the Desert, in Italy and in Normandy. It was General Montgomery's view that they should be given a spell in appointments or units where the vast experience they had gained could be turned to the training of the reinforcements who would shortly be coming overseas, or in posts where they would for a time be relieved of the strain of active service conditions in the front line.

With this in view, General Erskine gave up command of the Division after eighteen eventful months that had seen the capture of Tripoli and Tunis, the crossing of the Volturno and all the hardest fighting in Normandy. The Division was to see him again soon in charge of the Supreme Headquarters, Allied Expeditionary Force Mission to Belgium. He was succeeded by Major-General G. L. Verney who came from commanding the 6th Guards Tank Brigade, then in action not far to the west. Brigadier Hinde and Brigadier Mews the C.R.A., both of whom had seen a great deal of fighting in the Desert and since, were also posted to other commands. Among the units, over a hundred officers and men were posted to home commands or establishments, those selected being the ones who had served longest in the Field.

It was, therefore, a rather different Division, still much under strength, especially in infantry, that was to carry on the Normandy fighting and take part in the great advance to the Seine and Ghent before the month was out.

## August 4th to 6th

Continuous opposition was met down the Centre Line, so the Divisional Commander decided to move the 22nd Brigade, with the 5th Queens under command, in a loop to the left by way of a small village (La Poste, not shown on map) which lay three miles north of the Centre Line. From there they were to move across country during darkness in the hope of being able to by-pass Aunay to the north and gain the high ground beyond. The 11th Hussars sent one squadron even wider to the left to see if progress could be made through Villers Bocage. This squadron, "D", was much impeded by mines all day, but by the evening they had gained the outskirts of the town; the Flails of the Westminster Dragoons had been of much help to them. The Inniskillings, with one of the Rifle Brigade companies, carried out a successful attack and quite a fair amount of ground was cleared during the day.

On the 5th the Inniskillings led the 22nd Brigade, starting at 5.30 a.m., and during the morning, passing north of Aunay, they advanced fourteen miles along the new axis and reached Bonne-maison. In the afternoon they went on for another couple of miles until stopped by defences on the high ground north of Hamars. When night fell, the 1st Royal Tanks were supporting them from Bonnemaison. During the night advance Lieutenant-Colonel W. S. Stewart, commanding the Norfolk Yeomanry, was killed on a mine. He was one of the old experienced Desert leaders who had seen much fighting. Lieutenant-Colonel J. Goring took over command.

The ground which the leading troops had now reached was a fairly open plateau, but it was completely overlooked by the enemy from the slopes of Mont Pincon. Ahead of the Inniskillings lay a deep defile, four hundred feet below the level of the plateaux to north and south. The south sides of this ravine were very densely wooded and through these woods ran a good road up to the level ground beyond; from here, the ground was flat but very enclosed as far as Condé.

The 11th had reported in the morning that they found the streets of Villers Bocage so badly blocked by rubble and fallen masonry that they could not get through. Later in the day, "D" Squadron entered Aunay from the north and "C" from the west. This town was in an even worse state, being completely flattened; only the church and one building were standing and both were just empty shells. The Medical War Diary described the areas round Aunay as "full of dead and decomposing cattle and Germans—mines and booby traps very plentiful". It was clear that though armour and infantry could get forward, there was no Centre Line for the maintenance of the Division until the Royal Engineers and the Pioneer Corps could make diversions or clear a way through the mounds of rubble—the Division could not operate south of Aunay. Accordingly General Verney reckoned that the best way to make progress was to continue his move round Aunay with the whole D'vision and to make use of the good road that ran south through La Vallée so as to gain the level ground east of Mont Pincon. The 7th Queens were ordered to push on into La Vallée after dark, and just before midnight they reported their leading company in the village, which was densely mined.

The 6th was a fairly busy day. By 3.30 in the morning the 7th Queens had cleared the last of the enemy out of La Vallée, and they and the Sappers spent the remaining hours of darkness lifting the mines. Throughout the day the whole area was mortared and shelled and many of the Queens' carriers were destroyed. When the early morning mist drifted away, the enemy artillery busied themselves with targets on the high ground behind, for the weather was hot and dry and the least movement raised dense clouds of dust. Lieutenant-Colonel J. A. Norman's 3rd R.H.A. were in support of the forward troops and when the visibility improved they found that their Observation Posts looked right into the enemy's positions across the valley. "Some incredibly accurate shooting" was directed by Major P. Hilton and Captain Stokes.

Further to the west the 6th Queens were involved in some sharp fighting, at the end of which their four rifle companies were reduced to eight, fifteen, forty and fifty-five officers and men respectively, the total being the equivalent of about one full-strength company. Back at Bonnemaison the 1st Tanks were engaged with infantry and came in for much shelling. The 11th Hussars fanned out on a wide front to the east and south-east, but they found no alternative route to the high ground across the ravine. They met with a good deal of opposition and Major J. Turnbull, commanding "A" Squadron, was wounded.

*The Night Attack at La Vallée*                    *August 7th and 8th*

Any attempt to bring forward troops in daylight in order to carry
out an attack across the ravine would not only come under heavy
shell-fire but would also forfeit surprise, so the Divisional Commander ordered a night attack to be carried out so as to secure a
footing on the crest to the south. The objective was a small group of
houses about a mile and a half south of La Vallée at the top of
the steep hill.

The success of this night attack, which was afterwards described
as a "model" of its kind, turned on the most intimate co-operation
between the infantry and the artillery, and the plan devised by
Lieutenant-Colonel W. D. Griffiths, commanding the 7th Queens,
with Colonels Gregson and Norman, entailed an advance up
the hill inside a series of box-barrages, each having sides 300 yards
deep with a frontage of 600 yards, and each phase lasting for half
an hour.

At 2.30 a.m. on the 8th the Artillery laid down a sample
"box" for a few minutes for the infantry to see, and at 3.30 the
attack began. "D" Company, which was only sixty strong, were
divided into two platoons each of thirty, and they led the assault.
Some of the enemy were found half asleep in their trenches and
were roused by cries of "Wakey, wakey!", but others offered stiff
resistance and there was much hand-to-hand fighting, so the
barrage had to be continued for another twenty minutes. Fifty
prisoners were sent doubling to the rear. Close behind the infantry
came the Sappers clearing the mines off the main road. In the second
phase there was less opposition, so the same company continued into
the third phase where the bayonet work had to be resumed and
another twenty prisoners were taken.

"D" Company then consolidated and the advance was taken
up by "C", still inside the artillery "box". They gained the final
objective though held up for a short time by a strongly defended
house which was demolished by the guns of the Norfolk Yeomanry
who were following up closely. While this phase of the attack was
going on "B" Company came up and consolidated between "C"
and "D", so that when daylight came there were three company
defended areas up this important road.

The cost to the Battalion was only three killed and twenty-four
wounded; they had killed many Germans, taken 142 prisoners,
three guns, an ambulance and three other vehicles. There was much
praise for the Battalion stretcher-bearers who had to work under

unusually difficult and confusing conditions, and the whole attack was a tribute to the skilful control exercised by Colonel Griffiths and his Gunner associates and the excellence of the Signals personnel. At 7 o'clock the enemy launched the expected counter-attack; this was beaten off but at the cost of another sixteen casualties. Soon afterwards the 1st Royal Tanks arrived in support.

Away to the right, the 50th Division were advancing on Mont Pincon and the 43rd Division had reached the summit from the west side, supported by the 8th Armoured Brigade whose tanks were actually the first troops on the top.

*Last Days in the Bocage*                              *August 8th to 10th*

It was on the 7th that the Germans launched their ill-fated counter-offensive though Mortain towards Avranches, designed to cut off the American troops that had broken out of the Cherbourg Peninsula and were now streaming into the centre of France. Four Panzer Divisions were employed, and although they met with some success at first and captured Mortain, their attacks were held and the Allied Air Forces executed tremendous destruction on the few armoured troops that remained to the Germans in Normandy. The American advance was not checked for long, and as they began to swing round to their left the pocket developed that was to see the destruction of much of the German Army at Falaise.

An advance by the XXXth Corps to Condé would close the trap on the Divisions which were retreating from Mortain, so those of the enemy who were trying to hold back the north side of the salient put up fierce resistance in the area south of Mont Pincon, and they were helped by the ground, which was thick and difficult.

For the advance on Condé the 7th Armoured Division were ordered to move in two columns, one on the Aunay–Condé road and one from the foothold gained south of La Vallée. The left-hand column was to consist of the 1st Tanks and the 7th Queens who were already in position, and the other was made up of the Inniskillings, the 5th Tanks and the 5th and 6th Queens. The Inniskillings and the 5th Queens had to be moved from the high ground north of La Vallée; there was no trouble in moving the armour, but the infantry had to embus in broad daylight and full view of the Germans. Watchers on the slopes of Mont Pincon could see the cumbersome troop-carrying lorries which had been brought out of the positions where they had been hidden, manœuvring and backing and the enemy shells bursting round them. It seemed a miracle that so few were hit and that eventually the whole battalion was embussed and on the move. The coolness and steadiness of the drivers of 507 Company R.A.S.C., the troop-carrying Company, were magnificent.

On the 8th and 9th small gains were made but at heavy cost. The country was almost impassable for tanks and there were now too few infantry to give them adequate support; shelling and mortaring were continuous, and infantry and bazookas, supported by anti-tank guns, were numerous. The 5th Queens lost their Commanding Officer, Colonel Ashworth, and Major E. Jeffrey wounded, and another eighty casualties in this Battalion reduced them, like the 6th Queens, to little more than one company strong. The 6th Queens themselves lost another thirty-four officers and men, and among the casualties in the 7th Queens was Major P. Bosanquet killed. The Inniskillings sustained a severe loss when their Adjutant, Captain M. D. Williams, was killed while the Regiment were forming up for an attack on the 9th. Lieutenant-Colonel W. Furnivall, who had commanded the 131st Field Ambulance for a long time, was promoted to command No. 10 Casualty Clearing Station on the 9th and was succeeded by Lieutenant-Colonel W. Harvey.

By the evening of that day the Division no longer had the resources in infantry to go on fighting on such a scale. Since August 1st the losses in the Division had amounted to 523, by far the greater proportion of which had fallen on their one and only Infantry Brigade, which had suffered especially in casualties to the junior leaders, the Platoon and Section commanders. Since the start of operation "Goodwood" on July 18th the Division had been in close contact with the enemy throughout, with the exception of two days after they moved from that congested, shell-ridden area south of Caen where they had never been free from the enemy's fire. During those past three weeks nearly a thousand officers and men had been lost, most of them in the Rifle Brigade and the Queens Regiment. Such few reinforcements as had been sent up had had to go straight into action with no opportunity of settling down in their new Battalions—the officers did not know their men, nor the men their officers. All ranks were near exhaustion and General Horrocks, who was now commanding the XXXth Corps, urged that the Division be taken out for a rest. Throughout the 21st Army Group, and indeed further afield, there was a very serious shortage of infantry reinforcements; so bad was it that at the end of the fighting

in Normandy the 59th Division, who had greatly distinguished themselves as a hard-fighting formation, had to be broken up and their
troops distributed to other divisions so as to keep them up to strength.
For the armoured regiments, whose casualties were never so severe,
there was no great problem.

On the 10th, therefore, the bulk of the Division were relieved
and moved back a few miles. The Inniskillings and the 3rd and
5th R.H.A. were retained to work under the 43rd Division, and the
11th Hussars were again put under the XXXth Corps. The Inniskillings had a number of casualties during the next few days,
including Major the Marquess of Kildare, the commander of "B"
Squadron, dangerously wounded. The intention was that there
should be a fortnight out of the line; owing to the congestion in the
beach-head it was not possible to move far back and there was no
area in the Division's new location that was not apt to be shelled.
Indeed, the "rest" started badly, for on the first afternoon a salvo
of shells landed between the Divisional Commander's caravan and
the Headquarters of the Divisional Royal Engineers, killing and
wounding several men.

The administrative staff of the Corps were tireless in doing all
they could to help—Mobile Bath Units appeared like magic, there
were complete new outfits of clothing for every man, the Jerboa
Club re-opened and a Rest Camp that the Corps owned near the
sea gave generous allotments to the Desert Rats. In Brigadier G.
Webb, the chief administrative officer of the Corps, the Division had
an old friend of Desert days, and they owed him a lot for all he did.
Unhappily he was killed later in the Campaign. Some days previously
Brigadier T. Lyon-Smith had arrived as C.R.A.; he had held a
similar appointment in the 6th Armoured Division in North Africa.

On the night of August 7th/8th had occurred an operation of
much significance to armoured divisions. The 2nd Canadian Corps
had made an eight-mile penetration of the German defences south
of Caen with two armoured columns, each led by an armoured
brigade and followed by infantry in armoured personnel carriers,
which were S.P. guns with the armament removed. Here, under the
right conditions of ground, was the answer to the problem of how to
move the infantry of an armoured division in battle. Had it been
possible to make "Kangaroos", as they were called, available in
large numbers, the story of several battles in Normandy and later
might have been very different. One hopes that operation "Totalise"
has not been forgotten.

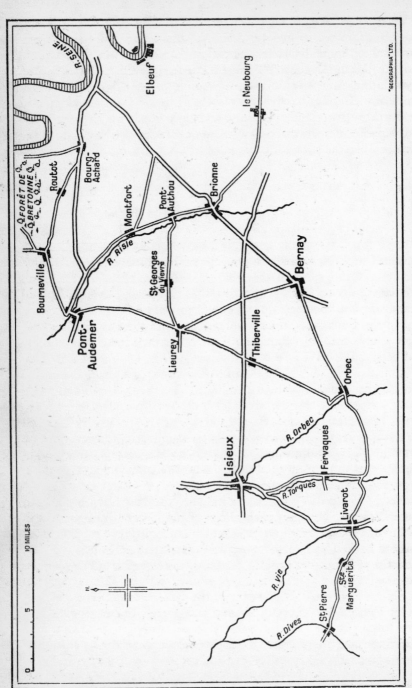

Map No. 15—The Advance to the Seine, August 17th to 28th, 1944

During the second week of August, following the failure of the Mortain counter-offensive, the United States troops fanned out over a wide area. Some divisions swung round and, while the Canadians and the Polish Armoured Division attacked south to Falaise and beyond, the Americans attacked north through Argentan. Large numbers of Germans were about to be encircled and trapped. On the north and west sides of the pocket the XXXth Corps pressed hard against desperate resistance as the enemy tried to keep a corridor open for his troops to escape.

## On to the Seine

### *August 17th to 28th*

The "rest" did not last long. Just before midnight on the 15th the Divisional Commander was roused and told that the Division was to move to the First Canadian Army (General H. D. G. Crerar) at dawn. This was a fairly tall order—men had to be fetched from Rest Camps on the coast, all units had to be alerted, liaison officers sent to the Canadians, routes worked out and the G.1 and several other senior staff officers fetched from Mont St. Michel where they had been sent for a couple of days' holiday. The Division was to join General Crocker's 1st Corps who were under the Canadian Army, and to lead the advance to the Seine. A concentration area was allotted to the east of the Caen–Falaise road and all units had a trying time getting there. The route lay across the supply lines of the Second Army, the heat was intense, the dust appalling and the traffic had never been worse. The new area was on the edge of an old battlefield and was described by the Medicals as: "This is a filthy leaguer; flies and mosquitoes very bad."

Now, for a few weeks, a very different type of fighting lay ahead of the Division. The days of the Bocage and of gains measured in a few hundred yards were gone, and instead of long-prepared defensive positions backed by large numbers of tanks and guns, opposition was to consist of small, but usually determined, rearguards taking quick advantage of the natural features of the country. From Caen to the Seine is about sixty-five miles and the route is intersected by the Rivers Dives, Vie, Touques, Orbec and Risle. The next ten days were to consist of four approach marches and four river-crossing operations, and there was a similarity about all of them; first, the following-up of the retreating enemy, delayed by mines and rearguards; then, the discovery that the main road bridge was blown and the fanning out of all available troops; a crossing place discovered, perhaps a bridge the enemy had forgotten to destroy or one overlooked and too weak to carry tanks; a small bridgehead formed, while the Sappers either built a new bridge or improved an existing one; the move of the main body of the Division across the river and the resumption of the pursuit. The reconnaissances along the river banks were often difficult, but every time a crossing-place was found and the 11th found three out of the four.

When the Division reached St Pierre sur Dives the 51st Division had already secured a crossing over the Dives and the 7th Armoured were directed on Livarot and then Lisieux. The advance began on the morning of the 17th, the Queens Brigade leading with the 8th Hussars under command, the 6th Queens on the north of the road and the 7th on the south, each with one squadron in support. Three squadrons of the 11th Hussars were fanned out on a very broad front. As there was no news as to what Allied troops, if any, were operating on the right, a screen of the Norfolk Yeomanry anti-tank guns was thrown out to the south. For the first three miles the country was fairly open and good progress was made, but as soon as the leading troops reached the higher ground, which was also more wooded, they came up against determined rearguards. Every bridge and culvert was blown, and the armoured cars could find no hole in the enemy's dispositions. For the next forty-eight hours progress was slow and the going became more and more difficult as far as Ste Marguerite and the high ground to the east of the village.

One of those accidents that is unavoidable in war occurred when low-flying R.A.F. planes mistook the leading troops of the Division for the Germans. In the confused circumstances of the enemy retreat and the thick country the error was understandable, but about twenty casualties were caused, including the Intelligence Officer of the 8th Hussars who was severely wounded while driving Colonel Goulburn, and the latter was badly shaken in the resulting smash of their Jeep. Three of the guns of the Norfolk Yeomanry were knocked out and other vehicles set on fire. During the first two nights of the advance, also, the German air force was unusually active. The 5th Tanks had six casualties, including their Chaplain, the Rev. A. H. Dickson, wounded, and ten vehicles destroyed, and the 1st Tanks, who were now commanded by Lieutenant-Colonel P. R. C. Hobart, lost thirteen men and two tanks; their Medical Officer, Captain Wainman, was killed. The 2nd Light Field

Ambulance had over twenty casualties. Altogether over 120 wounded passed through the Divisional medical units during these two days.

The village of Ste Marguerite which dominated the Centre Line was occupied by the 6th Queens on the 18th. Here the troops had first-hand evidence of enemy brutality—six civilians, men and women, were taken from their houses just before the Queens arrived and shot in cold blood. Their only crime was that they had been seen giving flowers to a Troop of the 8th Hussars. This case was fully reported and was investigated by the authorities with, it is hoped, satisfactory results.

On the morning of the 19th Lieutenant P. F. Chapman's Troop of the 11th got down to the River Vie about a mile north of Livarot and there found a rather rickety bridge which the enemy had overlooked. As soon as this news was wirelessed back General Verney changed the Centre Line of the Queens Brigade and ordered Brigadier Pepper to secure a bridgehead. By the early afternoon the 5th Queens, under Lieutenant-Colonel I. H. Freeland, were across. "B" Squadron of the 11th Hussars also crossed and fanned out to a depth of four miles. The Queens sent patrols into Livarot from the north and the enemy blew the main road bridge although he still had troops fighting on the west side. During the day the 1st Tanks lost two tanks and had over a dozen casualties.

It was not until the morning of the 20th that the main road was finally cleared and Colonel Mason led his 6th Queens into the town while the Sappers got to work repairing the damage. Livarot was the scene of "Liberation" for the first of many times, excited civilians, flags, fruit, flowers, kisses and wine—nothing was too good for the liberators. Another new experience which was to prove more valuable was the F.F.I., the Forces Françaises d'Intérieure, sometimes known also as the Maquis or the Resistance. It was their men who had helped Lieutenant Chapman and the Queens patrols. Throughout the advance they were to be of the greatest assistance, both men and women. Although their information was sometimes exaggerated, they performed many useful services and often showed great bravery. They interfered with enemy movements and defensive preparations, they prevented bridges being blown, they ambushed small parties, they took over prisoners, acted as guides, bicycled ahead into the next town or village to find out what the situation was and looked after the wounded when the Centre Line was cut and evacuation impossible. Their quality varied from district to district, and the Belgian Armée Blanche were outstanding. The 11th

P

always tried to have some "tame" ones with their leading armoured cars, and some stayed with the Regiment for a long time.

*Over the Touques*                              *August 20th and 21st*

In the afternoon of the 20th the Engineers had the bridge over the Vie ready for the passage of tanks, and the 22nd Brigade began to cross. Led by "C" Squadron of the 11th, the 5th Royal Tanks, carrying "I" Company of the Rifle Brigade, made for Fervaques. The armoured cars met a lot of opposition, but three Troops worked their way down to the river where they found two of the three bridges destroyed; the third, in the village, was intact and they held it until the arrival of the rest of the force. Just beyond, the enemy were using the main road to Lisieux and a number of lorries fell into the hands of the Rifle Brigade and the Tanks during the next thirty-six hours, including one which had breakfasts cooking on board. During the evening and night several counter-attacks were made in order to drive in this bridgehead, but they were all beaten off, at some cost, and over fifty prisoners were taken.

The rest of the 22nd Brigade, with "B" Squadron of the 11th Hussars and the 7th Queens, were ordered to make for Lisieux and to continue moving throughout the night, which was pitch dark and pouring with rain. There was a lot of confused small arms firing on the route, but the all-important bridge over the Touques two miles short of the town was taken before dawn and a small bridge-head secured.

The 21st was a difficult day, with the Division strung out over ten miles of road and fighting in three different places. Also, the Centre Line between Livarot and Lisieux was cut and this necessitated a battalion being kept along the main road to hold it open. The length of the lines of communication were beginning to worry the C.R.A.S.C., Lieutenant-Colonel E. G. Hazelton, whose lorries now had a turn-round of over 100 miles. Back at Livarot counter-attacks were made from both east and west, one attack consisting of a tank and a small party of Hitler Youth from the 12th S.S. Division, who rushed recklessly forward and appeared to have been drugged; they were eliminated and the Inniskillings knocked out their tank. The forward platoon of the 5th Queens here was cut off for a time and both the company commander, Major Young, and his second-in-command, Captain Groom, were wounded.

At Fervaques more counter-attacks and the presence of parties of the enemy behind the force there resulted in the 5th Tanks and the motor companies being more or less cut off all day; attempts by them to enlarge their bridgehead were unsuccessful. The area round Lisieux was strongly held, for the town was of great importance to the Germans' line of retreat. It lies in a steep wooded valley where three rivers converge. The bridgehead gained during the night advance was extended but progress up the main road proved impossible so the 7th Queens fanned out into the enclosed country to the right. Lieutenant Chapman succeeded in getting his armoured cars into the town but they were forced back. During the day a total of 200 prisoners was collected; they included a young man handcuffed to a French girl, and two military policemen who drove into Livarot with the intention of sign-posting the route of the 21st Panzer Division.

*The Battle of Lisieux*                     *August 22nd and 23rd*

By now the 51st Division were on the western outskirts of the town and General Crocker ordered them to clear up to the eastern side so that the 7th Armoured could break out; at the same time the 7th were to continue their pressure from the south. It was hoped that the troops at Livarot and Fervaques could be relieved during the day, but in the meantime General Verney tried to find some way round to the right. A company of the 7th Queens got down to the Orbec and forded the river, but then they came up against fierce opposition; reports made it clear that even if a bridgehead could be obtained here it would not be possible to get the main force of the Division across and up to the main road a mile and a half ahead, as the valley was very soft and the ground beyond wooded and dotted with houses that were occupied by the enemy. "A" Squadron of the 11th also got down to the river and upstream found five bridges all of which were blown immediately the armoured cars appeared.

At Fervaques the 5th Royal Tanks tried to break out but soon got held up and lost some tanks, but sufficient advance was made to enable "C" Squadron of the 11th Hussars to get out; they soon found themselves in thick forest country where they had to patrol on foot. Up-stream of Fervaques "D" Squadron, working due east from Livarot, found the only bridge over the Touques blown. The Canadians relieved the Fervaques force just before dark; the latter had just driven off another counter-attack and lost another tank and some more men.

At Lisieux, by the middle of the afternoon the 1st Tanks and the

5th Queens were well into the town. The infantry, under the temporary command of Major H. Nangle, moved forward to a start-line that was supposed to be clear in order to attack some high ground that would enable the armour to get through. The start-line, however, was not clear and some involved fighting took place which cost about twenty-five casualties, including Major P. Z. Henderson wounded.

During the early hours of the 23rd Lieutenant G. I. S. Burnett of the 7th Queens made a valuable reconnaissance of over a mile of the Orbec, but could find no crossing place. Throughout the day fighting went on in the streets, the 51st Division trying to break through from the west and the 7th Armoured from the south. The Inniskillings got their Reconnaissance Troop and "A" Squadron well in but found the streets blocked with rubble. In the afternoon a counter-attack was launched against the 5th Queens but this was driven back and in the evening the Battalion attacked towards the great church on the eastern outskirts of the town. At a cost of another twenty casualties, which included Major B. C. O'Brien wounded, they gained their objective against tanks and infantry.

*Lisieux to the Seine*                              *August 24th to 28th*
Early on the morning of the 24th Lieutenant W. G. G. Hunt's Troop of armoured cars reported that they had passed through Lisieux and were moving down the main road beyond; the 22nd Armoured Brigade were immediately ordered to follow up and were given the River Risle at Pont Authou as their objective. Two squadrons of the 11th were deployed in front of them and the Inniskillings led, with a company of the Rifle Brigade. For the first ten miles there were no enemy to be seen—only little groups of cheering French waving flags and throwing flowers, lining the sides of the magnificent Route Nationale along which all vehicles drove as hard as they could. With the sun shining, after a cold and very wet night, and the church bells ringing, it was more like a novel than real life.

The main road passed over the Division's right boundary near Thiberville so the leading troops swung left and moved by way of Lieurey, where some enemy posts were brushed aside, for St Georges du Vievre where the first serious opposition was met. Keen Resistance men appeared and were of great value. The Motor Company worked its way down to the river through very close country and reached the bank before nightfall, and the 11th Hussars, fanned out on a wide front as usual, found various alternative routes on all of which the bridges had been blown. All reconnaissance reports indicated that the line of the Risle was the enemy's next prepared rearguard position. When the troops leaguered the Division had advanced twenty-six miles and had over-run a few small parties of Germans. The only serious casualties were in the 6th Queens who had Major V. G. Spratt and Captains E. W. Walker and V. G. Docton wounded.

The Risle is an attractive trout stream and it flows close under steep wooded slopes on the west side of a little valley. The road winds down the hill, over a level-crossing at a small railway station and then over the bridge into the village of Pont Authou. Here, the buildings had been prepared for defence, and machine-guns were trained on the road and the approaches to the bridge across the fields. Early on the 25th the Scout Troop of "C" Squadron 11th Hussars managed to work their way to the bridge and found it in fairly good state, but the R.A.F. heavy bombers had done the Germans' work for them—for a hundred yards the road was reduced to a honeycomb of deep craters, and it was obviously going to take the Sappers a day to re-make some sort of route. As soon as the Divisional bulldozer could be brought up it was employed shovelling the remains of the station-master's house and other buildings into the gaping holes.

The bridge at Montfort had been destroyed, but the armoured cars found an unguarded, but very shaky-looking, wooden structure about a mile downstream. The Inniskillings got a squadron across with a Motor Company and formed a small bridgehead from which an attack drove the enemy from Pont Authou. Surprisingly, the bridge took the tanks of the rest of the Regiment and, later, of most of the Brigade. During the afternoon the bridgehead was expanded, but the Germans continued to hold the thickly-wooded high ground on the east side of the valley and the 11th could not get their cars out that day.

For the next three days the task of the Division was to clear the area up to the Seine and the southern border of the Forêt de Bretonne. Much scattered fighting took place over a wide area and cost the Division nearly a hundred casualties. Some of the Germans met with were stragglers and only too glad to give themselves up, but there were many small parties who had not had the hammering at Falaise and were full of fight and determined to cross the Seine and get away. They were well supplied with mines and anti-tank guns and there were many sharp actions over this wide area, particularly

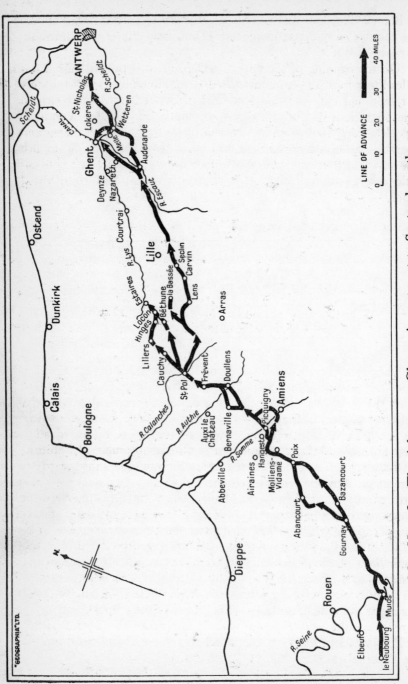

Map No. 16.—The Advance to Ghent, August 31st to September 5th, 1944

at Bourneville and Routot. The weather was exceedingly hot and the country very dense in places. There were scenes of enthusiasm in every village.

On the evening of the 28th the Division was pulled back a few miles for some rest and much-needed maintenance; unfortunately it rained hard all next day so work was particularly unpleasant. The operations of the past ten days, which had yielded a total of 980 prisoners, had been a pleasant contrast to the Bocage, and operating as an armoured division in mobile warfare during the last few days had had an encouraging effect on all, to which the enthusiastic and generous reception by the inhabitants had contributed much.

## The Advance to Ghent

*August 31st to September 5th*

*Reference Map—No. 16, page 230*

"When captains courageous whom death could not daunt
Did march to the siege of the City of Gaunt."

(Ancient Ballad)

The Battle of Normandy was over. With the gradual clearing up of the Falaise–Mortain pocket and the alignment of the Allies along the Seine, the extent of the crushing defeat suffered by the Germans became apparent. The enemy's losses in man-power were not far short of half a million, some 3,500 guns and 1,500 tanks had been taken or destroyed, and much other equipment. In spite of the heavy losses suffered, the German Command managed to get a great many men over the Seine by ferries, but owing to the destruction of all bridges west of Paris (which had been liberated on August 25th) no transport got across. This accounted for many stragglers being taken pushing their possessions in carts or even prams.

The immediate tasks confronting the 21st Army Group were the elimination of the enemy in Northern France, the clearance of the Pas de Calais where there were still many divisions, destruction of the V-bomb sites, the capture of airfields in Belgium and the seizure of the port of Antwerp. The United States First Army were to make for the country from Brussels to Namur, the Second Army for Antwerp and the First Canadian Army the coastal belt and all the Channel ports.

The Second Army plan was for two Corps to advance, the XXXth on the right led by the 11th Armoured Division directed on Antwerp, and the XIIth on the left led by the 7th Armoured directed on Ghent. Shortly before the advance began the Army right boundary was changed so as to include Brussels, and the Guards Armoured Division, who were resting near Flers, were brought up and moved forward on the right of the 11th Armoured. Several bridgeheads had been secured over the Seine, that on the XIIth Corps front being at Muids; the 15th (Scottish) Division had seized it on August 27th and three days later the 53rd (Welsh) Division and Brigadier Carver's 4th Armoured Brigade began to move across.

Within a week the 7th Armoured Division was to be in Ghent, having covered two hundred and twenty miles and taken ten thousand prisoners. Compared with the events of the previous three months, this represented victory on a scale that had not been experienced since the African Campaigns. The credit was to be shared between the fighting and the administrative portions of the Division. Unexampled demands were to be made on the endurance and efficiency of the latter, and the forward troops never lacked anything which it was in the power of the R.A.S.C. to obtain.

On August 29th Divisional Headquarters moved to a large château near Le Neuberg and on the next day the rest of the Division concentrated in this area and came under command of the XIIth Corps (Lieutenant-General N. M. Ritchie). Colonel Wall, after a long period with the Division, had been appointed G.1 (Training and Royal Armoured Corps) at G.H.Q. Home Forces a few days before, and his place as G.1 of the Division had been taken by Lieutenant-Colonel the Earl of Lewes. By now the 22nd Armoured Brigade were at less than two-thirds of their strength in Cromwell tanks and had only nine Light tanks, but they had enough men for the crews. The average shortage in each Battalion of the Queens Brigade was ten officers and two hundred men, the equivalent of two companies. On the morning before the advance was due to start General Dempsey had offered to replace the Queens Brigade with a Brigade from the 59th Division, but the Divisional Commander preferred to retain the officers and men who, though possibly few in numbers, had been so long in the Division and were so familiar with their armoured and other supporting arms, rather than try to absorb an entirely new formation unaccustomed to the workings and organization of an Armoured Division only eight hours, probably, before what was expected to be the decisive and

inal operation of the Campaign. General Verney was also influenced
by the feeling then universally held that the war was coming to an
end—only a couple of days before, a popular newspaper had quoted
in headlines a very distinguished General as saying "the end is in
sight". Below strength though they were, the Queens Battalions
were to play as great a part as they ever had.

On the afternoon of the 30th General Verney gave out the
orders for the advance and a gasp went round the room when he
said "Objective Ghent". There was an atmosphere of victory in the
air and few thought the German Army could ever recover from the
hammering it had had. As the orders were given out, a mood of
cheerfulness and optimism pervaded the great dining-room of the
Château d'Ecrosville, through the high windows of which could be
seen the A.C.V.s, tanks and all the other paraphernalia of modern
war drawn up under the ancient trees, with little groups of men
cooking their evening meal.

The 4th Armoured Brigade, the Royals (Lieutenant-Colonel H.
Lloyd) and the 10th Medium Regiment (Lieutenant-Colonel P.
Dunphie) were placed temporarily under the command of the 7th
Armoured Division and were already in action across the Seine.
Their orders had to go by liaison officers. The first task of the
Division was to secure the crossings over the Somme below Amiens
and above Abbeville and the Divisional Commander decided to
advance on a two-brigade front, the 4th Brigade and the Royals
on the right, the 22nd Brigade and the 11th Hussars on the left.
The Queens Brigade were to be in reserve and routed, if possible,
so as to be able to follow whichever Armoured Brigade made the
most progress.

Already administrative matters were beginning to cause worry.
There was no problem over rations as vehicles could carry all they
needed for a week if necessary, but petrol was obviously going to be
a difficulty. Each vehicle was ordered to load as much extra fuel as
could be obtained and each tank was to carry forty gallons in cans
tied onto the engine covers. Major G. S. Steven's 67 Company
R.A.S.C. who were responsible for petrol supply had to make two
consecutive journeys, each of a turn-round of 160 miles, and when
they got to their leaguer at 9 p.m. on the 31st they found orders to
form a petrol point on the other side of the Seine by dawn next day.
By the time they had done this, the drivers had been at the wheel for
72 hours and without sleep for 96 hours. There was to be no rest for
them for another fortnight.

*The Advance Begins*                                          *August 31st*

Long before it was light the whole Division was astir with higher hopes than had been felt for many a long day, and at three o'clock of a cold, pitch-dark night in pelting rain the move began. Early enthusiasm was soon damped by traffic congestion which was far the worst ever encountered, but as the first glimmer of dawn came the 11th Hussars were crossing one of the two bridges allotted to the Division. The 3rd R.H.A. recorded that it took them ten hours to cover the first eighteen miles. It was a trying, tiring start to an enterprise that was to tax the strength of the small proportion of the Division that were to go right through to the end.

As soon as they were across the river the 11th fanned out on a two-squadron front and by 9 o'clock Colonel Wainman and his men were half-way to the Somme. Like those who were following them, they were cheered almost the whole way. In every town and village the church bells were ringing and the flags were out; every inhabitant must have been by the roadside, waving and shouting. To stop was to be overwhelmed with flowers, fruit and gifts of eggs, to be embraced if one was unwise enough to leave one's vehicle and to be urged to come into the nearest house to share the bottle of wine that had been saved for four years for just this occasion. These scenes were to continue for the next week with increasing fervour when the Belgian frontier was crossed. It was about noon that the 11th first began to fall in with the German rearguards. Lieutenant W. G. G. Hunt was very badly wounded and several of his men killed in the first encounter. He himself fell into enemy hands but was fortunately handed over to some kindly nuns who tended him till the rest of his squadron could get through.

The Inniskillings led the 22nd Brigade and once clear of the traffic made good progress against slight opposition. When dark came, they had covered seventy-two miles and had been on the move for nineteen hours with no halt longer than a few minutes, and then they ran into opposition in several small villages just short of Abancourt. This they cleared away but they were held firmly at Abancourt itself, so the Rifle Brigade worked their way round and soon after midnight rounded up thirty of the garrison, the rest having got away in the dark.

The 4th Armoured Brigade made good progress and were less than twenty miles from the Somme at last light. They had met a lot of scattered resistance all the way. At one time in the morning their Headquarters at Bazancourt had been surrounded just as the

Divisional Commander was paying his first visit. The battle was a short one and soon beaming Maquis were marching a long column of prisoners down the village street. The Queens Brigade was the last formation across the Seine and by nightfall they had passed through Gournay which was the largest town liberated that day. The total number of prisoners amounted to 2,200. In the evening the 71st Infantry Brigade were put under command to come up next day and piquet the left flank.

*Over the Somme*                                      *September 1st*
    This was a busy day for the Divisional Staff with two Armoured Car Regiments and four Brigades under command and actions taking place on the whole Divisional front. Both the Royals and the 11th found all the main road bridges blown within the Division's boundaries. All the armoured car Troops met opposition and there were some sharp engagements. The only bridge discovered within the Divisional sector was little more than a farm bridge near Hangest. A company of the K.R.R.C. and a squadron of the Scots Greys managed to get across under heavy fire and the bridge collapsed under the last tank of the squadron. The 22nd Brigade, trying to get down to the river beyond Airaines, ran into a large rearguard, and their difficulties were further increased by an overflow of armoured troops from the Canadians on their left onto the Brigade Centre Line and they were brought to an abrupt halt.

    Just in the western outskirts of Amiens the 4th Brigade found another small bridge which was actually in the XXXth Corps area but not being used. Here the Royals and the 44th Royal Tanks crossed and went on for another ten miles. The rest of the Division looked like being badly hung up so General Verney got permission from the XXXth Corps to use the small Amiens bridge. At the same time he ordered Colonel Hunter to construct a bridge on the site of the blown one at Picquigny about five miles to the west of Amiens. He decided to move the Queens Brigade across behind the 4th Brigade as they were nearer, and in view of intelligence reports of large numbers of Germans on the left flank, he wanted some sort of flank guard to cover the run to the next river, the Authie.

    The Queens Brigade were now at Molliens Vidame and Brigadier Pepper was instructed to cross the Somme and push right on to the high ground near Bernaville, moving if necessary throughout the night; he was given the 5th Royal Tanks under command. All through the night of the 1st/2nd the tanks and the Queens Brigade troop-carriers rolled down the main road from Molliens Vidame, lurched off down a field track, through the narrow streets of a suburb of Amiens and across the quaking bridge which had certainly never before carried so much or such heavy traffic. It was a very black night, no lights were allowed and for much of the time the rain beat down; it says much for the skill of the drivers that the move went without a hitch and there were no mishaps. The bridge was a cause of much anxiety and as the last vehicle of Main Divisional Headquarters crossed in the early hours of the morning it quietly subsided into the river, its duty done.

Meanwhile the Sappers got busy at Picquigny as soon as the bridging material could get forward. They were overlooked from the high ground across the valley and were under artillery and small arms fire for most of the time, but the 4th Field Squadron worked on in spite of casualties and the bridge was completed by 11 p.m., one hour ahead of the time promised.

*Over the Authie*                                    *September 2nd*
From now on there was a constant threat to the left flank from the German divisions in the Pas de Calais. They threw out a line of defensive positions from Auxi-le-Chateau through St. Pol, Lillers and Béthune to La Bassée. Round Auxi the posts consisted of about 200 men with anti-tank and other guns, but further north they got stronger until they amounted to a battalion or more. The operations of the Division were now to consist of a series of right hooks. Between the rivers the country was open and lent itself admirably to fast cross-country movement by tanks, but all routes led eventually to the few river crossing-places situated in deep woody valleys. Soon, too, the Division was to run into the big coal-mining area south-west of Lille where movement was to be much restricted.

During the 2nd the Royals and the 4th Armoured Brigade, who had served the Division so well, reverted to command of the XIIth Corps under whom they operated on the left flank assisting the infantry divisions forward.

An unexpected difficulty suddenly appeared when the supply of maps ran out. There were so few that the commander of a leading squadron, whether of tanks or armoured cars, could consider himself lucky if there was one map in his squadron, and a small-scale one at that. This appreciably slowed down the gathering and passing of information and reduced the extent to which the Division could operate at night; much dependence had to be placed on the local

Resistance organizations. The Division was also beginning to run out of wireless touch with Corps, but this was not viewed so seriously.

The Queens had a couple of small battles on the way to Berna-ville and in these actions the 5th Queens and the 5th Tanks took a flying-bomb site, four 105-mm. guns and 400 prisoners. The 8th Hussars and the 5th Queens crossed the Authie north-west of Doullens, cleared Frévent and pushed on to St Pol where they came up against a defensive position that was too strong for such a small force. At one time the Division was in action in an area eighteen miles long. General Verney ordered the 22nd Brigade to come to the front, picking up the 7th Queens on the way, and to try to by-pass St Pol both to east and west. The Queens Brigade were to mask St Pol with the 5th Queens and the 8th Hussars, and to cover Auxi, where there was a large German force, with the 6th Queens. The situation was much complicated by the road often being cut behind the leading troops by small parties of Germans moving east and the forward movement of troops was delayed considerably—the tanks could travel across country, the troop-carrying lorries could not.

The Inniskillings attempted to find a route round St Pol to the east, but after covering several miles and losing four tanks they were held up by defensive positions, and when news came that better progress was being made to the west, they were halted. The other force consisted of the 1st Royal Tanks under Colonel Hobart, the 1st Rifle Brigade under Colonel Paley and C.C. Battery of the 5th R.H.A. They were not able to start until 5 p.m. as they were twenty-five miles south of St Pol, had to pass through most of the Division and were impeded by the enemy as well. However, they went well when once they got clear and as the night was not overcast they made good progress and eventually leaguered just beyond Cauchy.

During the day there was a serious petrol crisis and the situation was only saved by the prompt action of Major N. A. Smith, the second-in-command of the Divisional R.A.S.C., who sent the petrol lorries to the Second Army emergency reserve at Beauvais which entailed an extra journey after their very long routine journey. Already the Light Anti-Aircraft Regiment had been "grounded" on the Somme and their lorries taken to reinforce the R.A.S.C. Colonel Cardiff, the A.Q., had a daily and nightly problem to balance the amount of petrol likely to be available with the number of fighting troops that could be maintained forward. Fortunately the ammunition demands were small, but even so it was soon necessary to reduce the fighting strength of the Division in the forward area.

*Coal-mines and Canals*                    *September 3rd and 4th*

The right boundary originally given to the Division ran to the west side of Lille. General Verney had been here in 1940 and knew that the country was a maze of canals and large ditches, mostly crossed only by wooden bridges—the prospects of the Division getting to Ghent in less than a week across such country and against opposition were remote. On September 1st he had pressed to be allowed to move round the east of Lille, but it was not until noon on the 4th that Army assented to the desired change of boundary. Consequently, during the next couple of days the Division was involved in short probes, short advances and frequent changes of Centre Line so as to make some progress to the north-east. The adventures of Colonel Hobart's force show what the fate of the Division would have been if the boundary had not been changed. It is simpler to deal with the whole of their story and then to return to the doings of the remainder of the Division.

The force, which had leaguered near Cauchy at midnight on the 2nd/3rd, was soon cut off from the rest of the Division. At dawn they continued their advance and liberated the large town of Lillers where the Maquis were of great assistance in helping to drive the enemy out. A squadron of tanks and a motor company were left here to guard the Centre Line, and the force went on to the Aire Canal, three miles away, where the two remaining bridges were immediately blown in their faces. Back at Lillers the rearguard were hard pressed in street fighting—as soon as one street was cleared, more enemy would come in from the west, and both to north and south of the town more Germans appeared. A carrier patrol of "I" Company under Sergeant Meyer made contact with the Inniskillings to the east and, in co-operation with the Maquis, captured a battery of 105-mm. guns, a notable performance.

During the morning a patrol of the 11th Hussars found an intact bridge over the Aire Canal at Hinges, so the 1st Tanks were ordered to move east instead of north. This necessitated the abandonment of Lillers and it was feared that the Germans would wreck vengeance on the town. Luckily the Maquis were well enough organized to hold their own in the centre, but some civilians were killed in the outskirts. With the Rifle Brigade acting as rearguard the force crossed the Hinges bridge and pushed rapidly on to Locon, and when night fell they were well on their way to Estaires. They were in contact with the enemy on both sides of the road and in front, as also were their rearguard nine miles away. The guns of

CC Battery were at one time facing both north and south and firing in both directions.

Colonel Hobart halted at dark to let the rearguard close up. They then went on again and about midnight "C" Squadron of the 1st Tanks reached the bridge at Estaires which was at once blown. On the way they had destroyed two 88s and a lot of transport. In the morning patrols were sent out east and south. A carrier patrol directed on Béthune, after taking a lot of prisoners and some horse transport, received an urgent appeal from the Maquis who were being besieged in the prison in the centre of the town. The patrol was increased by the addition of a Troop of tanks, and by 2 p.m. had worked their way through the town and made contact with the 8th Hussars coming up from the south. By now better prospects had opened up and the time for the relief of this force had come. Their gallant exertions had shown that there was no future for the Division in that direction. Although the opposition could have been dealt with there were not the resources in bridging equipment to repair or replace the many bridges that had been blown. The Divisional Commander ordered them to return and stand down.

They well deserved a rest. For two days and two nights, largely cut off and unable to evacuate wounded or prisoners, let alone replenish or rest, they had been constantly moving and fighting. They had captured far more than their own strength in prisoners and had done much material damage. They solved the problem of disposing of their prisoners in two ways. When they left Lillers the prisoners were handed over to the Maquis as hostages in case the Germans should seize the town again. Later, the prisoners' boots were thrown into the nearest canal—this was preferred by the Germans to being handed over to the local inhabitants.

On the evening of the 2nd the rest of the Division were firmly held at St Pol, the Inniskillings having made some progress round by the east. At dawn on the 3rd the 11th fanned out on a three-squadron front over a wide area. Their most important discovery was a bridge over the La Bassée Canal at Cambrin. The enemy were in process of demolishing this but the Troop drove them away and held them off until, in the afternoon, "C" Squadron of the Inniskillings and "A" Company of the Rifle Brigade arrived, crossed it and made a small bridgehead. As the last tank went over, the bridge collapsed, but during the night a scissors bridge was brought up and launched at dawn. The other armoured car squadrons met with much opposition and in one of the engagements a well-known Troop leader, Lieutenant D. Creaton, was killed.

La Bassée was strongly held, but Lieutenant Chapman's Troop, working far out to the right, found their way not only into Lille but out again. They reported that, although the city was full of Germans, their principal difficulty had been with the inhabitants who went wild with joy at seeing the first Allied soldiers since 1940. The news of this exploit did not come in till late at night, but this important event was sufficient to show that with an adjustment of boundary the Division might yet get through to Ghent.

During the morning the Queens had to clear Frévent again, for the enemy had cut the Centre Line there once more. The Division disengaged from St Pol and moved up to the edge of the industrial area south of Béthune. About 2 o'clock in the morning on the 4th a general stand-to was ordered in consequence of some two hundred excited civilians rushing into Main Headquarters and reporting the imminent arrival of a thousand Germans with Tiger tanks following them down the road. Unwilling patrols, assembled hurriedly from the personnel of both Main and Rear Headquarters who were only a few miles apart, went out and found no cause for alarm. It was afterwards said that Rear Headquarters, who generally took three hours to pack up for a move, completed their arrangements for a hurried change to a less exposed locality on this occasion in well under an hour.

During the past few days events had moved swiftly on the right. The 11th Armoured Division, who had a two-day start of the 7th, had crossed the Seine on August 29th; they had met much opposition but, after a night advance on the 30th, had entered Amiens early on the 31st, capturing among others General Eberbach, the commander of the German Seventh Army, and entirely disrupting the enemy's plans for the defence of the Somme line. General Roberts' Division continued their rapid advance and, after covering seventy miles on the 3rd, halted just outside Antwerp which they entered early the next morning, securing intact the valuable port installations, "the major dividend of the great victory in Normandy and of the subsequent rapid advance", as Field Marshal Montgomery described it. The Guards Armoured Division, after a day and a night's halt at Douai, continued their run to Brussels, another sixty-five miles, the following day, meeting negligible opposition and passing some unfortunate American armoured cars which had run out of petrol a few hours before while making their way to the Belgian capital.

When morning came on the 4th the Division was still committed to moving west of Lille and all efforts were directed to enlarging the Cambrin bridgehead. What the Centre Line was to be after that was not an encouraging speculation, for wherever one looked to the north or north-east the map showed rivers, canals or large ditches. Even the optimistic C.R.E. could not forecast how many dozens of lorry-loads of bridging material might be needed, still less how many were likely to be available.

At noon came, at last, notification of the change of boundary, and General Verney immediately warned a force to prepare for what was hoped would be one last, long gallop for Ghent. The petrol consumption of the Division had been exceeding 70,000 gallons a day, which represented seventy lorry-loads, and it was out of the question to think of moving more than a composite brigade on this last 70-mile dash. The Ghent Force was made up of a reduced Main Divisional Headquarters, the 11th Hussars, Main Headquarters 22nd Armoured Brigade, the 5th R.H.A., the Inniskillings, the 5th Royal Tanks, the 6th Queens and "A" Company of the Rifle Brigade with additional lorries for petrol from the 8th Hussars, the 1st Tanks and the Rifle Brigade.

The remainder of the Division were ordered to stay in their locations near Béthune and keep open the Centre Line as far forward and back as their limited resources would permit.

*Full Speed for Ghent*                    *September 4th and 5th*
At half past three in the afternoon the 11th Hussars led the Force out. Their leading squadron, "A", was ordered to secure the valuable crossing over the Escaut at Audenarde, more famous as the scene of Marlborough's battle of Oudenarde, a "first bound" of fifty miles. "B" Squadron was directed to move by way of Courtrai in order to watch the always dangerous left flank and to report on the bridges over the Lys. "D" Squadron were to protect the left flank along the south and south-east suburbs of Lille.

The route lay at first through almost continuous small towns and villages south of Lille and then followed the main road past Audenarde, fairly open country with a few woods. "As far as Carvin," wrote a spectator, "there was no opposition. I stood in the square there and watched the column tearing through—it was a wonderful sight. This was a fine, straight main road and all the drivers really let themselves go, spurred on by the cheers of the frantic natives. The speed of the Cromwell tank was quite sufficient

Q

to enable it to hold its place with all the other vehicles, and the whole ground shook as the tanks roared past." To the left of the road between Carvin and Seclin was a body of German troops with guns which shelled the main road with a fair measure of accuracy at a range of less than a mile, but the road was never blocked, though a few blazing vehicles marked the place where a little extra speed was required.

Great as the reception had been in France, it was exceeded when the troops crossed the frontier into Belgium. As the 3rd R.H.A. War Diary said: "even more flowers, larger and better fruit, an even greater welcome". Besides flags on every church and almost every house, there were numerous banners strung across the roads: "*Vive les Anglais*", "Welcome", "Well Done" and other such greetings. At many places, also, were boards with chalked or painted inscriptions on them in the same vein; one said "You are quite welcome." Whatever the reason may be, there was an added warmth that struck everybody. Huge black, red and yellow flags took the place of the red, white and blue which had never been so large or numerous, and the enthusiasm of the people rose to a new pitch. Short though they must have been of food, they offered all they had, every vehicle was loaded with flowers and filled with apples and pears, the troops were embraced, thanked in broken English and thumped on the back; everyone seemed to have kept a bottle or two of brandy or wine which they insisted the nearest British soldiers should share. To those who were beginning to feel the strain it was a great encouragement, to all it is an unforgettable and cherished memory.

The 1st/5th and 1st/6th Queens were returning to the scenes of old triumphs, for it was near Audenarde that, in May, 1940, they had taken a prominent part in the desperate rear-guard fighting as the British Expeditionary Force made its successful withdrawal to Dunkirk.

Rather than be involved in street fighting in Ghent at night with a small force, the Divisional Commander ordered a halt when Audenarde had been secured, but it was not till long after dark that the tail of the column closed up, and the troops settled down to a few hours of badly-needed rest. Already the force was out of touch with Rear Headquarters at Béthune—the whole of that industrial area was a very bad one for wireless—and far out of touch with the extra-powerful sets at Corps Headquarters. Several "step-up" sets had to be sent back down the Centre Line next day to keep touch with Colonel Cardiff and the remainder of the

Division, and in view of the steady infiltration that went on for the next few days down the road behind, they all had to have an escort.

*Final Scenes*                                     *September 5th*

The advance was resumed at dawn. Eight miles short of the city, at Nazareth, there was an enemy force with guns; these were dealt with, but the 5th Royal Tanks found themselves embarrassed by 300 prisoners. Civilians reported large numbers of Germans to the south-west and west of Ghent and the 5th Tanks opened out so as to make use of all roads between the Escaut and the Lys. As they approached a road block in the suburbs a civilian came forward and said the German garrison wished to surrender. Then followed a series of unusual incidents. Colonel Holliman and Major A. H. Crickmay went forward to the road block and the German officer in command said that he and his Major would like to surrender. The Major then appeared, dramatically draped in a white sheet, and expressed the opinion that the General would probably surrender the city, together with its garrison of a thousand men, if a British officer would accompany him to the German Headquarters. Major Crickmay, therefore, was blindfolded and taken to see the German General.

A good deal of haggling went on, centred on the rank of the officer who was to accept the surrender. The General, Daser by name, was described as being "very aggressive about his honour". He was beautifully dressed, booted, spurred and bemedalled. Colonel Holliman then arrived and attempted to get over the rank difficulty by pretending to be a General himself, but unfortunately one of his officers addressed him as "colonel" and the Germans noticed it. Brigadier Mackeson then appeared and took up the running, but after a great deal more chaffering Daser stated that he had just heard that his Corps Commander had refused to authorize his surrender.

In the meantime, however, the enemy troops had withdrawn to the northern outskirts of Ghent, and although they escaped the prisoners' cage the old city was at least spared the destruction that street fighting would have caused. Subsequent German shelling did little damage but had the useful effect of discouraging an orgy of "liberation" such as went on in Brussels for some days.

At first light General Verney had sent "D" Squadron of the 11th and the Inniskillings across the bridge at Audenarde with orders to seize the bridges over the Scheldt at Wetteren and Melle. They were to approach the city from the east in the hopes of being able to enter if the other portion of the force could not get in from the south. The Melle bridge was blown and the one at Wetteren covered by fire from the opposite bank and raised into a vertical position. Under cover of fire from the squadron some gallant men of the Armée Blanche, the Belgian Resistance organization, lowered it, and the squadron crossed, drove off the enemy and swung left. They were soon in the north-east part of the city where the canal to the Scheldt Estuary leaves the docks. Part of the 6th Queens supported this move and helped to drive back a sharp counter-attack, taking twenty-five prisoners. "D" Squadron, meanwhile, had turned east and moved six miles towards Antwerp and were then held up by defended road blocks. They halted and covered the east flank of the Division. "B" Squadron of the 11th Hussars watched Deynze which Second-Lieutenant R. A. Flood, who went into the town, reported to be "stiff with Germans". This Troop took ninety-five prisoners during the day and the rest of the squadron fought several actions and received much help from the Belgians. Lieutenant E. A. I. Young's Troop had the assistance of a young lady who had parachuted into Lille two months before.

Even Divisional Tactical Headquarters got involved in a little battle on this busy day. On their way forward they were warned by a Resistance man of a German force ahead with which the local inhabitants were engaged, and this man kindly offered to guide them past. Perched on the front of the C.R.A.'s scout car, he then led the party straight to the scene of conflict, and it became apparent that his sole desire, which was not shared by his distinguished companions, was to join the fight. He was hurriedly thrown off.

Divisional Headquarters moved in the morning to Audenarde. "It was a remarkable sight, full of excited people singing and dancing and cheering. One enterprising man had erected a very loud amplifier to his gramophone and all day long and all through the night it played 'Tipperary' to a vociferous audience who never seemed to tire." Work at Headquarters was almost impossible for the mass of admirers crowding round; flowers, fruit and wine were pressed on all the troops, and when it was decided to move to a more peaceful location in the grounds of the Château at Sotteghem, some miles south-east of Ghent, General Verney was presented with an enormous bouquet by a young lady who was almost as embarrassed as he.

By 8 p.m. part of the force from the south had reached the Hôtel de Ville in the centre of the city and the Inniskillings force had a firm hold on the east side, including the valuable crossings of the river at Audenarde and Wetteren. Shortly after midnight the latter reported that an alarm of enemy approaching had been false and that "200 drunks have stumbled off elsewhere".

So ended an operation that will always stand out in the memories of those who had the good fortune to take part in it.

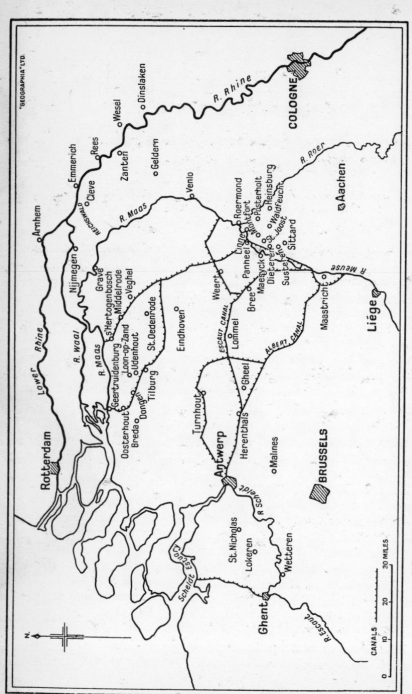

Map No. 17.—The Low Countries, September, 1944, to March, 1945

CHAPTER 9

*September 6th to November 30th, 1944*

# THE LOW COUNTRIES

*Reference Maps—No. 16, page 230. No. 17, page 246*

"Embosom'd in the deep where Holland lies.
That water-land of Dutchmen and of ditches."

*Consolidation Round Ghent*                    *September 6th to 13th*

THE next few days were spent securing the positions gained in and around Ghent and in protecting the Centre Line. The city itself was clear except for shelling that went on for a few more days, but the only serious damage caused was when a troop-carrying lorry filled with men of the Queens was hit. The enemy were held in the dock and factory area to the north where there was much sniping and mortaring. The activities of the Germans did not prevent the inhabitants from showing their enthusiasm for their Liberators, and the 3rd R.H.A. recorded on the 9th that there were "at all times swarms of civilians of all ages round the guns in action and nearly all cartridge cases disappear as souvenirs as soon as fired". About this time, too, there were strong rumours of Hitler's abdication and "fini la guerre" which spread like wildfire.

On the east side of Ghent the bridge at Wetteren required improvement by the Royal Engineers and on the 6th the 4th Field Squadron set to work. Hardly had they begun than they were attacked by a company of S.S. troops supported by mortars and anti-tank guns. A fierce fight followed in which the Sappers were assisted by the transport drivers of the Inniskillings who were nearby. "C" Squadron of the Regiment hurried to the scene and this finally turned the scale, but the Sappers had done great execution among the enemy of whom twenty-five were killed, including their commander, and ten taken prisoner.

The principal anxiety, however, lay to the south of Ghent. General von Zangen, who was now commanding the German

Fifteenth Army, had altogether eleven divisions under his command, some very battered, and it was his intention to concentrate them at Audenarde and fight his way through to the east. Not only did this move threaten to cut the 7th Armoured Division in pieces but it also menaced the lines of communication of the 11th Armoured Division and the other Allied troops from Brussels to Namur and beyond.

The 11th Hussars, watching the line of the River Lys, reported large concentrations of the enemy assembling beyond Deynze, and others who had crossed the river and already collected in the area behind them and between Deynze and Audenarde. Accordingly the Divisional Commander ordered the destruction of the bridges over the Lys and the preparation of the Escaut bridges for blowing should he be hard pressed. "This," said the C.R.E. in a report later, "entailed frantic reconnaissances of the whole river line in a great hurry by all the officers of the Field Squadrons. As these were the first bridges we had ever blown, there was a considerable flutter in the Royal Engineers' dovecot. As a result of much anxious calculation we came to the conclusion that we had just enough explosive in the whole Divisional Engineers to make some sort of a gap in all the bridges." This operation was somewhat disheartening for Lieutenant J. D. Burridge's Troop of the 11th who had spent all day fighting the enemy, taking fifty prisoners and trying, as they thought, to prevent the bridge being blown by the Germans, only to find their own Sappers blowing it in the evening.

After the gapping of the Lys bridges the covering troops fell back to the Escaut line with the hope of keeping the main road open for as long as possible. Gradually the troops who had been halted round Béthune were relieved by others moving up and were able to come forward where they were badly needed, not only to complete the clearing of Ghent but to avert a second Battle of Oudenarde, this time a defensive one. On September 6th, however, the German Commander-in-Chief ordered the Fifteenth Army to withdraw across the Scheldt Estuary instead of fighting their way eastwards. This order took a couple of days to get through and much difficulty was caused to the 7th Armoured in that time.

The Centre Line was cut in many places and on many occasions. Colonel L. R. H. Keatinge, the new A.D.M.S. in place of Colonel E. C. Eccles who had gone to command No. 79 General Hospital, was ordered not to evacuate wounded down the Centre Line, but to make use of the civilian hospitals in Audenarde and Ghent; this turned out to be a very satisfactory arrangement especially as the line of evacuation was eighty miles long, but it was unfortunate that the Division was temporarily deprived of the use of its admirable No. 29 Field Dressing Station (Major K. Borland), which could always rise to any emergency. As it was also impossible to evacuate the several thousand prisoners which the Division now held, they were concentrated in the gaol at Audenarde—here they complained that they had little or nothing to eat, which was true, but there was nothing to give them till the Centre Line was opened permanently.

A very heavy strain fell upon the Military Police, and this seems a suitable opportunity to make mention of this Corps whose services to the Army were so indispensable. In the Division they were controlled by Major E. P. Wedlake-Lewis the A.P.M., and comprised about a hundred men under Captain E. Clarke's command. It was their duty to mark the Divisional and Brigade Centre Lines with the Divisional sign on a metal plate bearing an arrow and the number of the formation or unit beneath. The Police were always to be found right up amongst the forward troops, controlling traffic and ready to put any wanderer on the right road. General Dempsey summed up their work in these words: "The Military Policeman became so well-known a figure on every road to the battlefield that his presence was taken for granted. Few soldiers as they hurried over a bridge which was a regular target for enemy aircraft or artillery gave much thought to the man whose duty it was to be there for hours on end directing the traffic and ensuring its rapid passage." During the long advances when the road was so often cut for a few hours by small bodies of the enemy they had a nerve-racking and arduous task, often alone on their posts and never sure who the next arrival might be. Just north of Audenarde one was killed on his post and inevitably they suffered a high proportion of casualties. Many a weary officer and N.C.O. seeking his destination must often have blessed them as he led his convoy forward to his leaguer.

For the R.A.S.C. the heavy strain continued, and it was fortunate that so many of the officers and men were veterans of Africa and Italy and knew their jobs so well. By the time the head of the Division reached Ghent the turn-round was over 120 miles a day; for the nine-day period it averaged more than 90 miles a day and on one day it had been 150. The petrol requirements were met by a hundred lorries from Major Steven's 67 Company, the normal Petrol-carrying Company, augmented by fifty lorries from 58 Company under Major L. J. Aspland, who normally worked for the Queens Brigade, and twenty lorries from the 15th Light Anti-Aircraft Regiment who had been "grounded". Not only were all current requirements met, but when the Division was able to concentrate round Ghent there was a reserve built up of enough petrol to move the whole Division eighty miles and spare artillery ammunition for 150 rounds per gun. There were many incidents on the road; on one occasion one of the platoons of 67 Company, driving as hard as it could from La Bassée to Ghent, had to run the gauntlet of enemy on the road and then found the petrol point at Audenarde being attacked. At some cost, Captain H. Jennings and his 67 Company men drove the Germans off. It is worth recording that this particular platoon, during the whole Campaign, covered 462,000 miles, an average of 14,000 miles per vehicle.

Thanks to the foresight of Colonel A. C. Lusty the R.A.O.C. carried sufficient spare parts and other stores to meet all demands, and there was no case of a weapon or vehicle being kept out of action for want of spares. The R.E.M.E. were also faced with a difficult task for it was not possible to send the Workshops forward. However, Colonel J. D. Berryman sent his recovery sections with the most forward troops and they did good work in clearing roads and collecting vehicle casualties in localities whence they could easily be recovered. Praise, too, should be given to the Divisional Signals (Lieutenant-Colonel G. S. Knox), for they were required to operate sets at ranges far longer than had ever been contemplated or practised. It had to be accepted that touch would be lost with Corps for much of the time, but it was never impossible to communicate between Main and Rear Divisional Headquarters with the use of "step-up" sets and by asking the Signal operators to work almost continuously with no rest. The success of the operation was due, in no small degree, to the skill and devotion of Colonel Knox and his officers and men.

This is a suitable place in which to make special mention of wireless communications, the development of which made remarkable strides during the war, greater advances possibly than any other type of equipment. By 1944 every armoured vehicle in an Armoured Division and many wheeled vehicles were permanently fitted with their own wireless sets; these had a range of between ten and fifteen miles in North-West Europe and between five and ten miles in the mountains of Italy. With a standing order that speech was always to be officer-to-officer except in the smallest sub-units, it was possible for the Divisional Commander to obtain accurate information from any part of the Division's forward or rear area in a matter of a few minutes. At any time he could speak to his immediate subordinates or their chief Staff officers, whether on the move or not. As he motored along, he could receive or send out information or orders; the subordinate commanders were equally well served. The experience and skill of the Royal Signals, and of the officers and men in all units who were responsible for the upkeep and "netting" of the wireless, were of the highest. They reached and maintained the standard of "The Wireless Always Works". It never failed.

After several days travelling through liberated territory vehicles had taken on rather an unusual appearance. They were bedecked with flowers and thousands of people seemed to have run riot with chalk, writing "Vive" or the V-sign. It was also the custom of the inhabitants of all towns and villages to write the name of the place on any vehicle they could approach. It was, too, by no means unusual to see a name and a short message for some missing member of the family chalked on in the hope that it might be seen by the person for whom it was intended. By the time the Army reached Belgium it was an interesting study to examine all those names going back, perhaps, to some place south of the Seine.

*The Division Closes Up*

The 7th Queens were the first Battalion to come forward to Ghent from Béthune and on their way they had a sharp fight with a force of Germans making for the Escaut—over a hundred of the enemy were killed and wounded. The Rifle Brigade, who followed, had not been wasting their time at Béthune and Colonel Paley had enlisted a number of French and Belgian volunteers, thus following the precedent set by the Regiment in 1813 when they had enrolled Spaniards during the Peninsular War. These twentieth-century volunteers proved to be as great a success, even though, on one occasion, the Adjutant inspecting a parade found one of them wearing trousers of a very violent check below his battle-dress blouse. Most units of the Division at this time were allotted Liaison Officers of Belgian or Dutch nationality. They were all of the greatest value, not only in co-operating with the local Resistance movements and acting as interpreters, but also, when hard weather necessitated billeting on a big scale, in arranging accommodation and smoothing over difficulties. Many lasting friendships were made with these officers and N.C.O.s, and the Division owes them much.

To the east side of Ghent the Division gradually spread out, cleared Lokeren and St Nicholas and various small villages, but operations could not be continued over the canal that runs east and west a mile or two north of St Nicholas; beyond there lay an area of polder country and it would have required far larger numbers of infantry than were available to clear the country up to the Scheldt Estuary. A Troop of "D" Squadron 11th Hussars reached the western end of the Antwerp Tunnel which passes beneath the Scheldt, but found it blocked. For several days there was a good deal of fighting on the west side of Antwerp and it was apparent that the Germans were determined to maintain a foothold there. On the 7th the 5th Royal Tanks took 450 prisoners and on the next day the armoured cars took over 800.

On the north side of Ghent the Glasgow Highlanders were brought up from the 15th Division to assist the Queens Brigade in clearing the dock and factory area. The 6th Queens were held up owing to a swing bridge being opened and swung to the wrong side of the basin. Some of the 4th Field Squadron R.E. swam over and fixed a cable to the bridge and to one of the 5th Royal Tanks' tanks, which then pulled the bridge back. Under cover of fire from "A" Squadron, "C" Squadron then crossed, followed by the infantry who cleared the warehouses on the far side. There was a good deal of enemy shelling and mortaring, and a certain number of casualties were sustained, including Captain B. L. Butler of the 5th Tanks who was killed. Forty prisoners were taken. Some valuable support was given by rocket-firing aircraft in spite of the difficulty of the enclosed locality.

On the 11th the Polish Armoured Division arrived to take over the area. In the main square they assembled large numbers of prisoners and picked them over—those who came from Polish territories were at once changed into British uniforms and shipped to England to be trained for the Polish Army. On the same day the Division started to move to the Malines area, "an extremely pleasant march", said the 3rd R.H.A.; "grand reception everywhere and all vehicles finished laden with fruit and tomatoes". During the last two days in Ghent the Division had lost forty-seven men, most of them from the Queens Brigade. When General Verney took his leave of the Burgomaster he was presented with an inscribed plaque to commemorate the Liberation of Ghent from the Germans; this is now in the Royal Armoured Corps Museum at Bovington. At Malines Brigadier H. J. B. Cracroft arrived to take command of the 22nd Armoured Brigade.

## THE BATTLE OF ARNHEM

*September 13th to 24th*

During the ten days following the arrival of the Second Army in Belgium there was a steady move eastwards of the Armoured Divisions as the Infantry Divisions came forward and as ground was gained for the next operation. The 7th Armoured moved to Malines and then took over a long line on the canal between Herenthals and Antwerp where, after a few days, the Canadians arrived in relief. It was not a period of great activity. The Division had not the resources to gain ground across the canal nor were they required to do so. There was patrol activity, shelling and mortaring, and the 7th Queens, who occupied a large factory near Herenthals, did much execution with their snipers from the upper windows—on one day, the 21st, they claimed a bag of sixteen Germans killed and four wounded. During all this period, and indeed for another two and a half months, the 7th Armoured suffered from an acute shortage of infantry. Many who were not trained or intended for use as ordinary infantry had to be employed as such—near Herenthals, for example, the machine-gunners and anti-tank men of the Rifle Brigade went into the line as Riflemen. Frequently the armoured car and tank crews had to be used on foot patrols and later on even the Royal Engineers had to take their place in the line as infantrymen.

This country in which the Division now found itself was not attractive and it became still less so as autumn and winter closed in. All of it was flat and much of it consisted of scattered fir trees, marsh, sandy wastes and scrub, intersected by numerous canals and large drainage ditches. The roads for the most part were raised above the surrounding country and movement off them was frequently impossible. It was a depressing landscape and the only warm thing about it was the greeting of the Dutch folk when the troops crossed the frontier; their kindness, like that of the Belgians, endured for many months.

The Guards Armoured Division made substantial advances and gained bridgeheads over the important Albert and Escaut Canals. The 11th Armoured were moved to the east of them, and the 50th Division came up on the left of the Guards and crossed the Albert Canal south of Gheel, following which the 15th Division crossed the Escaut Canal north of that village. All these crossings were very strongly opposed, especially that at Gheel where the enemy seemed determined to drive the Scottish back.

On September 17th began Operation "Market Garden", the purpose of which was to establish the three Armoured Divisions of the Second Army in the area Hamm, Munster and Osnabruck whence the Army was to advance eastwards and occupy the Ruhr. There were three obstacles, German resistance, administrative difficulties and the ground. The first-named turned on the extent to which the German Army could be rallied after its shattering defeats in Normandy and France. The administrative difficulty lay in whether such a force could be maintained at the end of a long and slender line of communication which was, initially at least, no more than one rather indifferent road, and several hundred miles from the base area whence all supplies had to come in motor transport. The ground problem was posed by the Rivers Maas, Waal and Lower Rhine and the many canals between them.

Lieutenant-General F. A. M. Browning's 1st Airborne Corps was to be dropped on a line from Eindhoven to Arnhem, the American 101st Airborne Division being responsible between Eindhoven and Grave, the American 82nd Airborne Division were to deal with the Maas at Grave, the Waal at Nijmegen and the wooded country south-east of Nijmegen, and the British 1st Airborne Division with the Polish Parachute Brigade were to gain the cross-ings of the Lower Rhine at Arnhem. The advance by the ground troops was entrusted to the XXXth Corps who had the Guards Armoured Division in the lead with the 43rd and 50th Divisions to follow up. The VIIIth Corps, which included the 11th Armoured Division, were to guard the right flank of the XXXth Corps and clear the country to the east of the corridor, while the XIIth Corps, with the 7th Armoured Division under command, were to act similarly on the west flank. In both cases the nature of the ground on either side of the corridor and the resistance put up by the enemy were far harder than had been anticipated; long after the Arnhem operation was concluded much hard fighting had to be put in before this narrow corridor could be cleared.

The 7th Armoured were not directly concerned during the first week of the operation, but as the aircraft carrying the troops flew over the Divisional area the artillery fired on such German anti-aircraft batteries as were within reach. On the 19th the Division was given the task of carrying out the evacuation of the Gheel northern bridgehead. The 15th Division were required to move

further east and the resistance here had been so strong and the
losses so heavy that it was decided to abandon the positions gained.
This task was carried out in one night at a cost of only twenty
casualties, much less than had been expected.

*Trouble on the Centre Line*                       *September 24th to 27th*
    On the 19th the Guards Armoured Division had reached
Nijmegen which they found strongly defended and it was not until
the evening of the 20th that they and the 82nd Airborne Division
gained possession of the two bridges over the Waal. A further attempt
to advance, using the main road in daylight, was held up almost as
soon as it started; but a squadron of the Household Cavalry on the
22nd found a way through to the Polish Parachute Brigade which
had been dropped south of the Lower Rhine almost opposite Arnhem.
On the same day, the Centre Line was cut by an enemy force at the
village of Veghel where the road runs through flat country with small
fields and hedges. During the next day this force was driven off by
some of the Guards and 50th Division, but twenty-four hours later
the Centre Line was cut again, this time between St Oedenrode
and Veghel where there are woods on both sides, and this time the
force was a much stronger one, with tanks and artillery.
    During the evening the Division received orders to move up at
once and Brigadier Pepper went forward to find out what he could,
for the situation was obscure and information vague and con-
tradictory. It was a wet, cold, blustery evening and turned out to
be a nasty night. By dawn the Division was concentrated about six
miles south of Eindhoven. From there General Verney went on to
join Brigadier Pepper at the Headquarters of the 50th Division in the
woods about two miles south of St Oedenrode.
    The road from Eindhoven up to the scene of the "cut" was an
amazing sight with the transport of the Guards and other Divisions,
Corps and Army Troops and lorries of bridging equipment, all
double-banked on the road and nose-to-tail. They had sat there for
a day and a night already, and with only a narrow track between
them they looked like sitting there for a long time to come. Some-
how, however, the Military Police managed to keep a lane clear
and to shepherd forward the Army Group and Army Commanders
to join a gathering at 50th Divisional Headquarters of the Commanders of the VIIIth, XIIth and XXXth Corps and a representative
of the 101st Airborne Division. One of the decisions arrived at was
to put the Queens Brigade and the Inniskillings under the command

of the 50th; by superhuman endeavours the Police got them through, and by one o'clock on the next day the enemy had been driven back sufficiently far to allow the vast stream of transport to move forward, speeded up by occasional shell bursts on the way.

During the night of the 25th/26th, the survivors of the 1st Airborne Division were withdrawn from Arnhem covered by troops of the 43rd Division who had gone forward by the route found by the Household Cavalry.

*Holding the Line*                    *September 28th to October 21st*

The Division continued to drive the enemy back on the north-west side of the main road for about two miles, at the cost of some casualties and then moved forward across the canal at Veghel. The 11th Hussars worked towards s'Hertogenbosch but found the town protected by a ring of defensive positions. The 1st Tanks reached Veghel on the 27th and cleared two villages to the north-west, and gradually the Division took up a line that extended from Veghel to the Maas north of Oss.[1] Here they settled down to nearly a month of static warfare on a front fourteen miles long. This was a great strain on the Division's resources; already their strength was low, in the last three days of September they lost another seventy-five men and during the first three weeks of October another hundred and sixty-two officers and men were killed or wounded. It was never possible to pull a company or squadron further back than the reserve line which, in this open warfare, meant a state of continual alertness; the most that could be done was to send men for forty-eight hours' leave to the Jerboa Club in Eindhoven where everything the administrative staff could think of was done to make them comfortable.

The right portion of the front consisted of polder, large open fields cut up by wide and deep dykes; this was held by the 11th Hussars. The rest of the front was small copses and woods, heath and scrub, marshy and dead flat. The 22nd Armoured Brigade held the right sector here and the Queens Brigade the left. The life consisted of a never-ending succession of day and night patrols, mortaring and shelling, and no day passed without casualties; on the 20th Lieutenant J. W. Crocker of the Inniskillings was killed—he was the son of the Commander of the 1st Corps. There were two engagements of note. One was an enemy attack on Heesch[1] by a force at least a battalion strong; this was driven off and 250 prisoners were taken. The other was an attack by the Germans on the church at Geffen,[1]

[1] Not shown on Map 17.

the tower of which was an outstanding observation-post; this cost
the enemy twenty-five prisoners. Standing as it did, a landmark for
miles, it was always an enemy target but their artillery failed to do
it any harm and attempts were made to get a party into it so as to
blow down the tower. Generally defended by the Rifle Brigade, it
withstood all attempts and when the Division moved away later in
the month it was still standing. On the other parts of the front
there were engagements between patrols almost every day and night,
and an unattractive life was not made better by the cold, damp,
foggy weather which persisted throughout the month.

Early in October both the Brigade Commanders left. Brigadier
Pepper was appointed to command the Battle School in England
and Brigadier Cracroft had to go to hospital. One of the old Desert
fighters, he had been wounded in Normandy but had managed to
get past the doctors before he was fully fit; now his wounds broke
out and there was no alternative but for him to go to hospital.
Brigadier W. R. Cox came from the 50th Division to command the
Queens Brigade and Brigadier A. D. R. Wingfield, another with
much Desert experience, took command of the 22nd Brigade.
Another departure about this period was that of the Rev. F. W.
Synnott, the veteran Irish Chaplain of the 5th R.H.A. He had
reached high rank as a combatant officer in the First World War
and had seen much action in the Second. He was a well-loved man
whose departure was widely regretted.

Oss was a remarkable place and deserves special mention. A
small industrial town about the size of Horsham, it contained a vast
German Army food store with hundreds of tons of frozen beef,
mutton, bacon, butter, cheese and many other commodities. For
some weeks most of the Second Army was fed on rations from this
store—there was even an issue of cigars. It was said that just before the 11th arrived, when the town was in No-Man's-Land, a
Dutch storeman used to issue to the Second Army in the morning
and to the Germans from s'Hertogenbosch in the afternoon—he
seemed indifferent as to who drew the rations so long as there was a
signature in his book.

During the day the armoured car squadrons were spread out in
the polder and in the evening they closed into a ring round the town
supported by the guns of the Norfolk Yeomanry. They also had
under command a hundred men of the well-organized Dutch
Resistance Army. Commanded by a remarkable character known
as Tom of Lith, of whose daring there were innumerable tales,

R

these men spent the nights lying out and watching all likely avenues of approach or carrying out raids of their own; by day they operated with the squadrons on the banks of the Maas. The Regimental news-letter of the 11th describes the highly complicated telephone system that was used by the Resistance to send reports to s'Hertogen-bosch, Nijmegen and other places further afield: "The Oss telephone exchange was a model of courtesy and efficiency enabling us to ring up towns still in German hands—an easy, if unorthodox, way of reconnaissance. Twice the Germans tumbled to this and rang up Oss to ask the "form," but they got no change from the telephone girls at our end, and eventually at the end of their three minutes cut the line and called it quits."

The Burgomaster, M. de Bombac, was another remarkable character who was untiring in the help he gave the Regiment—there were shower baths, football matches, even dances arranged by him, and he took care that as many men as possible should be billeted in houses and small farms. His care and kindness will long be remembered.

## THE SOUTH-WEST HOLLAND OPERATIONS

### October 22nd to 31st, 1944

Although the port of Antwerp had been captured undamaged it had not been possible to bring it into use as the north and south banks of the Scheldt Estuary were still held by the Germans. Nor had it yet been possible to make much use of the Channel Ports. When the enemy retreated strong garrisons had been left in them and the capture of each had necessitated a special siege operation. Until the approaches of Antwerp were clear the Second Army could not develop any more full-scale offensive operations. Accordingly, in the latter part of October all resources were devoted to clearing the approaches to Antwerp, both by land and sea.

The First Canadian Army, with whom were the 1st Corps, were to drive back the Germans on both the south and north sides of the Estuary, and the right flank of this Army was to advance up to the estuary of the Maas. The XIIth Corps was to be on the right of this manœuvre and was to advance westwards from the positions occupied in the Oss–Eindhoven area.

The 53rd (Welsh) Division came up into the 22nd Armoured Brigade's area in great secrecy just before the operation began, and their task, with the Inniskillings, was to capture s'Hertogenbosch. On the left of the 7th Armoured Division, the 51st Division was to advance north-west from the Veghel–St Oedenrode road, and on their left the 15th Division was to take Tilburg. The 7th Armoured was to advance to within two miles of s'Hertogenbosch and then to pass between the 51st and 15th Divisions and establish themselves at Geertruidenburg near the mouth of the Maas, thirty miles away.

The country through which the Division was to operate was typical of Brabant. For the first part there were thick woods alternating with large stretches of pine-covered sand-dunes. Further south it was slightly more cultivated but again intersected by thick woods. West of the road from Tilburg to Loon-op-Zand the woods gave way to polder, very large fields divided by dykes. Over the whole area the roads were few and poor, embanked for the most part and very liable to collapse under the weight of armoured vehicles. The operations were to a certain extent hampered by the lengthening nights and, owing to the bad weather, were more extended than would have been the case in summer. It was nearly always wet and often very cold.

The battle began at 4 a.m. on October 22nd with heavy artillery concentrations on all known enemy positions and these continued until, at 6.30, the Queens Brigade advanced, supported by the 8th Hussars and by mine-sweeping "Flail" and flame-throwing "Crocodile" tanks. The enemy defences consisted of strong points surrounded by minefields which caused considerable delays, but the first two villages were taken by the 5th Queens without much trouble, and in the afternoon the 1st Royal Tanks carried out a wide and successful sweep of the surrounding country. The 7th Queens, however, were up against much more determined opposition at Middelrode which held out till early the next morning. During the day the Division lost four tanks of the 8th Hussars destroyed and sustained about sixty casualties—over a hundred prisoners were taken.

On the right the 53rd Division made good progress to within four miles of s'Hertogenbosch, their leading Brigades being supported by the Inniskillings and some of the 5th Royal Tanks, whose work received high praise afterwards. The 11th Hussars covered their right flank.

During the night of the 22nd/23rd the 7th Queens cleared Middelrode and took 130 prisoners. The Division then concentrated, waiting while the 51st Division secured crossings over the Rivers Dommel and Aa (not shown on map) and it was not until the 25th that they were able to move up to the bridge over the Aa—even then the move forward was much hampered by the 51st Division's traffic on the narrow roads. On the morning of the 26th, the 22nd Brigade crossed with the 5th Tanks in the lead and the 11th Hussars operating as far ahead as the country permitted. The former met much opposition but the 1st Tanks, moving round the north flank, made good progress and reached Udenhout in the evening, clearing the town and taking eighty prisoners.

On the following day the advance was directed on Loon-op-Zand which was found to be very strongly defended and surrounded by many minefields; also, the ground was very wet and boggy. Here, the attackers were held up all day. On the left the 15th Division reached Tilburg and the 11th Hussars got as far as the canal on the north side of this large town where they found all the bridges blown.

On the 29th the 5th Queens cleared Loon-op-Zand from the west and the 1st Tanks pressed on for Oosterhout, ten miles further on. At Dongen there was a strong enemy position in the woods to the east of the town, held by infantry amply supplied with mines, artillery and bazookas. Lieutenant J. A. M. Cousins and his Troop of the 11th Hussars made a gallant dash for the important cross-roads short of the woods, but came under a torrent of fire which knocked out two of the three vehicles and killed several of the Troop including the intrepid Troop Leader himself. The position was attacked by the Inniskillings carrying some of the Rifle Brigade on their tanks but this attack was halted by boggy ground on one flank and by mines on the other. However, the 1st Tanks and "C" Company of the Rifle Brigade worked further round the flank and eventually the attack was successful and the position was taken together with 120 prisoners.

When the 8th Hussars and the 5th Queens entered Dongen they got "the best welcome in Holland". The 11th Hussars said: "For once the stolid Dutch gave full vent to their emotions, and the armoured cars entered under a panoply of flags with one long roar of cheering ringing in their ears. The small town was almost undamaged, so that officers and men were soon installed inside comfortable billets. It was just as well, for the day was bitterly cold and the weather experts were predicting snow."

Next, the 1st Tanks and the 7th Queens attacked and captured Oosterhout, and the Rifle Brigade pushed patrols on to a village just short of Geertruidenburg, receiving some assistance from the Polish Armoured Division who were advancing from Breda on the west side of the canal from Tilburg. The total of prisoners for the day was 200.

By now the Division was up to the Maas and a quiet period followed while the area was cleared of the few remaining enemy and a defensive line formed along the river. The operations during the last week of October had cost the Division 110 casualties and the loss of twenty-two tanks; the prisoners taken numbered nearly 900.

## NOVEMBER 1944

For the first ten days of November the Division enjoyed a quiet period. Except for the outpost positions on the Maas there was no contact with the enemy and the men had a chance of resting and training, and the tank crews could overhaul their Cromwells which, as usual, had gone supremely well. There were villages and farms where the troops could be billeted and Divisional Headquarters took up its leaguer in some gardens in Tilburg. This was a large modern town and quite undamaged. The people appeared rich and prosperous and, as in most parts of Holland, they were generous and hospitable. Only one untoward incident occurred. A cinema in the town had been placed at the disposal of the troops and there had been performances on two successive nights, but on the third night the projector broke down so the performance was cancelled. Later, at an hour when the theatre would have been full of men enjoying a film, the place blew up. Whether a time-bomb had been left there or a saboteur had got in was never discovered.

By now the American Armies were lined up on the frontiers of Germany from Switzerland to Aachen, twenty-five miles east of Liège, where they were actually on German soil. All of France, Belgium and Luxemburg had been freed. The British Second Army had cleared Holland up to the line of the Maas and held a salient jutting out towards Arnhem.

A spell of bitter weather in the middle of the month coincided with the issue of special winter clothing for the crews of all armoured vehicles. These were known to the troops as "zoot suits" and the 11th Hussars described them as "a mass of zip fasteners joined together by windproof and waterproof material". Cunning manipulation of the zips turned them into sleeping bags. They were a valuable addition to the troops' kits.

On November 10th the Division moved to the eastern portion of the Second Army sector and took over a line along the Maas and the Wessem Canal. This was very unattractive country, wooded, sodden with water and abounding in mines. The 11th Hussars were centred on Maesyck and maintained standing patrols along the Maas, and the infantry held the remainder of the front.

On the 14th the XIIth Corps launched a small offensive to clear an area of ground east of Weert. The Division had but a small part to play but, as sometimes happens in war, it turned out to be a very expensive operation. The requirement was to seize the lock gates at Panheel before the enemy could destroy them and drain the water out of the canal, an occurrence that would greatly hamper the movements of the Division on the left. The task was undertaken by the 7th Queens supported by "C" Squadron of the 8th Hussars. The lock was taken in three-quarters of an hour, but during that short time the Queens lost one officer killed and six wounded, five men killed and twenty-five wounded. The Germans brought down intense defensive fire; both the leading platoon commanders were at once hit and so were the commanders of the two leading companies and the reserve company; the adjutant and the intelligence officer were also wounded, the latter fatally. Almost the only surviving officer among the forward troops was Lieutenant Wilkinson-Cox who had only just joined the Battalion; he led his platoon in an assault of the lock buildings covered by close support fire from the 8th Hussars' tanks, of which seven were bogged on the way forward, and the enemy were driven off and the lock gates taken intact.

By the end of November the reinforcement situation in the 21st Army Group was so serious that one Division had to be disbanded, and the man-power problem was aggravated by the introduction of a scheme under which all officers and men who had served for five years overseas were sent back to England, either permanently or, if they volunteered, on a period of leave instead. This hit the R.H.A. and the 8th and 11th Hussars particularly hard, and altogether a good many men in the Division were affected.

The 50th Division, which was now temporarily commanded by Major-General L. O. Lyne in place of Major-General D. A. H. Graham who had been injured, was the Division selected for disbandment, but in recognition of its great fighting record it was re-constituted in England as a Training Division. Some of its units and personnel were retained in the 21st Army Group, however, and two of these units, the 2nd Battalion Devonshire Regiment (Lieutenant-Colonel P. H. W. Brind) and the 9th Battalion Durham Light Infantry (Lieutenant-Colonel H. J. Mogg) were transferred to the 7th Armoured. This meant the end of the two-year association of the Queens Brigade with the Division, an association that had taken part in so many great events and which was severed with reluctance. All three of the Battalions were very seriously depleted by casualties and under the new organization the Queens Royal Regiment was to be represented only by the 1st/5th Battalion, which was now to be made up for the most part of officers and men who had not served abroad for so long as had many of their comrades. No other units were affected *in toto*, but all had the gaps in their ranks filled. General Lyne came as the new Divisional Commander and General Verney soon after went to the 6th Armoured Division in Italy. Brigadier Cox went to command the 69th Infantry Brigade and his place was taken by Brigadier J. M. K. Spurling from the 50th Division. General Lyne had not been altogether lucky hitherto, for the 59th Division which he had commanded in Normandy had had to be broken up in August, and he had been only a short time with the 50th when it, too, ceased to be an active force.

With the Division up to strength, it was now possible to form a Divisional Battle School, a luxury that shortage of men and operational commitments had hitherto made impossible. Since D-Day every available man had been required in the fighting line and there had never been a time when instructors and students could have been spared from active operations. The School was situated near Brussels where there was a good training area as well as adequate facilities for recreation, and it remained there till the end of the Campaign. A Divisional Convalescent Depot was set up on the same premises and proved invaluable.

During the first week of December the Division took over a six-mile sector of line from the Guards Armoured Division between Maesyck and Sittard. The front was held as lightly as possible and the principal activity was patrolling across waterlogged fields towards enemy defences that lay on the other side of a small stream. On this part of the front the enemy had more artillery than usual and the villages in the forward area were frequently shelled, but the Divisional Artillery gave the customary quick and accurate support and exacted retribution on enemy batteries on a scale of ten rounds for every one fired by the Germans. There was also a certain amount of air activity on the enemy's part and on one occasion the 15th Light Anti-Aircraft Regiment brought down seven German planes, and they had successes on other days too.

On the 16th the Ardennes Offensive began when the Germans attacked on a forty-mile front with two Panzer Armies. The right of the attack was at Monschau, thirty miles east of Liège, and the front, which was held by the Americans, was penetrated to a considerable depth. Bad weather for some days previously had prevented the Allied Air Forces from carrying out the usual reconnaissances, so complete surprise was obtained.

The Offensive had the ambitious object of breaking right through to Antwerp and separating the British and American Armies. The 21st Army Group moved a number of divisions down to act as a covering force in case the Germans should succeed in crossing the Meuse, as the Maas is known in Belgium, but the 7th Armoured Division was not involved. The Allied Air Forces were able to go into action on the 24th and from then the tide began to turn. The enemy reached the furthest point of their advance on the 25th by which time they were only a short distance east of the Meuse. The Allied counter-attack began on January 3rd and by the 16th the salient had been eliminated.

The weather was bitterly cold all this time and the most elaborate precautions had to be taken to keep vehicles in running order. Not only was there the risk of engines freezing, but tank tracks froze to the ground, instruments inside turrets became unusable and the mud on wheels and tracks froze so hard that it had to be chipped off before the vehicle could be taken out. Christmas was celebrated with the usual ample fare that Quartermasters are always able to produce on such occasions, but the most notable event was the performance of the Divisional Choir, who, organized by Mr. Wingfield Digby, provided the musical setting for Field Marshal Montgomery's Christmas broadcast. The only disturbance was that caused by a sharp attack on one of the 11th Hussars' forward Troops early on the 26th—this was a short but spirited engagement in which the enemy got the worst of it.

CHAPTER 10

# THE ADVANCE INTO GERMANY

*Reference Maps—No. 17, page 246. No. 18, page 268. Back Endpaper*

## OPERATION "BLACKCOCK"

*January 13th to 31st, 1945*

THE intention of this Operation, which was under control of the XIIth Corps, was to clear the territory up to the River Roer. The plan was to drive a salient into the enemy's positions on the left of the 7th Armoured Division's sector, to gain the main road that runs from Sittard to Roermond, and then to outflank the German defences on the right so that the 43rd and 52nd Divisions could advance. Additional troops were placed under the command of the 7th Armoured and consisted of the 8th Armoured Brigade and the 155th Brigade from the 52nd Division for the early stages and the 1st Commando Brigade for the later period.

The ground was frost-bound and covered with snow and it was essential to success that there should be no thaw—otherwise the tanks would not be able to operate freely across country and the roads would break up under the density of the traffic. A further essential was that the slender line of communications, which consisted of one narrow road, should be kept free from traffic congestion, for along it had to pass the best part of two Armoured Brigades as well as all other vehicles. The freedom of this road was ensured by the provision of traffic-control posts manned by officers and signallers. Under conditions of extreme cold, with little sleep and subjected often to heavy shelling, these posts carried out their tasks magnificently and it was largely due to them that the operation went so well.

On the 13th the 5th Queens carried out a preliminary attack to take a small village a thousand yards in front of the line. This operation, aided by Flails and an artillery barrage, was successful at a cost of seventeen casualties. The main attack was due to start early on the 16th but it had to be postponed for twelve hours as a smoke-screen, put down to cover movement on the left flank, froze in the air and created a very dense fog. When, however, the fog dispersed the first attack was by the Durhams who, carrying ladders to cross the twenty-foot stream in front of the German posts, captured Dieteren and took many prisoners.

Throughout the afternoon and night the 621st Field Squadron worked furiously to make a causeway so that vehicles could get up to the Durhams—thick mist, accurate and continuous shelling and the repeated bogging of their vehicles did nothing to daunt them. Then, in the pitch dark of the freezing early hours of the 17th, the Queens moved forward to attack another village, Susteren. On their way forward they were themselves attacked from the flank, but the fire of Colonel Norman's 3rd R.H.A. shattered the enemy before he could get to close quarters and the Queens went on. Once in Susteren, they were counter-attacked by infantry and tanks, and they knocked out two tanks before "B" Squadron of the 1st Tanks arrived in their support. The Queens lost sixty-eight officers and men and the 1st Tanks lost seven tanks during the battle. So bad was the mud that wheeled vehicles could not get forward and the scout cars of the 1st Tanks had to be towed. Lieutenant-Colonel Harvey's 131st Field Ambulance faced great difficulties and two Sections under Major J. Watt and Lieutenant Pleasants, R.A.M.C., had to man-handle all their equipment forward. Other gains were made by the Devons using armoured troop carriers and they were supported by "C" Squadron of the 1st Tanks and "Crocodile" flame-throwers.

There followed several days of hard fighting. The Germans were well supported by artillery and fought fiercely from village to village, but a series of attacks by infantry, generally a battalion strong, with the support of tanks and flame-throwing Churchills, gradually drove them back. The slight thaw that threatened at the beginning of the operation turned to renewed hard frost—otherwise movement would have been brought to a standstill. During the morning of the 18th the Devons and the 1st Royal Tanks captured Echt[1] and the advance continued to the north-east with the 8th Armoured Brigade coming up on the right; the rapid advance of this Brigade enabled the 52nd Division to reach the high ground about Waldfeucht.

On the 20th and 21st very fierce fighting took place in St Joost

[1] Not shown on Map 17.

where "I" Company of the Rifle Brigade and the 8th Hussars were at first involved. The enemy, who were parachutists and fought desperately, held every house, and after "I" Company had lost twenty-six men, a high proportion of the strength of a Motor Company, the Durham Light Infantry came up to carry on the house-to-house fighting. They, too, had many casualties, including Major McCartney of "A" Company killed and Major Anderson of "C" Company missing. Then more of the Rifle Brigade arrived and finally the place was cleared. It was near here that Colonel Holliman, who had commanded the 5th Royal Tanks for so long and with such distinction, was killed. He was one of the old-timers of the Division who had seen a great deal of fighting and had always been in the thick of it.

On the 22nd the Inniskillings, with "C" Company of the Rifle Brigade, moved forward to take Montfort and with the use of scissors bridges made good progress until dark against increasing resistance. During the night the 5th Queens came up and the force, with the support of the 5th Tanks, captured the village together with many prisoners. On the 24th the Division pushed forward on three axes. On the right, the Queens and the 1st Tanks moved east to Posterholt which they took next day. They were preceded by "D" Squadron of the Eleventh, three of whose Troops, under Lieutenants R. E. Alton, A. S. Hunter and Nation-Tellery, carried out some valuable reconnaissances. In the centre were the Devons and the Inniskillings who advanced north-east to the Roer, and on their left were the 8th Hussars and the Commando Brigade advancing towards Linne. By now the enemy was falling back fast, covering his retreat with machine-gun posts and a multitude of mines.

With the gaining of these objectives Operation "Blackcock" was concluded, and until well into February the Division held the areas gained. It was not a period of great activity except on the part of patrols. The Commandos on the left carried out a number of raids round the Maas and in one of these Lance-Corporal Harden of the Commando's R.A.M.C. greatly distinguished himself in succouring the wounded; unhappily, he was killed, but a posthumous Victoria Cross was awarded later. Towards the end of January, Colonel Goulburn, who had commanded the 8th Hussars for a very long time, was given another appointment; he was succeeded by Lieutenant-Colonel G. R. D. FitzPatrick.

On February 6th an attack was launched southwards through the Reichswald by British troops under the command of the 1st

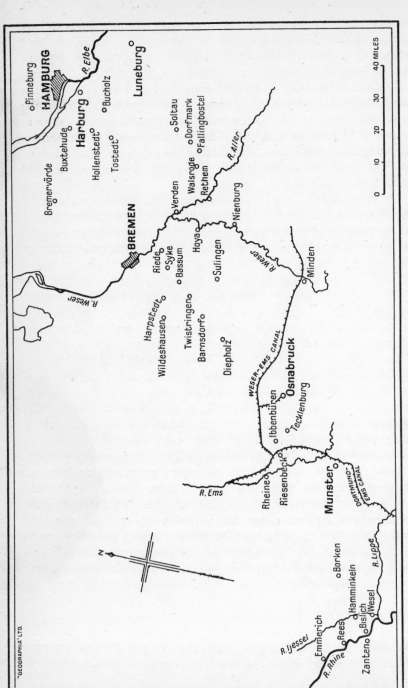

Map No. 18.—The Advance into Germany, March to May, 1945

Canadian Army with the object of clearing the left bank of the Rhine, and shortly afterwards the American Ninth Army attacked northwards to join up with them. There was a great deal of very hard fighting under appalling weather conditions and it was not until March 10th that these operations ended. Further south the Americans took Cologne on March 7th and a few days later the whole west bank of the Rhine had been cleared as far south as the River Moselle at Coblenz. Thirty miles south of Cologne a firm bridgehead had been established at Remagen where the bridge had been seized by a *coup-de-main*. The stage was now set for the final act of the war.

On February 21st the Division was withdrawn from the line and concentrated round Bree and Weert, a depressing part of the country which was crowded with troops. Here much training was done and the Staff planned for Operation "Plunder", the crossing of the Rhine.

## OVER THE RHINE

*The Plan*                                              *March, 1945*

The Second Army was to cross the Rhine at three main points: at Rees with the XXXth Corps, and at Zanten and Wesel with the XIIth Corps under which was to be the 7th Armoured Division. The 6th British and 17th United States Airborne Divisions were to land on the far side of the river and, amongst other tasks, were to seize crossings over the Rivers Lippe and Ijessel. Seven miles upstream at Dinslaken the American Ninth Army was to cross. Within the XIIth Corps the plan was for the 15th Division to cross at Zanten and they were to construct three bridges, one suitable for tanks, and a number of ferries. On the right, Commandos were to land at Wesel. The operations were to start on the night 23rd/24th. As soon as the ferries were in position the 4th Armoured Brigade was to cross in support of the 15th Division, and the 7th Armoured Division was to cross as soon as there was a bridge for them and to exploit eastwards, the 53rd Division coming up on their left and taking the 4th Brigade under their command. The ultimate objective of the 7th Armoured was Hamburg, 190 miles away.

*Operation "Plunder"*

The Division remained back in a concentration area a hundred miles away on the evening of the attack, except the 3rd and 5th R.H.A. who were supporting the Commandos. The assault went successfully and by the end of the day the Commandos had secured most of Wesel and the important bridge at Hamminkeln, and the 15th Division had a good footing in Bislich, but the 51st Division had not yet taken Rees. Operations went satisfactorily on the next two days, the 25th and 26th, and by the morning of the following day a tank bridge was in position between Zanten and Bislich with a lighter bridge further downstream.

On the morning of the 27th the 11th Hussars led the Division across the Rhine. On the east side there was but one secondary road to serve two bridges and progress was very slow to begin with. Every village was a mass of rubble, a tribute to the accurate bombing of the R.A.F., and the ways through them were so narrow that it took a long time for vehicles to get forward, while the boggy state of the ground prevented cross-country movement. The fields all round were dotted with empty gliders and ruined, burned-out aircraft, but brightened amid the gaunt debris of war by the gaily coloured silks of the discarded parachutes of the 6th Airborne men. The 22nd Brigade moved on a two-Regimental front with the Inniskilling group on the right and the 5th Royal Tanks group on the left. By the evening of the 28th the Inniskillings were in the outskirts of Borken; this village the Inniskillings and the Durhams occupied in the evening without much opposition, and the advance pressed on for another four miles until, at nightfall, the cavalry were held up by a position too strong for them to deal with without substantial infantry support.

So the advance continued for the next few days with the 22nd Brigade, commanding the leading troops, often fighting three separate actions at a time up to the River Ems and the important group of airfields at Rheine. There was scarcely a village that had not to be fought for hard. The story of all this fighting, which is far too detailed to be fully recorded in a Divisional History, is of small actions by squadrons and companies or of battalion actions supported by regiments of tanks, of villages cleared, road blocks stormed or by-passed, innumerable bridges built and miles of road opened up by the Royal Engineers, and all the time a few more casualties every day and a steadily mounting bag of prisoners. Sometimes the infantry would be carried in armoured troop-carriers, and these fully proved their worth. Always there were the wide and fruitful reconnaissances by the 11th Hussars out to the flanks and as far as it was possible to get ahead, with a never-ending stream of valuable information.

On the right the 11th Armoured Division had crossed the Rhine on the 29th and made good progress. They were now equipped with the new and most successful Comet tank which mounted an improved 17-pounder gun. Further to their right the 6th Airborne men, carried on the Churchill tanks of the 6th Guards Tank Brigade, were making even longer advances. On the left progress was slow, and gradually the 7th Armoured developed a longer and longer open left flank. The 155th Brigade of the 52nd Division was placed under command and generally used to cover this flank.

Resistance, too, was stronger on this flank and the men with bazookas were the chief menace to the armour. They would lie in wait by the roadside or near a road block, and with one discharge from their cheap single-shooters could immobilize or destroy a tank. Spraying the sides of the road with machine-gun fire as the tank moved forward was all the crew could do unless the going permitted the tanks to travel at full speed which greatly reduced the enemy's chances of scoring a hit. At other places resistance would be composed of groups, perhaps fifty or a hundred strong, with a few 88s or S.P. guns, and these were usually sufficiently determined to require a planned attack by infantry with tank and artillery support. Much of the country over which the fighting of the next few weeks was to take place consisted of woodlands, and here the bazooka-men and small enemy groups had natural advantages over the armour. As time went on, the state of disorganization among the German forces became more apparent. Reinforcements no longer went to build up existing units—instead, they became just more battle-groups some of which, though hastily assembled, often fought very well indeed.

On April 1st the Inniskillings and the Durhams battled their way into Rheine against much opposition and there found all the bridges over the Ems blown. They had had a twenty-mile advance, "the first good 'swan' since crossing the Rhine". On the way they had passed German hospitals, the patients of which are described by the 11th as having come to the roadside to watch the passage of the troops, "most of them silent and grim, a few excited and a few sneering". The inhabitants of the towns where there had been no fighting seemed amazed at the huge procession of tanks, guns, cars and lorries; they "stared sourly" or hurried into their houses. In one of these towns Colonel Wainman is noted as having come up to give fresh orders and "in a moment he was off again, scattering sheets of paper behind him as he went, for it was his custom to carry his maps stuck together in a vast billowing sheet from which he would tear off and discard a map as soon as we were off it—a splendid gesture which indicated that we would never have to retrace our steps". Rheine was cleared on the 2nd by the 157th Brigade, and the 131st Brigade concentrated for the next move forward.

*Over the Dortmund-Ems Canal*

By April 1st the 11th Armoured Division had crossed the Dortmund-Ems Canal, captured Tecklenburg and were well on their way to Osnabruck. Making use of the 11th Armoured's bridgehead, General Lyne hoped to break through the Teutoburger Wald, a wooded ridge that rises sharply above the plain, at Ibbenburen and then go on to the River Weser south of Bremen. By the morning of the 3rd the 131st Brigade was concentrated at Riesenbeck ready to attack through the 11th Armoured's bridgehead, the 155th Brigade of the 52nd Division was coming up behind to safeguard the Centre Line and the 22nd Armoured Brigade was in reserve south of Rheine. The first task was the capture of Ibbenburen, the approaches to which lay in narrow gorges and then crossed a small river. Very severe fighting was to follow, reminiscent of the bad days in Normandy, for a large force of officer-cadets and N.C.O.s from a tactical school had been moved to defend this town—their standard of training was high and their courage fanatical. They were aided by thick woods which made observation and artillery support for the attackers difficult and the ensuing fighting was close and hard.

After a successful preliminary operation on the left by the Devons, who took a hundred prisoners and established themselves on the high ground, the attack on the town was led by "A" Squadron (Major A. C. Gibson) of the Inniskillings and "A" Company of the 9th Durhams. Progress was slow against snipers, bazooka-men, and numerous roaming machine-gun teams, and when night fell the attack had been brought to a standstill. The Cavalry and Light Infantry resumed their attack in the morning and steadily gained ground, while the 155th Brigade put in an attack on the flank. The tactics of the training school were most skilful—some men would lie low and allow the Durhams to pass, then rise and shoot them from behind. The marksmanship of the snipers was of a high order, and several tank commanders and drivers fell victims to their accuracy. House after house was set on fire, but the Germans fought back from the blazing ruins like men possessed and many perished in the flames. This fierce fighting went on all day and it was not until troops of the 53rd Division came up that the final resistance was overcome.

Meanwhile, news had been received that the 11th Armoured Division had captured an intact bridge over the Osnabruck Canal, so General Lyne obtained permission to move the 22nd Brigade along the other Division's Centre Line. During the next two nights this move went on, along execrable roads with very bad traffic congestion, while away to the left the sky was aglow from the flames of Ibbenburen. By the evening of the 4th, the 5th Royal Tanks, now commanded by Lieutenant-Colonel A. R. Leakey, had seized a bridge over the Weser-Ems Canal and had made a long advance, and on the next day they went on to Diepholz, where an unusual event was a sharp attack by the German air force. Some opposition met with just short of this town was dealt with by the Rifle Brigade, the tanks and Lieutenant-Colonel Moore's 5th R.H.A., and it was entered on the morning of the 6th.

*To the Weser*                                                                 *April*

In this area the left flank was protected by a large expanse of marsh and it was a relief not to have to position small groups at important points along the Centre Line. Brigadier Wingfield was now leading with his 22nd Armoured Brigade and on April 5th he made for the crossing over the Weser at Hoya. Throughout the night 5th/6th the 1st Tanks and the 2nd Devons kept up the advance, " 'A' Squadron in the lead, flat out, with guns blazing", and before dawn on the 6th they reached Hoya, nearly forty miles from Diepholz, but as the leading tank approached the bridge the demolition charges were set off. Further to the left was a bridge west of Verden and the 8th Hussars made for that, supported by "K" Battery, now commanded by Major G. T. A. Armitage who till recently had been G.2 of the Division. However, it was strongly protected by infantry and guns and it was clear that until much larger forces could be brought forward there was no hope of crossing the Weser, so the Division, with the 155th Brigade under command, turned north in order to cut off from Bremen the German First Parachute Army which was retreating before the XXXth Corps.

The 131st Brigade concentrated between Diepholz and Sulingen, and then moved north to Twistringen and Bassum. The former town was taken by a company of the Durhams and "C" Squadron of the Inniskillings, but there was much resistance at Bassum, which was reached on the evening of the 7th but not taken till next day,

s

when converging attacks by "A" Squadron of the Inniskillings and "A" Company of the Rifle Brigade from the north-west, and by a company of the Durhams with "B" Squadron of the Inniskillings, finally drove the enemy out.

The 155th Brigade advanced north from Diepholz, captured Barnstorf and linked up with the 131st Brigade at Bassum on the 9th. At the same time the 22nd Brigade advanced towards the southern approaches to Bremen, and the 8th Hussars and the Queens took Riede which was set alight during the fighting. Among the fifteen casualties of the Queens here was Lieutenant Wilkinson-Cox, killed, who had so distinguished himself at Panheel lock in November. The 11th Hussars and the 5th Royal Tanks took Syke. Here an act of treachery on the part of a group of Germans who had surrendered resulted in the death of Lieutenant W. Newton of the 5th Tanks. Later, there was a sharp counter-attack on Syke by three companies of infantry with two Tigers; they were driven off by Major Burdon's "C" Squadron of the 11th, a company of the Rifle Brigade and a battery of the Norfolk Yeomanry who knocked out one of the Tigers.

By the evening of the 9th the Durham Light Infantry with the Inniskillings and a battery of the Norfolk Yeomanry had reached Harpstedt and Wildeshausen, and the latter town was occupied during the 10th. That evening, about 10.30 p.m., when everyone had settled down quite happily, some German lorries carrying S.S. troops slipped into the town on the tail of some British transport and a fierce fight suddenly broke out in the dark. The Durhams' Aid Post was over-run and several medical orderlies were taken prisoner, the Regimental Headquarters of the Inniskillings found themselves in the forefront of the battle, and both the Rifle Brigade and the Norfolk Yeomanry were also soon engaged. The enemy were driven out, but they had destroyed four tanks and several other vehicles. On the same day the 8th Hussars got within four miles of Bremen and the R.H.A. shelled the city.

About this time Colonel Paley, who had commanded the 1st Battalion Rifle Brigade since June, 1943, left to take up an appointment on the Staff of the VIIIth Corps, and Lieutenant-Colonel Phelan, who had commanded the 2nd Light Field Ambulance for a very long time, went to command No. 33 Casualty Clearing Station. Command of the Rifle Brigade Battalion went to Lieutenant-Colonel P. A. D. Boden, and Lieutenant-Colonel C. Levy took over the Light Field Ambulance.

By the evening of the 10th it was apparent that the battle for Bremen would be a long business and one for which an Armoured Division was not suitable, so the 3rd Division, commanded by Major-General Whistler, took over the 7th Armoured Division's sector and the latter moved south-east to Nienburg. Here the 53rd Division had crossed the Weser unopposed but they had met very strong opposition on the Aller at Rethem which was stoutly defended by marines. On the 11th the 5th Royal Tanks were sent to support the 53rd and after destroying eight 88s and some other guns they and the infantry with them fought their way into the town. On the night of the 13th/14th the 53rd Division secured a crossing over the Aller and on the following day the 4th Armoured Brigade crossed and the 2nd Devons went with them.

*The Last Lap*                                    *April 15th to May 7th*
During this final phase the Division was to advance to the Elbe at Harburg, to cut the Autobahn between Bremen and Hamburg which large numbers of the enemy were using, to clear a wide tract of country between Soltau and Harburg, and finally to take the surrender of the great city of Hamburg. There were to be ten days of fighting in almost every village and town on the routes which the various columns followed and, inevitably, the story has to be rather a disconnected one.

Gradually the Rethem bridgehead was enlarged and on the 15th the 22nd Armoured Brigade were able to cross, and by that evening Walsrode had been occupied by the 8th Hussars, "A" Company of the Rifle Brigade and the 5th Queens. A bombing raid that night did some damage to the bridge at Rethem but the rest of the Division were able to cross on the 16th. Much damage had been done to all the roads by the Germans blowing large craters in them, and this slowed down movement a lot, for the Sappers had either to fill in the craters or to construct by-passes before the wheeled vehicles could get forward.

The Division was now directed on Soltau and the 22nd Brigade led the advance in two columns—one, with the 8th Hussars along the main road to Soltau, and the other with the 1st Tanks further to the north. The country was much wooded and in addition progress was hampered by numerous road blocks of felled and booby-trapped trees, mines, and blown culverts and bridges, but by dusk on the 16th the 1st tanks were only two miles west of Soltau. On the other route, the 8th Hussars met opposition at

Fallingbostel where the town was held by infantry with mortars and some artillery. The place was cleared by the Queens in house-to-house fighting but they found that the enemy had blown the bridge at the end of the main street "which was now burning well". It was, however, possible to by-pass the gap and the column pushed on, and by nightfall foot patrols of the Rifle Brigade were in Dorfmark.

The most notable event of the 16th was the liberation of a large Prisoners-of-War Camp at Fallingbostel which was first entered by Major P. H. Huth, the second-in-command of the 8th Hussars, and the Reconnaissance Troop. Here were 6,500 British and American prisoners in one camp and 3,500 in another. Already the British prisoners had taken over control and the main gate was guarded by sentries "immaculate in scrubbed belts and gaiters and well-ironed battledress". All who visited the camp were immensely impressed by the good order and discipline of the men, some of whom had been there for four or five years and had suffered much hardship. The credit for this state of affairs lay with Regimental-Sergeant-Major Lord, Grenadier Guards, of the 1st Airborne Division, whose magnificent leadership not only sustained the morale and the self-respect of the prisoners but averted many difficulties that the sudden transition from captivity to freedom might have created. The Sergeant-Major was found calmly waiting in the Commandant's Office for the reports of his orderly Warrant Officers and for such orders as the British Army might give for the evacuation of the men. Lieutenant-Colonel H. Moore, who had succeeded Colonel Cardiff not long before as the principal administrative staff officer of the Division, sent up rations, cigarettes and the latest newspapers. The camp contained some men of the 7th Armoured who had been taken in the Desert and others who had been lost at Villers Bocage in June, 1944, and more recently.

One of the senior officers of the Division visited at this time the notorious Concentration Camp at Belsen which had recently been surrendered to the 11th Armoured Division. He recorded: "No pictures or words can ever adequately portray the horror of what I saw. Of the 40,000 or 60,000 political prisoners of all nationalities, one could only hope for a quick death for the majority. The awful cloying stench of death was everywhere. There were piles of dead bodies, mere bags of bones from years of systematic starvation, but worst of all was the animal look and habits of so many of the prisoners still alive; all spark of human intellect seemed to have departed. The haunting memory of it will be with me till my dying day."

On the 17th the 22nd Armoured Brigade by-passed Soltau and the town was left to the 155th Brigade to deal with, supported by the Inniskillings. At 5 a.m. that morning they launched their attack and "C" Squadron and the flame-throwers of the 7th Royal Tanks did fine work in the streets. When night came the town had been taken, and next morning the Inniskillings and the 7th Tanks cleared the enemy away for some miles to the north. This enabled the 131st Brigade to push through, and the next task for the Division was to gain bridges over the Elbe at Harburg. Meanwhile, the rest of the 22nd Brigade had met very bad going over extremely boggy roads, but Tostedt was taken on the 18th and the next day Bucholz fell to the 131st. By now Bremen had been captured and the German First Parachute Army was being squeezed into a pocket between that city and Hamburg.

The Division was now undertaking two quite separate tasks— one, to cut the Autobahn between Bremen and Hamburg and if possible to capture Harburg, and the other to clear away the large numbers of the enemy in the forests to the northwards of Soltau. This latter proved to be a long and tedious task, for the Germans were lavishly supplied with ammunition and food from the many dumps in the woods. There was now a wide gap between the 11th Armoured on the right and the 7th Armoured, and this was only lightly covered by armoured car patrols of the Inns of Court Regiment and the 11th Hussars. The left flank of the 7th Armoured was completely open, but the Guards Armoured Division were coming up there, directed towards Bremervörde.

Harburg lies at the end of a series of ridges running north and south, an area about ten miles by seventeen which is mostly wooded, and the Germans, who included S.S. troops, parachutists, submarine crews, stevedores from the Hamburg docks and even policemen and firemen from Hamburg, soon made it plain that they were going to contest every acre of ground. It was a good defensive area, for nature had provided the Elbe at the defenders' backs, the Harburg Forest on their right and a line of marshes on their left, and it was impossible for them to be out-flanked.

The Autobahn was cut at Hollenstedt on the 19th by the 8th Hussars and the Queens who attacked the village with the support of rocket-firing aircraft of the R.A.F. The group then turned east and worked their way to the Elbe valley against continuous opposition—in one village "A" Company of the Rifle Brigade used their new flame-throwers mounted in carriers for the first time with great success, and "C" Company also did good work with them in the forest country. By the 20th the Inniskillings had reached the outer defences of Harburg where there was much shelling and every indication that the town was held in strength by a determined force. On the next day the 131st Brigade got close to the town, advancing with the 5th Tanks and a company of the Rifle Brigade on one route and the 9th Durhams on another, but as they approached the last bridge over the Elbe was blown.

On the 21st a squadron of the Inniskillings, a Troop of the 11th Hussars, a company of the Rifle Brigade and a detachment of Naval Commandos attacked Buxtehude. The garrison surrendered without much trouble and included an admiral and several hundred of the German Navy's women's service. These last were of forbidding appearance and of pronounced Nazi ideas; no one seemed willing to take these Amazons off the Division's hands and they showed no inclination whatever to return to their own homes, if they still had any.

By now the VIIIth Corps were over the Elbe and the 11th Armoured Division and the 6th Airborne Division had reached the Baltic Sea. The 1st and 2nd Canadian Corps had over-run Holland. The Russians had broken through on the Berlin front, the German front opposite the Americans in Bavaria and Czecho-slovakia was disintegrating, and in Italy German emissaries were discussing terms with Field Marshal Alexander. The end was near.

From now until the German Army capitulated the Division was occupied in clearing up the area south and south-west of Harburg. In the north of the area, some troops watched the enemy's peri-meter round Harburg while others patrolled east and west; there were a few counter-attacks and some patrol activity. In the enemy pocket near Soltau the 1st Tanks and the Household Cavalry, with the 160th Brigade of the 53rd Division, gradually swept the country and took many prisoners.

## The Surrender of Hamburg

Towards the end of April the air was filled with rumours of German surrender. Hitler had apparently made up his mind to make his final fight in Berlin rather than flee to the mountains of Southern Germany; others of the German leaders were reported to be deserting him, and already peace feelers were known to have been put out both in Switzerland and to Count Bernadotte in Sweden.

On April 29th a small enemy deputation, consisting of two

staff officers and a civilian, approached our lines under a white flag and were taken to the Headquarters of the 131st Brigade. While the situation, which largely turned on the prospects of immunity for German hospitals, was being discussed, the civilian engaged the Divisional Intelligence Officer in conversation, and he introduced, first, the question of securing immunity for his own concern, the Phoenix Rubber Works, and secondly the possibility of the surrender of Hamburg itself. He explained that this matter had been favourably received at a recent meeting of the Hamburg Chamber of Commerce, although the police and the S.S. were thought to be opposed to it. All this information was passed back to General Lyne who, after communicating with the Corps Commander, wrote to the General commanding in Hamburg, General Wolz, a letter demanding the surrender of the city, and this was carried back by the civilian; the two German officers had already departed and had blown themselves up in one of their own minefields.

Amongst other things, the letter contained a threat of a further air-raid and this was too much for the recipient, for the recollection of the last raid was fresh in the minds of all the citizens—it was thought that 10,000 people had been killed or burned to death in that raid alone. General Wolz was agreeable to negotiations and was told, through a staff officer whom he sent on the evening of May 1st, that the city must be surrendered unconditionally within forty-eight hours. Just as the officer was about to leave, the first announcement of Hitler's death came through on the B.B.C. Thinking that this item of news would encourage General Wolz in his surrender project, one of the Staff told the German that his "Führer" had been "bumped off". After the latter term had been translated, the German burst into tears and asked for British advice as to whether he should follow his "Führer's" lead and "bump himself off". The answer was that under no circumstances would he do any such thing till he had delivered his message to his commander; after that, he had an entirely free hand. A little light humour was introduced by the German interpreter whose scarf colours seemed to be familiar to one of the British party. "Isn't that a Brasenose scarf?" he was asked. "No, Christ Church," replied the German. "I was there studying the House of Lords."

On May 2nd General Wolz appeared at Divisional Headquarters and was ready to discuss immediately the arrangements for the surrender of Hamburg, and early the following morning he was one of a party that included a delegation from Admiral Doenitz who had succeeded Hitler as Head of the State. This delegation was

sent on to the Second Army and owing to a slight hitch Wolz
was sent too. However, he was returned later and everything
proceeded according to the plan the Staff had worked out, though
with some delay, so on the afternoon of May 3rd Brigadier Spurling
went to the Town Hall and received the capitulation of this great
port. The dock area was an awe-inspiring sight. The mass of twisted
metal and mountains of rubble made observers wonder whether
the port facilities could ever come into action again. The damage
was very concentrated and testified to the accuracy of the R.A.F.'s
bombing. The Germans had succeeded, by what must have been
almost super-human efforts, in keeping open one rough track through
the devastation, and over that passed the main body of the Division.

On May 4th the 11th Hussars moved out to Pinneburg, twelve
miles to the north-west. By now, the surrender of Germany, though
not yet officially declared, was a reality. Down every road patrols
met streams of German soldiers and sailors who only asked to be
relieved of their arms—they poured along in their thousands, mostly
on foot but some packed in big ten-ton lorries and their trailers, or
in horse-drawn transport, all making their way west to surrender.
That night the news was received that hostilities would cease at
eight o'clock the next morning. During the next few days the disarming of the German forces continued and the Division advanced
to the Kiel Canal, forty-five miles north-west of Hamburg, where ten
thousand sailors formally surrendered to the Divisional Commander.

"V.E. Day" was celebrated with the inevitable bonfires and
other signs of rejoicing, and the Prime Minister's speech was followed by a short Service at Divisional Headquarters which, for
some who had been in the Division for six years, was better attuned
to their feelings than much merry-making.

Then, for several months, the Division settled down to the
tasks of an Army of Occupation. The area for which they were
responsible stretched from Hamburg nearly to the Danish frontier
eighty miles away, but this is no place to tell of the post-war problems
with which they were then confronted, of the 300,000 German
prisoners who had to be evacuated, of the incalculable numbers of
refugees from eastern and southern Germany, of the 100,000
Displaced Persons, many from Eastern Europe, most of whom
could not, or would not, return home, and all of whom were in a
pitiable state of moral and physical decrepitude.

The last chapter of the war story of the 7th Armoured Division
was set in Berlin in July 1944.

# EPILOGUE

## THE GREATEST DAY

*"Thou in the van first took the field*
*And gotten hast the Victory."*

ON July 21st, 1945, at 10 o'clock in the morning, a roar of guns broke out over the ruins of Berlin as the 3rd Regiment Royal Horse Artillery fired a 19-gun salute in honour of the Right Honourable Winston Churchill who had arrived to hold the Victory Parade.

It was the 7th Armoured Division that was given the honour of playing the principal part in a Parade that was to set the seal on the Second World War.

And during the past few weeks the troops of the Division had been assembling in Berlin, that scarred and blackened ruin for so long the scene of Nazi pageantry. Flag-poles had been erected, stands built, vehicles painted and equipment polished for what was surely to be the greatest of many triumphs that the Division had enjoyed since they had first gone into action almost exactly five years before.

With Field Marshals Sir Alan Brooke and Sir Bernard Montgomery, the Prime Minister drove down the Charlottenburg Chausée which was lined by troops, and at the Grosse Sterne the inspection started. The 3rd R.H.A. were drawn up by the Monument, then each side of the Chausée stretching almost to the Brandenburg Gate were the 5th R.H.A., the 8th and 11th Hussars, the Royal Engineers and the massed carriers of the Infantry.

After passing the mounted portion of the Parade the Prime Minister came to the Infantry of the Division and the men of the Royal Navy, the 1st Battalion Grenadier Guards, the composite Battalion from the Canadian Army, the Royal Air Force and the R.A.F. Regiment.

The Inspection over, the March Past began. First came the 3rd R.H.A., then the 5th R.H.A., the 8th Hussars, the 11th Hussars, the Royal Engineers and the Infantry carriers, their vehicles so polished and painted that they might have come from some jeweller's shop rather than the stern fields of battle. Here were two Regiments who had hardly missed an action in all the years of fighting, one whose guns had never failed to meet every demand of courage and skill no matter how exacting, and one whose armoured cars had ever been first in the advance and last in the retreat, two Regiments whose standards can seldom have been equalled and never surpassed.

As the thunder and roar of the armoured vehicles faded and died away in the distance twenty minutes later, the battered walls echoed to the music of the Bands leading the marching contingents. Their bayonets glinting in the light, the long columns came swinging down the broad processional way to the old familiar and traditional tunes that have played the British Army past on ceremonial parades the world over, but never, surely, on such an occasion as this.

What thoughts must have passed through the minds of the veterans as they saluted their great War Leader! Of that first venture through the wire of the Egyptian frontier and the overwhelming victory of Beda Fomm and Sidi Saleh; of Sidi Rezegh in November 1941, and the desperate fighting in that same area a few months later; Alam Halfa and Alamein; Tripoli and Tunis; the crossing of the Volturno; the bloody fighting in the Bocage and on the Plains of Caen; the exhilarating scenes of "Liberation" on that long road to Ghent; the harsh winter battles and the last long advance into the heart of the enemy's country.

So many scenes, good times and bad, savage heat and extreme cold, sand-storms and snow, rain and sunshine, and perhaps, too, so many names—O'Connor and Creagh, the first architects of victory: Gott and Campbell; Pinney, Ward Gunn and Beeley; Holliman and Wainman; and all those others whose names find no written record but who gave their whole endeavours to their comrades and their Regiments, who died in battle or afterwards, who will be honoured and remembered for all time by those who served with them.

All too soon the moments of triumph passed, a spectacle unique and one which, in the dark days not so long before, had seemed unattainable. From Mersa Matruh to the Baltic, "a march unsurpassed through all the story of war", said the Prime Minister to the Division. "May the fathers long tell the children about this tale! May your glory ever shine! May your laurels never fade! May the memory of this pilgrimage never die!"

# THE ORDER OF BATTLE

## AFRICA

NOTE— During operations many changes of a temporary nature took place. They are mentioned in the text as they occur.

### NOVEMBER, 1940

*4th Armoured Brigade*
7th Hussars
2nd Royal Tank Regiment (less one squadron with the 3rd Hussars)
6th Royal Tank Regiment
One Battery 3rd R.H.A.
One squadron 3rd Hussars (with the 2nd R.T.R.)

*7th Armoured Brigade*
3rd Hussars (less one squadron with the 2nd R.T.R.)
8th Hussars
1st Royal Tank Regiment
One Battery 3rd R.H.A.
One squadron 2nd Royal Tank Regiment (with the 3rd Hussars)

*Support Group*
4th R.H.A.
1st K.R.R.C.
2nd Rifle Brigade

*Divisional Troops*
3rd R.H.A. (less two batteries)
106th R.H.A.
11th Hussars
Divisional Signals[1]

*Royal Engineers*
2nd Field Squadron
141st Field Park Troop

[1] From 1940 officers and men of the Middlesex Yeomanry formed part of the Divisional Signals.

*R.A.S.C.*
No. 5 Company
No. 58 „
No. 65 „
No. 550 „
4th New Zealand Reserve Company
1st Supply Issue Section R.I.A.S.C.

*R.A.M.C.*
2nd/3rd Cavalry Field Ambulance
3rd/3rd „ „ „

*R.A.O.C.*
Divisional Workshops
„ Ordnance Field Park
„ Forward Delivery Workshop Section
1st Light Repair Section
2nd „ „ „
3rd „ „ „

NOVEMBER, 1941

*4th Armoured Brigade*
2nd R.H.A.
8th Hussars
3rd R.T.R.
5th R.T.R.
2nd Scots Guards

*7th Armoured Brigade*
7th Hussars
2nd R.T.R.
6th R.T.R.

*22nd Armoured Brigade*
2nd Royal Gloucestershire Hussars
3rd County of London Yeomanry (Sharpshooters)
4th County of London Yeomanry (Sharpshooters)

*Support Group*
3rd R.H.A.
4th R.H.A.
1st K.R.R.C.
2nd Rifle Brigade
60th Field Regiment R.A.
One battery 51st Field Regiment R.A.

*Divisional Troops*
102nd R.H.A.
King's Dragoon Guards
11th Hussars
4th South African Armoured Car Regiment
1st Light Anti-Aircraft Regiment R.A.
Divisional Signals

*Royal Engineers*
4th Field Squadron
143rd Field Park Squadron

*R.A.S.C.*
No. 5 Company
No. 30     „
No. 58     „
No. 65     „
No. 67     „
No. 550    „

*R.A.M.C.*
2nd Light Field Ambulance
13th   „       „       „
15th   „       „       „
7th Light Field Hygiene Section

*R.A.O.C.*
Divisional Workshops
      „      Ordnance Field Park
In each Brigade and Support Group:
   One Light Repair Section
   One Light Recovery Section
   One Ordnance Field Park
Light A.A. Regiment Workshops

APRIL, 1942

*4th Armoured Brigade*
1st R.H.A.
8th Hussars
3rd R.T.R.
5th R.T.R.
1st K.R.R.C.

*7th Motor Brigade*
4th R.H.A.
9th K.R.R.C.
2nd Rifle Brigade
9th Rifle Brigade

*Divisional Troops*
102nd R.H.A.
K.D.G.
15th Light A.A. Regiment R.A.
Divisional Signals

*Royal Engineers*
4th Field Squadron
143rd Field Park Squadron

*R.A.S.C.*
No. 5 Company
No. 30 ,,
No. 58 ,,
No. 67 ,,
No. 432 ,,
No. 550 ,,

*R.A.M.C.*
2nd Light Field Ambulance
7th ,, ,, ,,
14th ,, ,, ,,
15th ,, ,, ,,

*R.A.O.C.*
Divisional Workshops
     ,,      Ordnance Field Park
15th Light A.A. Workshops
In each Brigade—one Workshop

OCTOBER–NOVEMBER, 1942

*4th Light Armoured Brigade*
3rd R.H.A.
Royal Scots Greys
4th Hussars and one squadron 8th Hussars
2nd Derbyshire Yeomanry
1st K.R.R.C.

*22nd Armoured Brigade*
1st R.T.R.
5th R.T.R.
4th C.L.Y.
4th Field Regiment R.A.
97th     „          „          „
1st Rifle Brigade

131*st (Queens) Brigade*
1st/5th Queens Royal Regiment
1st/6th     „          „          „
1st/7th     „          „          „
53rd Field Regiment R.A.
Two batteries 57th Anti-Tank Regiment R.A.
11th Field Company R.E.

*Divisional Troops*
11th Hussars
15th Light A.A. Regiment R.A.
65th Anti-Tank Regiment R.A. (Norfolk Yeomanry)
Divisional Signals

*Royal Engineers*
4th Field Squadron
21st     „          „
143rd Field Park Squadron

*R.A.S.C.*
No. 5 Company
No. 10      „
No. 58      „
No. 67      „
No. 287     „
No. 432     „
No. 507     „

*R.A.M.C.*
2nd Light Field Ambulance
7th     „          „          „
14th     „          „          „
15th     „          „          „

*R.A.O.C.*
Divisional Ordnance Field Park
15th Light A.A. Workshop
In each Brigade—one Ordnance Field Park and one Workshop

SEPTEMBER 15TH, 1943

## ITALY

*22nd Armoured Brigade*
1st R.T.R.
5th R.T.R.
4th C.L.Y.
1st Rifle Brigade

*131st (Queens) Brigade*
1st/5th Queens Royal Regiment
1st/6th  ,,      ,,      ,,
1st/7th  ,,      ,,      ,,
"C" Company, 1st Cheshire Regiment

*Divisional Troops*
11th Hussars
Divisional Signals

*Royal Artillery*
3rd R.H.A.
5th R.H.A.
15th Light A.A. Regiment R.A.
24th Field Regiment R.A.
65th Anti-Tank Regiment R.A. (Norfolk Yeomanry)
69th Medium Regiment R.A.
146th Field Regiment R.A.

*Royal Engineers*
4th Field Squadron
621st  ,,      ,,
143rd Field Park Squadron

*R.A.S.C.*
No. 5 Company
No. 58    ,,
No. 67    ,,
No. 287   ,,
No. 432   ,,
No. 507   ,,

*R.A.M.C.*
2nd Light Field Ambulance
131st Field Ambulance
70th Field Hygiene Section
21st Mobile Casualty Clearing Station
3rd Field Surgical Unit
7th Field Transfusion Unit
132nd Mobile Dental Unit
135th    ,,     ,,     ,,

*R.A.O.C.*
Divisional Ordnance Field Park

*R.E.M.E.*
22nd Armoured Brigade Workshops
131st Brigade Workshop
15th Light A.A. Workshop

## JUNE, 1944

## NORTH-WEST EUROPE

*22nd Armoured Brigade*
1st R.T.R.
5th R.T.R.
4th C.L.Y. (until July, 1944)
5th Royal Inniskilling Dragoon Guards (from July 1944)

*131st (Queens) Brigade* (until November, 1944)
1st/5th Queens Royal Regiment
1st/6th    ,,     ,,     ,,
1st/7th    ,,     ,,     ,,
No. 3 Support Company, Royal Northumberland Fusiliers

*Divisional Troops*
8th Hussars
11th    ,,
Divisional Signals

*Royal Artillery*
3rd R.H.A.
5th R.H.A.
15th Light A.A. Regiment R.A.
65th Anti-Tank Regiment R.A. (Norfolk Yeomanry)

T

*Royal Engineers*
4th Field Squadron
621st ,,        ,,
143rd Field Park Squadron

*R.A.S.C.*
No. 58 Company
No. 67     ,,
No. 507    ,,
No. 133    ,,    (from January, 1945)

*R.A.M.C.*
2nd Light Field Ambulance
131st Field Ambulance
29th Field Dressing Station
70th Field Hygiene Section
134th Mobile Dental Unit

*R.A.O.C.*
Divisional Ordnance Field Park
22nd Armoured Brigade Ordnance Field Park
131st Brigade Ordnance Field Park

*R.E.M.E.*
7th Armoured Troops Workshop
22nd Armoured Brigade Workshop
131st Brigade Workshop
15th Light A.A. Workshop

*Royal Armoured Corps*
No. 263 Forward Delivery Squadron

NOVEMBER, 1944

*131st Brigade*
1st/5th Queens Royal Regiment
2nd Devonshire Regiment
9th Durham Light Infantry
No. 3 Support Company, Royal Northumberland Fusiliers

APPENDIX 2

# COMMANDERS, SENIOR STAFF OFFICERS AND HEADS OF SERVICES

### DIVISIONAL COMMANDERS

Major-General P. C. S. Hobart
,, ,, M. O'M. Creagh
,, ,, W. H. E. Gott
,, ,, J. C. Campbell, V.C.
,, ,, F. W. Messervy
,, ,, J. M. L. Renton
,, ,, A. F. Harding
,, ,, G. W. E. J. Erskine
,, ,, G. L. Verney
,, ,, L. O. Lyne

### G.S.O. I's

Lieutenant-Colonel W. H. E. Gott, K.R.R.C.
Colonel H. L. Birks, Royal Tank Regiment
Colonel C. H. Gairdner, 10th Hussars
,, ,, G. W. Richards, Royal Tank Regiment
,, ,, H. E. Pyman, Royal Tank Regiment
,, ,, R. M. P. Carver, Royal Tank Regiment
,, ,, P. R. C. Hobart, Royal Tank Regiment
,, ,, N. M. H. Wall, 7th Hussars
,, ,, The Earl of Lewes, Life Guards

### A.A. & Q.M.G.S

Lieutenant-Colonel C. M. Smith, R.A.S.C.
,, ,, J. L. C. Napier, Royal Tank Regiment
,, ,, J. R. Bowring, 9th Lancers
,, ,, G. S. Hatton, R.E.
,, ,, J. G. Cowley, R.E.
,, ,, C. E. F. Turner, R.E.
,, ,, E. B. W. Cardiff, Scots Guards
,, ,, H. Moore, Royal Fusiliers

291

### COMMANDERS, ROYAL ARTILLERY

Brigadier S. Williams
,,      C. B. Vaughan-Hughes
,,      R. Mews
,,      T. Lyon-Smith

### COMMANDERS, ROYAL ENGINEERS

Lieutenant-Colonel A. C. Mitchell
,,            ,,      J. F. Farewell
,,            ,,      P. A. Clauson
,,            ,,      H. H. C. Withers
,,            ,,      W. R. G. Walker
,,            ,,      A. D. Hunter
,,            ,,      B. S. Armitage

### OFFICERS COMMANDING DIVISIONAL SIGNALS

Lieutenant-Colonel F. A. H. Matthew
,,            ,,      C. Knowles
,,            ,,      H. N. Crawford
,,            ,,      The Hon. S. A. Maxwell
,,            ,,      P. Hyde
,,            ,,      R. Seddon
,,            ,,      G. S. Knox

### COMMANDERS, ROYAL ARMY SERVICE CORPS

Lieutenant-Colonel W. J. F. Eassie
,,            ,,      H. J. Gilman
,,            ,,      E. Marshall
,,            ,,      P. Cahill
,,            ,,      E. G. Hazelton

### ASSISTANT DIRECTORS MEDICAL SERVICES

Colonel Q. V. B. Wallace
,,      B. J. Daunt
,,      E. C. Eccles
,,      L. R. H. Keatinge

### ASSISTANT DIRECTORS ORDNANCE SERVICES

Lieutenant-Colonel L. H. Howard-Jones
,,            ,,      J. J. Walsh
,,            ,,      F. Morris
,,            ,,      J. Orr
,,            ,,      R. L. Bellamy
,,            ,,      G. C. Pritchett
,,            ,,      A. C. Lusty

COMMANDERS, ROYAL ELECTRICAL AND MECHANICAL ENGINEERS
Lieutenant-Colonel R. L. Bellamy
      ,,       ,,    J. D. Berryman

## SENIOR CHAPLAINS
The Reverend E. J. Dodge
   ,,    ,,    S. F. Woodhouse
   ,,    ,,    A. V. Kingston
   ,,    ,,    K. Meiklejohn
   ,,    ,,    S. B. Wingfield Digby

## BRIGADE COMMANDERS
*Heavy Armoured Brigade*
Brigadier H. R. B. Watkins, Royal Tank Regiment

*Light Armoured Brigade*
Brigadier H. E. Russell, 12th Lancers

*4th Armoured Brigade*
Brigadier J. A. L. Caunter, Royal Tank Regiment
    ,,    A. H. Gatehouse, Royal Tank Regiment
    ,,    G. W. Richards, Royal Tank Regiment

*7th Armoured Brigade*
Brigadier H. E. Russell, 12th Lancers
    ,,    G. M. O. Davy, 3rd Hussars

*Pivot Group*
Lieutenant-Colonel H. R. B. Mirrless, R.A.
    ,,       ,,    W. H. E. Gott, K.R.R.C.

*Support Group*
Brigadier E. S. B. Williams, Rifle Brigade
    ,,    W. H. E. Gott, K.R.R.C.
    ,,    J. C. Campbell, V.C., R.H.A.

*4th Light Armoured Brigade*
Brigadier W. G. Carr, 12th Lancers
    ,,    M. G. Roddick, 10th Hussars
    ,,    C. B. Harvey, 10th Hussars
    ,,    D. S. Newton-King, South African Forces
    ,,    J. C. Currie, R.H.A.

*7th Motor Brigade*

Brigadier J. M. L. Renton, Rifle Brigade
    ,,      Viscount Garmoyle, Rifle Brigade
    ,,      T. J. B. Bosvile, Rifle Brigade

*22nd Armoured Brigade*

Brigadier J. Scott Cockburn, 4th Hussars
    ,,      W. G. Carr, 12th Lancers
    ,,      G. P. B. Roberts, Royal Tank Regiment
    ,,      W. R. N. Hinde, 15th/19th Hussars
    ,,      H. Mackeson, Royal Scots Greys
    ,,      B. Cracroft, Royal Tank Regiment
    ,,      A. D. R. Wingfield, 10th Hussars

*131st (Queens) Brigade*

Brigadier W. D. Stamer, North Staffordshire Regiment
    ,,      L. H. Whistler, Royal Sussex Regiment
    ,,      M. S. Ekins, Royal Fusiliers
    ,,      E. C. Pepper, Bedfordshire and Hertfordshire Regiment
    ,,      W. R. Cox, King's Shropshire Light Infantry

*131st Brigade*

Brigadier J. M. J. Spurling, Leicestershire Regiment

# THE EARLIEST DAYS

*(For most of the information contained in this Appendix the author is indebted to Major-General Sir Cecil Smith.)*

FEW Divisions can have had such small beginnings as the 7th Armoured. When General Hobart arrived in Egypt in September 1938 to be the Commander Mobile Force (Egypt), he found the troops of which it was composed in the Desert round Mersa Matruh to which they had been hurriedly despatched because of the Munich crisis. Divisional Headquarters was improvised from Headquarters 3rd R.H.A., with some attached officers. The D.A.A. and Q.M.G. was extracted from Headquarters British Troops in Egypt who were under the impression that his primary duty lay in Abbassia Area. Later a G.2, G.3 and Staff Captain arrived from home.

When the force was withdrawn from the Desert in October 1938, Divisional Headquarters had time to look round and see what the Division consisted of. They found a Headquarters composed of a Major-General and four Staff Officers plus a few clerks (not yet posted), Headquarters of a Cavalry Brigade, three Cavalry Regiments (mechanized, with a mixed bag of vehicles), the 3rd R.H.A., two Tank Regiments, indifferently equipped, and that was all. Of Services there were none. Such Services—Engineer, Signal, Supply and Transport, Medical and Ordnance—as had been available at Mersa Matruh had been provided from the normal garrison of Egypt and were withdrawn from Divisional control on return from the Desert.

The Divisional Staff may well have felt discouraged. But one great asset they had, a Divisional Commander of great initiative, drive and leadership who was prepared to try to make bricks without straw. Although he was not destined to lead this Division in the Field, his spirit was to remain with them long after he had gone and many were the times when his views were quoted—" 'Hobo' always used to say . . . "

On the administrative side the tasks to be performed, and the difficulties to be overcome before the formation could be regarded as in any way fit to take the Field, appeared well nigh insuperable. There were some Heads of Services, but no Services. The fighting units had inadequate. and in some cases unsuitable, transport; there was a general lack of cooking and other administrative equipment suitable for Desert conditions; service in cantonments in Egypt did not lead to "active-service minded-ness", particularly in administrative matters.

Inspired by their commander, the small administrative staff set out to overcome these difficulties. This was not a leisurely matter and up to that time the D.A.A. and Q.M.G. had not thought it likely that he would work from 9 a.m. to 6 p.m. on Christmas Day in peace-time; but he did.

Although the Divisional Commander did not relish the fact that he was Commander Abbassia Area in addition to Commander "Mobile Force", this extra task had certain assets on the administrative side. Such administrative elements as there were in Cairo came under his command and, although none was definitely allotted to the Division on mobilization, it became generally recognized that the Division would have prior claim on certain elements. From no source was more help received than from the elements themselves, all of whom were only too eager to be associated with a formation which would obviously go to war when the occasion arose rather than remain in barracks in Cairo.

Thus, as time went on it became recognized that Major W. J. F. Eassie would command any R.A.S.C. that might be allotted, Captain J. J. Walsh was stolen from the 1st Royal Tank Regiment and attached to Divisional Headquarters as Divisional Ordnance Mechanical Engineer, while Major L. H. Howard-Jones, R.A.O.C., kept sequestrated in Ordnance Workshops such meagre recovery and repair resources as he could scrape together as a nucleus of an Armoured Division Workshop. A Cavalry Field Ambulance, on which had been bestowed the title "1st/3rd", was always available for training. It was believed that this fractional title in fact indicated that it was one-third of a Field Ambulance, but it became known as "1st/3rd".

Such administrative resources, inadequate though they might seem and attached to the Division by such slender threads, were not in fact completely out of proportion to the fighting part of the Division, even when eventually a Support Group of two Greenjacket Battalions and the 4th R.H.A. was added. The main trouble was the obsolescence of the majority of the armoured fighting vehicles, their inadequate numbers, the lack of replacements, and the shortage of administrative vehicles. One of the biggest problems, which always exists with armour, was the lack of "mileage" for training. Outstanding among the matters studied were the recovery of damaged vehicles, daily maintenance of food, water, petrol and ammunition, and the evacuation of wounded. The study was domin-ated by the probability that the enemy would enjoy air superiority.

It was clear that the system of supply suitable for warfare on the Continent of Europe, working, that is, from railheads fairly close at hand, would not meet the needs of troops in the Desert widely scattered over long distances. A detailed practical study of the problems was made by Major Eassie and Major C. S. Grenville-Grey of the K.R.R.C., and they

had as their assistants Lieutenant P. G. Turpin, R.A.S.C., and Lieutenant
R. M. P. Carver, R.T.R., both of whom were to rise to the rank of Brigadier before the end of the war.

In pre-war planning it was envisaged that the Division would have to
be maintained in the Desert south-west of Mersa Matruh, but when Italy
entered the war it found itself on the Libyan frontier. With railhead 150
miles away, an additional transport echelon was necessary; none was
available from Egypt so use had to be made of the R.I.A.S.C. of the 4th
Indian Division who delivered to the 7th Armoured's second-line transport.
This latter was adequate for a short time only, and soon a daily turn-
round of eighty miles of very bad going proved too much for men and
vehicles and a strong detachment of New Zealand A.S.C. had to be called
in to assist.

The R.A.O.C. resources were almost enough for the static conditions
which fortunately prevailed for some months. The R.A.M.C. established
a chain of staging-posts at which wounded could recover from the exhausting conditions of travel in an ambulance over the Desert. Air was
used when available for the evacuation of serious cases. The Division was
fortunate in having by then as A.D.M.S. Colonel Q. V. B. Wallace, whose
acquisitive ingenuity was at the disposal of his patients to their very great
benefit.

Water was a major difficulty. In the Desert it is found in "Birs", which
are stone-lined tanks, many of them constructed by the Romans. Most
depended for their supply on surface drainage from the slight annual
rainfall and, though sufficient to provide the wandering Bedouin with his
scanty needs, they were far from enough for the needs of an Army,
besides being unpopular with the medical authorities. Later, water was
pumped from the Nile and the Royal Engineers developed wells at Bagush
and Mersa Matruh which had also originally been driven by the Romans.
Distribution of water was an R.A.S.C. responsibility. The target aimed
at in the first instance was two gallons per man per day. In the early days
when the Division's strength was about 7,500 this meant delivering
15,000 gallons, or nearly 70 tons, exclusive of the weight of the containers. As the 3-ton lorry could only carry about $2\frac{1}{2}$ tons normal load in
the Desert, water at this rate, even for a Division only at half-strength,
required nearly an extra platoon of transport, which was not available, so
the ration soon had to be reduced to one gallon a man per day, and in this
was included vehicle requirements, which were unusually heavy with
certain types.

Distribution was not easy. There were not enough water trucks and
in any case they were not very suitable for detailed distribution. The
peace-time $12\frac{1}{2}$-gallon copper camel water tanks were tried, but these
were exceptionally heavy as well as expensive to make. The 4-gallon
"flimsy" was a failure for petrol and was even less satisfactory for water,
which is heavier. In the end, the commercial 2-gallon petrol tin was

U

adopted, but as it was not in normal use in the Middle East it had to be manufactured specially.

Water came forward from Mersa Matruh in 350-gallon tankers or in 40-gallon drums. At the water-point, it was either transferred into the 2-gallon cans, a process that was wasteful and extravagant, or the water was decanted into canvas containers from which the 2-gallon cans were filled. These containers were called "Sportapools", but whether this was because they had been used as children's play pools, or because they were supported by the weight of their contents, has never been satisfactorily decided. What was quite certain was that they were a menace. Much water was lost by spilling and evaporation; the "pool" was at the mercy of sand-storms; and no really satisfactory and sanitary means was ever devised for filling the cans. The "end product" had a sand content which made it a matter of indifference whether it was subsequently used for tea, coffee, lime juice or rum—they all looked the same.

Colonel Marshall, who was then commanding No 5 Company, R.A.S.C., has recorded: "The distances covered by the Companies took up every hour of the day and night. Much of the time was spent in filling 2-gallon water containers for our Brigade which had a strength of about 6,000. This meant that 3,000 containers had to be filled from 'Sportapools' by hand which, in the dark and on a bitterly cold night, was not the soldiers' idea of an exciting war. Lack of sleep and improvised meals made tempers very short from Driver to C.O."

It is worth recording that even one gallon of water is a very small ration when it has to cover, not merely tea-making, but cooking, washing-up, shaving, personal ablution and laundry, as well as radiator-filling. At times, in the Desert, the ration had to be reduced to half a gallon per man per day.

An extra item, not in a driver's normal curriculum of training, was navigation. Compasses were generally scarce and administrative vehicles frequently got lost, with the result that they ran out of petrol and drivers had to walk north until they reached the coast road. It is to be feared that some never got back.

Such reputation as the Division may later have gained for fighting and administrative efficiency owed much to its early experiences when it had to "make do" with what was available, and when all Heads of Services had to look round for themselves in order to get their Service functioning satisfactorily. The Desert has been described as the administrator's hell, but it was not really as bad as all that. Given sound, Desert-worthy vehicles, trained and experienced drivers, keen and competent officers and N.C.O.s, ample wireless sets and compasses, and enough defensive weapons, administration in the Desert should be no more difficult than anywhere else. But in the early days the 7th Armoured Division had none of these, save the keen officers and men. That they managed well was due to the British talent for improvisation—that, and a fine Divisional spirit.

# A FEW STATISTICS

NOTE.—*For the figures given below, the author is indebted to the Rev. E. G. Hazelton who, as Officer Commanding the Divisional Royal Army Service Corps during 1944–45, compiled the Divisional R.A.S.C. History in which the fullest details can be found.*

## Petrol and Ammunition Loads

During periods of heavy fighting the R.A.S.C. carried 300 tons of ammunition and 150 tons of petrol per day.

During periods of fast movement, ammunition was reduced to 150 tons per day and petrol raised to 360 tons per day.

## Petrol

During completely static periods the Divisions used 30,000 gallons of petrol per day.

The average consumption during the period of the advance to Ghent was 70,000 gallons a day, when for part of the time more than half the Division was stationary while only a proportion carried on the advance.

The Petrol Company lifted 69,245 tons of petrol between D-Day and May 5th, which was an average of 466 lifts per lorry. "B" Platoon of the Petrol Company, which was equipped with $4\frac{1}{2}$-ton Mack lorries, covered 462,000 miles, which was an average of 14,000 miles per vehicle.

## One Day's Work

On one occasion this "B" Platoon of the Petrol Company was used on an ammunition lift, Eindhoven—Louvain—Waterloo—Eindhoven—Nijmegen. At Louvain they collected 25-pounder cartridges and at Waterloo the drivers had to dig out of a wood (where they had been hidden since 1940) a large number of shells which had to be carried forty yards to the vehicles. Each driver loaded $4\frac{1}{2}$ tons and then had himself to unload them at Nijmegen. On this trip the Platoon covered 240 miles in 19 hours over roads that were crowded with transport and in many places almost ruined by pot-holes and collapsed verges.

## APPENDICES

## AMMUNITION EXPENDITURE

*June 6th*, 1944, *to May 5th*, 1945

| Type | Period and Total | Average per gun per day | Maximum per gun per day |
|---|---|---|---|
| 1. R.H.A. 25-pr. H.E. | June to Sept.: 295,700<br>Oct. to Dec.: 104,400<br>Jan. to May: 149,168 | 51<br>28<br>26 | 600*<br>—<br>130 |

Grand Total 549,268

| | June to Sept. | Average per month | Oct. to Dec. | Average per month | Jan. to May | Average per month | Grand Totals |
|---|---|---|---|---|---|---|---|
| 2. Tanks 75-mm. H.E. | 13,000 | 3,250 | 19,807 | 6,602 | 18,918 | 4,729 | 51,725 |
| 3. Tanks 17-pr. A.P. | 3,989 | 997 | 2,436 | 812 | 3,428 | 857 | 9,855 |
| 4. 7·92 Besa | 947,230 | 236,807 | 149,000 | 47,500 | 1,688,600 | 417,500 | 2,784,830 |
| 5. ·30 Browning | 428,000 | 107,000 | no record | no record | 999,000 | 248,750 | — |
| 6. 4·2-in. H.E. Mortar | 5,248 | 1,312 | 5,024 | 1,674 | 10,056 | 2,514 | 20,328 |
| 7. 3-in. H.E. Mortar | 14,070 | 3,517 | 12,556 | 4,185 | 25,524 | 6,331 | 52,150 |
| 8. ·303 | 306,300 | 76,575 | 376,000 | 125,333 | 464,300 | 116,075 | 1,146,600 |

SOME MONTHLY EXPENDITURES FROM A BATTERY OF THE 3RD R.H.A.

July, 1944 .. .. 11,030  December, 1944 .. 4,654
August .. .. 23,089  February, 1945 .. 4,723
October .. .. 11,941  April .. .. 7,523
November .. .. 7,947

* The author is assured that this figure is correct. This quantity is recorded as having been fired in one period of twelve hours during the Mont Pincon battle in August, 1944.

# THE DIVISIONAL SIGN

SOON after General Creagh took command of the Division, in early 1940, the Divisional emblem, the Jerboa or Desert Rat, was born. The Division's background was the Desert, as it had to be in those early days when the defence of Egypt depended largely on them—they were proud of their freedom of it and their mobility in it. To them, it was a little of what the sea is to a sailor, something to be respected but not unfamiliar or alarming. To many of them, for all its manifold disadvantages and discomforts, the Desert held a certain charm, and one enthusiast, a pioneer of early mechanical Desert travel, even affirmed that the sand-dunes were alive—that they moved, sang and even reproduced their young.

So, therefore, the men of the Division were proud to think of themselves as Desert Rats after the hardy, highly mobile little denizens of the Desert's most inhospitable fastnesses.

Up to this time the Divisional emblem had consisted of a plain white circle on a scarlet ground. It was decided that the circle should carry a Jerboa. After much searching of the Cairo Zoo, the Divisional Commander's wife produced on a sheet of hotel notepaper a Desert Rat rampant. This was transferred, in flaming scarlet, to the white circle of the Divisional Commander's flag and thence it spread onto every vehicle and eventually onto every topee flash.

When the 7th Armoured Brigade left the Division and went to Burma at the end of 1941 they kept the Divisional Sign but changed the colour to green. It was not until the Division was resting in the Homs-Tripoli area in the summer of 1943 that the shoulder-patch was produced; this was the original red Jerboa on a khaki square. The white circle and the red square remained on vehicles, but were omitted from the shoulder-patch.

When the Division left Italy at the end of 1943, Brigadier G. Webb, who had been on the Divisional Staff and was then on the Staff of the XXXth Corps, was commissioned by General Erskine to order shoulder-patches for the whole Division, to be ready for issue when the troops arrived. The result was an animal more like a kangaroo than a Jerboa, on a black background, which is still the Divisional Sign. When General Erskine got back they had all been produced and the War Office refused to sanction a new and different issue, so the altered one had to be accepted.

On vehicles the red square and white circle persisted, although the Jerboa tended to change his shape. For a long time the Queens Brigade carried a black Jerboa in a red oval on their vehicles, the red oval having been the sign of the 44th Division to which they had originally belonged.

When the 4th Armoured Brigade finally left the Division permanently after the capture of Tunis, they kept the Jerboa and the white background, but changed the colour to black and put his tail over his head instead of between his legs.

Whatever his shape, his colour or his attitude, the Jerboa remains the farthest-travelled animal with the longest fighting record. Long may he be honoured.

## FLOREAT JERBOA

# BIBLIOGRAPHY

CHURCHILL, Rt. Hon. Winston: *The Second World War* (Cassell).

CLARKE, Brig. Dudley: *The Eleventh at War* (Michael Joseph).

CLAY, Maj. E. W.: *The Path of the 50th* (Gale & Polden).

COLLINS, Maj.-Gen.: *Lord Wavell* (Hodder & Stoughton).

DE GUINGAND, Maj.-Gen. Sir F.: *Operation Victory* (Hodder & Stoughton).

EISENHOWER, Gen.: *Crusade in Europe* (Heinemann).

ESSAME, Maj.-Gen.: *43rd Wessex Division, 1944–45* (Clowes).

EVANS, Maj.-Gen.: *The 5th Inniskilling Dragoon Guards* (Gale & Polden).

E.W.I.P.: *Taurus Persuant* (Rhine Army Press).

GILL and GROVES: *Club Route* (Hanover Press).

HART, B. Liddell: *The Rommel Papers* (Collins).

HASTINGS, Maj.: *The Rifle Brigade in the Second World War* (Gale & Polden).

JACKSON, Lt.-Col.: *Operations, VIIIth Corps* (St. Clements Press).

LONG: *Australia in the War of 1939–45* (Canberra Official Press).

MARTIN and JOHNSTON: *Short History of the 7th Armoured Division* (Private).

MARTIN, Lt.-Gen.: *The 15th Scottish Division, 1939–45* (Blackwood).

MONK: *History of the 7th Medium Regiment* (Loxley).

MONTGOMERY, F.-M. Visc't: *El Alamein to the River Sangro* (Hutchinson).

MONTGOMERY, F.-M. Visc't; *Normandy to the Baltic* (Hutchinson).

SHULMAN, M.: *Defeat in the West* (Secker & Warburg).

STACEY, Col. C. P.: *The Canadian Army, 1939–45* (King's Printer, Ottawa).

STEWART, P. F.: *History of the XIIth Royal Lancers* (Oxford University Press).

WILMOT, Chester: *The Struggle for Europe* (Collins).

WOOZLEY, Maj. A. D.: *History of the K.D.G.s* (McCorquodale).

YOUNG, Brig. D.: *Rommel* (Collins).

# INDEX

AA, River, 259, 260
Aachen, 261
Abancourt, 234
Abbeville, 233
Acroma, 88, 91, 94, 108, 113
Agedabia, 48, 51, 96–98, 137, 138
Agnena, River, 177
Ainsworth, Lt. J. B. L., 175
Airaines, 235
Aird, Maj. I. B., 194
Aire Canal, 238
Akarit, Wadi, 155
Alam Halfa, 122 et seq., 127, 282
Alam Hamza, 96, 110
Albert Canal, 253
Alexander, F.-M. Viscount, 122, 156
Alexander, Maj. K., 52
Aller, River, 275
Alton, Lt. R. E., 267
Amaye, 195–197, 199, 214
Amiens, 186, 233 et seq.
Anderson, Maj., 267
Andrews, Sgt., 153
Antelat, 42, 98, 100, 137, 138
Antwerp, 185, 231 et seq., 252 et seq., 264
Apsey, Maj. W. J., 171, 195, 206
Argentan, 223
Arkwright, Maj.-Gen. H., 168
Armitage, Lt.-Col. B. S., 292
Armitage, Maj. G. T. A., 273
Arnhem, 253 et seq.
Ashworth, Lt.-Col. J. B., 200, 220
Ashworth, Lt. R. J., 174
Aspland, Maj. L. J., 249
Auchinleck, F.-M. Sir C., 60, 65, 85, 100, 116, 119, 122
Audenarde, 241 et seq., 248 et seq.
Aunay, 214 et seq.
Authie, River, 236
Auxi-le-Chateau, 236, 237
Aversa, 170, 178
Avranches, 213, 219

Baldwin, Capt. J. N. A., 104
Bardia, 23, 24, 31, 35, 56, 74, 83, 90, 136
Barne, Lt.-Col. A. M., 138
Barnstorf, 274
Bassum, 273, 274
Battipaglia, 167

"Battleaxe", Op., 49–59
Bayeux, 183, 184, 186, 188, 189, 191, 211
Bazancourt, 234
Beard, Capt., 194
Beauvais, 237
Beda Fomm, 36–47, 282
Beeley, Rfm., 71, 282
Belhamed, 84, 88, 89, 115
Bellamy, Brig. R. L., 292, 293
Belsen, 276
Ben Gardane, 150
Benghazi, 36, 37–48, 51, 53, 97, 98, 100, 137 et seq., 150
Benina, 97
Beresford-Peirse, Lt.-Gen. Sir N., 27, 55, 59
Bernaville, 235, 237
Bernay, 186
Berryman, Lt.-Col. J. D., 250, 293
Béthune, 236, 239–242, 248, 251
Bingham, Capt. J. K. W., 57
Bir Berraneb, 85, 91
Bir Chetla, 80
Bir el Reghem, 85, 88, 89
Bir Enba, 28–30
Bir Hacheim, 101 et seq.
Bir Harmat, 108
Birks, Maj.-Gen. H. L., 32, 291
Birley, Lt.-Col. N. A., 67, 111
Bir Regeit, 33
Bir Temerad, 96
Bislich, 270
Bizerta, 159
"Blackcock", Op., 265 et seq.
Bloomer, Maj. B. G., 169
"Bluecoat", Op., 211 et seq.
Boden, Lt.-Col. P. A. D., 118, 274
Bolton, Brig. L., 62
Bonnemaison, 216, 217
Borken, 270
Borland, Maj. K., 249
Bosanquet, Maj. P., 220
Bosvile, Brig. T. J. B., 121, 294
Bou Arada, 162
Bourguebus, 201 et seq.
Bourneville, 231
Bowring, Lt.-Col. J. R., 291
Brammall, Sgt., 194
Bras, 204 et seq.

Bray, Sgt., 193
Breda, 260
Bree, 269
Bremen, 272–275, 277
Bremervörde, 277
Brezzia, 177
Brind, Lt.-Col. P. H. W., 262
Briquessard, 192, 195, 198, 199, 213
Brooke, F.-M. Sir A., 281
Brown, Air-Marshal, 20
Brown, Maj. J. B., 30
Browning, Lt.-Gen. F. A. M., 254
Brussels, 231, 232, 248, 263
Bucéals, 191
Bucholz, 277
Bucknall, Lt.-Gen. G. C., 180, 192, 197
Buq Buq, 30
Burdon, Maj. W. V., 196, 274
Burnett, Lt. G. I. S., 228
Burridge, Lt. J. D., 248
Burton, Maj., 38
Butler, Capt. B. L., 252
Buxtehude, 278
Byass, Lt.-Col. F. W., 44, 72

CAEN, 183, 185, 200 et seq., 211 et seq.,
    220 et seq., 282
Caesar, Lt. J. V., 199
Cagny, 204 et seq.
Cahagnes, 196, 213 et seq.
Cahill, Brig. P., 292
Camarelle, 168
Cambrin, 239, 241
Campbell, Maj.-Gen. J. C., 25, 38, 39,
    43, 62, 73–75, 77, 78, 95, 100, 101,
    282, 291, 293
Canale di Fiumerelle, 173
Cancello, 171
Cap Bon, 159
Capri, 178
Capua, 168, 171, 177
Capuzzo, Fort, 23, 24, 35, 53, 56, 57,
    68, 116, 136
Cardiff, Lt.-Col. E. B. W., 237, 242,
    276, 291
Cardito, 171
Carlton, Maj. J. R. D., 57
Carr, Brig. W. G., 67, 75, 78, 86, 121,
    293, 294
Carr, Maj., 194, 196
Carver, Brig. R. M. P., 13, 15, 125
    159, 170, 196, 206, 232, 291, 297
Carvin, 241, 242
Castle, Maj. E. R. S., 111
Cauchy, 237, 238
"Cauldron", The, 103 et seq.

Caumont, 185, 192, 193, 198–200, 207,
    209, 211 et seq.
Caunter, Brig. J. A. L., 19, 23, 42, 47,
    293
Chance, Maj. R. F. L., 23, 68
Chapman, Lt. P. F., 225, 227, 240
Chapman, Lt.-Col. P. G., 112
Cherbourg, 200
Christopher, Lt.-Col. J. C., 112
Churchill, Rt. Hon. W. S., 15, 31, 47,
    60, 85, 100, 119, 122, 149, 281, 282
Chute, Lt.-Col. R. F. E., 57, 72
Cicola, 178
Clark, Lt.-Gen. M. W., 165
Clarke, Brig. D., 15
Clarke, Capt. E., 249
Clauson, Lt.-Col. P. A., 125, 292
Clifton, Col. G. H., 86
Clive, Brig. A. F. L., 154
Coblenz, 269
Collishaw, Air Marshal, 20
Cologne, 269
Colombelles, 204 et seq.
Combe, Maj.-Gen. J. F. B., 23, 30, 38,
    39, 42, 45–47, 51
Conde, 211, 212, 216 et seq.
Congreve, Maj. J., 71
Coningham, Air Marshal, 127
Consett, Lt.-Col. C. d'A. P., 105
Cook, Capt., 41
Copeland, Lt. R. G. G., 137
Corbett-Winder, Lt.-Col. J. L., 14, 130
Cormelles, 204 et seq.
Cosgrave, Capt. H., 133
Cotton, Lt., 194
Courtrai, 241
Cousins, Lt. J. A. M., 260
Cowley, Lt.-Col. J. G., 125, 291
Cox, Brig. W. R., 257, 263, 294
Cracroft, Brig. H. J. B., 252, 257, 294
Crangles, Sgt., 153
Crankshaw, Maj. J. A. N., 48, 196
Cranley, Lt.-Col. Viscount, 170, 193,
    196
Crawford, Brig. H. N., 106, 107, 125,
    292
Creagh, Maj.-Gen. Sir M. O'M., 19,
    23, 27, 30, 37, 39, 47, 52, 57, 62,
    282, 291, 301
Creaton, Lt. D., 240
Crerar, Gen. H. G. D., 223
Crickmay, Maj. A. H., 243
Cripps, Lt.-Col. D. S., 68, 76
Crocker, Lt.-Gen. Sir J., 156, 183, 223,
    227
Crocker, Lt. J. W., 256

Crossley, Lt.-Col. A. B. C., 39
"Crusader", Op., 65–98
Cunningham, Lt.-Gen. Sir A., 61, 65
Currie, Brig. J. C., 70, 83, 84, 87, 95, 293
Custance, Brig. N., 141, 147
Cuverville, 204 et seq.

DABA, 130, 134, 136
Daunt, Col. B. J., 292
Davy, Brig. G. M. O., 15, 62, 83, 293
de Bombac, Mons, 258
de Bruyne, Lt.-Col. G., 105
Demouville, 204 et seq.
Dempsey, Lt.-Gen. Sir M., 183, 201, 232, 249
Derna, 36, 51, 52, 56
de Salis, Lt.-Col. S. C. F., 52, 70, 71, 74, 75, 90
Deynze, 244, 248
Dickson, Rev. A. H., 224
Diepholz, 273, 274
Dieteren, 266
Dinslaken, 269
Dives, River, 203, 223
Docton, Capt. V. G., 229
Dodge, Rev. E. J., 60, 293
Dommel, River, 259
Dongen, 260
Dorfmark, 276
Dorrien-Smith, Maj. F. A., 199
Dortmund-Ems Canal, 272
Douglas, Brig. A. S. G., 52, 84
Doullens, 237
Doyle, Capt., 88
Drew, Lt.-Col. H. D., 68
Dunne, Maj. N. G. F., 198
Dunphie, Lt.-Col. P., 233
Dyas, Capt., 194

EASSIE, Brig. W. J. F., 292, 296
Eccles, Col. E. C., 248, 292
Echt, 266
Eden, Maj. R. A., 75
Edwardes, Maj. Hon. M. G., 112, 118
Eindhoven, 254 et seq., 299
Eisenhower, Gen. D., 144, 166, 187
Ekins, Brig. M. S., 196, 200, 294
el Adem, 66, 69, 91, 92, 94, 101, 102, 108, 113 et seq., 137 et seq.
el Agheila, 48, 100, 142, 143
el Alamein, 11, 60, 116 et seq., 127 et seq., 160, 282
Elbe, River, 11, 275 et seq.
el Duda, 76, 85, 87, 88, 91, 105
Eleut et Tamar, 110

el Gubi, 67, 69, 77, 84, 85, 91–93, 105, 106, 108, 110, 117
el Hamma, 155
el Hammam, 53, 55
el Krib, 156
Elliott, Capt. C. S., 107
Elrington, Lt.-Col. M., 174
Elton, Brig. H. G., 142
Emieville, 204 et seq.
Ems, River, 270, 271
Enfidaville, 156
Erskine, Maj.-Gen. G. W. E. J., 15, 149, 156–158, 163, 165, 170, 187, 192, 199, 215, 291, 301
Escaut Canal, 253
Escaut, River, 241, 243, 248, 251
Estaires, 238, 239
Ewin, Lt.-Col. A. A. H., 67

FALAISE, 185, 186, 201, 207, 208, 219, 229
Falkiner, Lt.-Col. Sir T., 154
Fallingbostel, 276
Farewell, Lt.-Col. J. F., 292
Fawcett, Maj. J., 113
Fellows, Maj. N. C. B., 45
Fervaques, 226 et seq.
Fielden, Lt.-Col. G., 24, 44
Filose, Maj.-Gen. A. A. E., 103
Firth, Capt. H. H., 104
FitzGerald, Maj. D. J. O., 176
FitzPatrick, Lt.-Col. G. R. D., 267
Flers, 212, 232
Flood, Lt. R. A., 244
Floyd, Maj.-Gen. Sir H., 212
Foggia, 169
Foliot, Cmdt., 31
Forester, Lt.-Col. M., 168, 199
Foret de Bretonne, 229
Fosdick, Lt.-Col. F. R. C., 72
Foster, Capt., 73, 77
Four, 205, 207
Francolise, 177
Freeland, Lt.-Col. I. H., 225
French, Maj., 194
Frénouville, 207
Frévent, 237, 240
Freyburg, Lt.-Gen. Sir B., 84, 89, 95, 117, 143
Fuka, 27, 134
Furnivall, Lt.-Col. L. T., 220

GABES, 155
Gabr Saleh, 68, 70, 80, 85
Gairdner, Lt.-Gen. C. H., 291
Gambut, 35, 80, 88, 137

Gape, Lt. W. H. V., 24
Garigliano, River, 177, 178
Garmoyle, Brig. Viscount, 74, 95, 113, 118, 121, 294
Garnett, Lt., 191
Gatehouse, Maj.-Gen. A. H., 55, 88, 101, 293
Gazala, 88, 94–96, 100 et seq.
Gebel Akhdar, 35, 36
Geertruidenburg, 259
Geffen, 256
Gheel, 253, 254
Ghemines, 46
Ghent, 231 et seq., 247 et seq., 282
Ghirba, 24, 58
Gibbon, Lt.-Col. E. H., 206
Gibson, Maj. A. C., 272
Gilman, Brig. H. J., 292
Godwin-Austen, Lt.-Gen. Sir A., 65
"Goodwood", Op., 201 et seq.
Gordon, Lt.-Col. D. S., 174, 194
Goring, Lt.-Col. J., 216
Goschen, Maj., 41
Gott, Lt.-Gen. W. H. E., 18, 19, 52, 61, 62, 73, 74, 80, 87, 91, 95, 101, 122, 123, 282, 291, 293
Goulburn, Lt.-Col. C., 181, 224, 267
Gournay, 235
Graham, Maj.-Gen. D. A. H., 262
Gray, Sgt., 72
Grave, 254
Grazzanise, 173, 174
Gregson, Lt.-Col. G. P., 195, 198, 218
Grentheville, 205
Grenville-Grey, Lt.-Col. C. E. M., 105, 296
Griffiths, Lt.-Col. W. D., 218
Groom, Capt., 226
Gunn, Lt. G. Ward, 72, 73, 282

HACKETT, Brig. C. J. W., 104
Hafid Ridge, 57
Halfaya Pass, 25, 52, 53, 56, 57, 65, 90
Hamamet, 156
Hamars, 216
Hamburg, 269, 275 et seq.
Hamm, 254
Hamminkeln, 270
Hangest, 235
Harburg, 275 et seq.
Harcourt, Lt.-Col. A. C., 42
Harden, Cpl., 267
Harding, Lt.-Gen. Sir John, 11, 15, 125, 130–133, 136–138, 143, 146, 147, 291
Harpstedt, 274

Hartigan, Lt., 31
Harvey, Brig. C. B., 141, 149
Harvey, Lt.-Col. W. S., 220, 266, 293
Hatton, Brig. G. S., 291
Hazelton, Lt.-Col. E. G., 226, 292, 299
Heesch, 256
Hely, Lt.-Col. A. F., 70
Henderson, Maj. P. Z., 228
Herenthals, 253
Hermon, Lt.-Col. R. A., 119
Heycock, Capt. J., 76
Hilton, Maj. P., 217
Himeimat, 123, 130, 131
Hinde, Brig. W. R. N., 15, 149, 189, 196–198, 215, 294
Hinges, 238
Hobart, Maj.-Gen. Sir P., 18, 19, 186, 291, 295
Hobart, Lt.-Col. P. R. C., 163, 181, 224, 237–239, 291
Hobbs, Maj. P., 107
Hogg, Maj. J. N., 105
Hollenstedt, 277
Holliman, Lt.-Col. C. H., 197, 243, 267, 282
Homs, 162 et seq.
Hope, Maj. H. A., 70
Horrocks, Lt.-Gen. B. G., 130, 156, 165, 220
Hottot, 213
Howard-Jones, Brig. L. H., 292, 296
Hoya, 273
Hubert-Folie, 206 et seq.
Hughes, Tpr. E., 42
Hunt, Lt. W. G. G., 228, 234
Hunter, Lt.-Col. A. D., 150, 151, 176, 235, 241, 248, 292
Hunter, Lt. A. S., 267
Hunter, Maj. J. A., 108
Huth, Maj. P. H., 104, 276
Hutton, Lt.-Col. W. M., 159
Hyde, Lt.-Col. P., 292
Hynes, Maj. L. G., 45

IBBENBUREN, 272, 273
Ijessel, River, 269
Inglis, Brig., 117

JAGO, Lt.-Col., 67, 87
Jarvis, P.-S.-M., 44
Jeffrey, Maj. E., 220
Jennings, Capt. H., 250
Jerram, Brig. R., 29
Jerusalem, 191, 192, 200, 205
Johnston, Capt. M. E., 14
Jones, Maj. V. H., 27

KAIROUAN, 156
"Kangaroos", 221
Keatinge, Col. L. R. H., 248, 292
Kidston, Lt.-Col. G. J., 78, 87, 110, 119
Kildare, Maj. Marquess of, 221
Kilkelly, Lt.-Col. G., 104
Kingston, Rev. A. V., 293
Knightsbridge, 94, 108 et seq.
Knowles, Lt.-Col. C., 292
Knox, Lt.-Col. G. S., 250, 292
Koenig, Gen., 103, 110

LA Bassée, 236, 240, 250
Lagni, River, 171
La Hogue, 204 et seq.
La Lande, 214
La Poste, 216
Latham, Brig. H., 15
La Vallée, 217 et seq.
Lawson, Maj. J., 131
Leakey, Lt.-Col. A. R., 273
Le Beny Bocage, 211, 213
Leclerc, Gen., 155
Leese, Lt.-Gen. Sir O., 129, 142, 143
Leetham, Lt.-Col. W. I., 52, 125
Le Neuburg, 232
Le Poirier, 205
Levy, Lt.-Col. C., 274
Lewes, Lt.-Col. the Earl of, 232, 291
Liardet, Lt.-Col. H. M., 112
Liège, 261, 263
Lieurey, 228
Lille, 236, 238 et seq.
Lillers, 236, 238, 239
Lindsay, Capt. Hon. M., 14
Linne, 267
Lippe, River, 269
Lisieux, 224 et seq.
Lister, Lt.-Col. M. D. B., 57, 67, 71
Livarot, 224 et seq.
Livry, 192, 193, 196
Lloyd, Lt.-Col. H., 233
Lockett, Capt. R. R., 177
Locon, 238
Loire, River, 185, 186
Lokeren, 252
Loon-op-Zand, 259, 260
Lord, R.-S.-M., 276
Louvain, 299
Low, Brig. A. R. W., 105
Lower Rhine, River, 254
Lumsden, Lt.-Gen. H., 100, 101, 114, 130, 142
Lusty, Lt -Col. A. C., 250, 292
Lyne, Maj.-Gen. L. O., 262, 263, 272, 273, 279, 291

Lyons, Sgt. H., 148
Lyon-Smith, Brig. T., 221, 244, 292
Lys, River, 241, 243, 248

MAAS, River, 254, 261, 262, 267
McCartney, Maj., 267
McCreery, Lt.-Gen. Sir R., 165
Macdonald, Maj., 192
Macdonnell, Lt.-Col. J. R., 115
Mackeson, Brig. H., 243, 294
Maclaren, Maj. R. N., 17
McSwiney, Lt. P., 72
Madalena, Fort, 23, 24
Maesyck, 262, 263
Maktila, 28, 29
Malines, 252, 253
Marble Arch, 143
Mareth, 152 et seq.
"Market Garden", Op., 254 et seq.
Marriott, Maj.-Gen. J. C. O., 91, 114
Marsh, Capt., 31
Marshall, Lt.-Col. E., 292, 298
Mason, Lt.-Col. J. H., 199, 225
Massico, Monte, 177, 178
Matthew, Lt.-Col. F. A. H., 292
Maxwell, Lt.-Col. Hon. S. A., 125, 139, 292
Mayfield, Lt.-Col. B., 84
May-sur-Orne, 208 et seq.
Mechili, 35–37, 51, 56, 97
Medenine, 151 et seq.
Medjerda, R., 159
Medjez el Bab, 156
Meiklejohn, Rev. K., 293
Melle, 244
Melville, Lt., 78
Mersa Brega, 48, 138, 139
Mersa Matruh, 17, 18, 20–25, 27–29, 52, 66, 117, 135, 282, 295 et seq.
Messervy, Gen. Sir F., 100, 101, 106, 107–111, 114, 118, 291
Messina, 165
Meuse, River, 264
Mews, Brig. R., 125, 133, 168, 195, 215, 292
Meyer, Sgt., 238
Middelrode, 259
Miller, Maj. A. G., 24, 29
Milner, Capt. C. F., 196
Mirrlees, Lt.-Col. H. R. B., 19, 293
Mitchell, Lt.-Col. A. C., 292
Mogg, Lt.-Col. H. J., 262
Molliens Vidame, 236
Mondragone, 178
Monschau, 263
Montfort (Normandy), 229

Montfort (near Roermond), 267
Montgomery, F.-M. Viscount, 122, 124, 129, 154, 156, 181, 187, 201, 264, 281
Mont Pincon, 185, 212 *et seq.*
Moore, Lt.-Col. H., 276, 291
Moore, Lt.-Col. (R.H.A.), 273
Morris, Lt.-Col. F., 292
Mortain, 219, 223
Moselle, River, 269
Mosley, Capt. M. H., 41
Moubray, Lt.-Col. J., 24
Msus, 37, 39, 98, 100, 138
Mteifel, 109
Muids, 232
Muir, Capt. H. M., 111
Munster, 254
Murray-Smith, Lt., 42

Namur, 231, 248
Nangle, Maj. H., 228
Napier, Brig. J. L. C., 25, 291
Naples, 165 *et seq.*, 178
Nation-Tellery, Lt., 267
Nazareth, 243
Neame, Lt.-Gen. Sir P., 50, 51
Newton, Maj. O. H., 74
Newton, Lt. W.. 274
Newton-King, Brig. D. S., 88, 149, 293
Nibeiwa, 28, 29
Nienburg, 275
Nijmegen, 254, 299
Noble, Capt., 191
Nofilia, 143
Norman, Lt.-Col. J. A., 217, 218, 266
Norrie, Lt.-Gen. Sir W., 65, 68
Northey, Maj. E. G. V., 68

O'Brien, Maj. B. C., 228
O'Brien, Rfm., 44
O'Connor, Lt.-Gen. Sir R., 20, 27, 30, 33, 37, 38, 49–51, 125, 201, 203, 204, 212, 282
Oosterhout, 260
Orbec, River, 223, 227
Orne, River, 183, 185, 188, 203 *et seq.*, 212 *et seq.*
Orr, Lt.-Col. J., 292
Osnabruck, 254, 272
Osnabruck Canal, 273
Oss, 256
O'Sullivan, Lt., 31

Paine, Lt. R. F., 70
Paley, Brig. A. G. V., 171, 237, 251, 274

Palmer, Maj., 110, 115, 169
Panheel, 262, 274
Parker, Maj. M. E., 176
Payne-Gallwey, Lt.-Col. P., 29, 39, 52, 156
Pearson, Lt.-Col. T. C. H., 41, 46
Peaseley, Lt., 174
Pepper, Brig. E. C., 188, 200, 225, 255, 257, 294
Pepys, Lt.-Col. A., 97, 98, 138
Petherick, Lt.-Col. W. G., 30
Phelan, Lt.-Col. P., 274
Phillips, Maj. J. W., 88, 104
Phillips, Lt. P. G. W., 168
Picquigny, 235, 236
Pinneburg, 280
Pinney, Maj. B., 72, 73, 282
Pleasants, Lt., 266
"Plunder", Op., 269 *et seq.*
Plunkett, Lt.-Col. Hon. R., 118
Point *309*, 185, 205, 213
Point *361*, 212
Pompeii, 178
Pont Authou, 228, 229
Porto Farina, 159
Posterholt, 267
Pritchett, Lt.-Col. G. C., 292
Prittie, Maj. Hon. H. D. G., 171
Pyman, Maj.-Gen. H. E., 107, 125, 291

Qattara Depression, 118, 123

Rankin, Lt.-Col. W., 200
Raper, Maj. W., 178
Rapp, Lt. R. A., 144
Rees, 269, 270
Regi Lagni, 171
Reichswald, 267
Reid, Capt. D. G. R., 107
Reid-Scott, Maj. A., 30, 205
Remagen, 269
Renton, Maj.-Gen. J. M. L., 38, 43, 101, 103, 105, 118, 125, 291, 294
Rethem, 275
Retma, 103 *et seq.*
Rheine, 270–272
Rhine, River, 269 *et seq.*
Richards, Maj.-Gen. G. W., 101, 291, 293
Richardson, Maj. J. A., 107
Richardson, Maj. J. H. C., 44
Riede, 274
Riesenbeck, 272
Rigel Ridge, 114
Risle, River, 223, 228, 229
Ritchie, Lt.-Gen. N. M., 100, 116, 232

Ritson, Maj. W. V., 31
Robarts, Maj. A. V. C., 52
Roberts, Maj.-Gen. G. P. B., 112, 137, 147, 149, 156, 201, 240, 294
Roberts, Maj., 177
Roddick, Brig. M. G., 141, 293
Roermond, 265
Roer, River, 265
Roquancourt, 204 *et seq.*
Rosekilly, Capt., 79
Routot, 231
Russell, Brig. H. E., 17, 19, 30, 62, 293
Ruweisat Ridge, 119, 123, 132

St Georges du Vièvre, 228
Sainthill, Lt.-Col. H. M., 116
St Joost, 266
St Lô, 201, 211
Ste Marguerite, 224, 225
St Martin des Besaces, 213
St Nicholas, 252
St Oedenrode, 255 *et seq.*
St Paul du Vernay, 192, 193
St Pierre sur Dives, 224
St Pol, 236, 237, 239, 240
Salerno, 165 *et seq.*
Sandbach, Maj. P., 76
Santa Maria la Fossa, 171
Sarno, River, 168
Sauques, 214
Scafati, 168, 169
Scheldt, River, 244
Scott, Brig. H. M., 159
Scott, Maj., 196
Scott Cockburn, Brig. J., 294
Seclin, 242
Seddon, Lt.-Col. R., 292
Segnali, 103, 110, 115
Seine, River, 185, 223 *et seq.*, 232 *et seq.*
Sessa Aurunca, 178
Seymour-Evans, Maj., 24
Sfax, 156
Sheferzen, 58, 81, 83, 84, 136
Shepherd, Lt.-Col., 85
s'Hertogenbosch, 256, 259
Shiffner, Maj. Sir H., 74
Sicily, 162, 163, 165
Sidi Azeiz, 24, 86
Sidi Barrani, 20, 23, 25, 28, 29, 33
Sidi Bregisc, 96
Sidi Omar, 32, 56, 58, 65, 74, 84, 136
Sidi Rezegh, 14, 66–92, 95, 101, 102, 108, 115, 282
Sidi Saleh, 39–47, 282
Sidi Sulieman, 24
Simonds, Lt.-Gen. G. G., 208

Sinclair, Maj. T. C., 41, 70
Sirte, 143
Sittard, 263, 265
Smail, Lt.-Col. A. T., 125, 148, 177
Smith, Maj.-Gen. Sir C., 18, 25, 27, 291, 295
Smith, Maj. N. A., 237
Sofafi, 28, 31
Soliers, 205 *et seq.*
Sollum, 22, 23, 29, 52, 56–58, 68
Soltau, 275, 277
Soluch, 137
Somma Vesuviana, 170
Somme, River, 233 *et seq.*
Sorrento, 178
Soulevre, River, 213
Sparanise, 177
Speke, Maj. N. H. R., 124
Spratt, Maj. V. G., 229
"Spring", Op., 208 *et seq.*
Spurling, Brig. J. M. J., 263, 280, 294
Stamer, Brig. W. D., 294
Steven, Maj. G. S., 233, 249
Stewart, Lt.-Col. W. S., 79, 176, 216
Stokes, Capt., 217
Straker, Lt., 38
Sulingen, 273
Summerlin, Lt., 107
Susteren, 266
Swetenham, Lt.-Col. J. E., 213
Syke, 274
Synnott, Rev. F. W., 257

Taieb el Essem, 84
Talbot, Capt. G. S. W., 199
Taranto, 165
Tarhuna, 145–147, 149
Tecklenburg, 272
Tel el Aisa Ridge, 119
Tengeder, 103, 138
Teutoburger Wald, 272
Thiberville, 228
Thompson, Lt., 175
Thomson, Maj., 215
Threlfall, Capt., 76
Thury-Harcourt, 212
Tilburg, 259 *et seq.*
Tilly-la-Campagne, 208 *et seq.*
Tilly (near Bayeux), 189, 191, 200
Tmimi, 96
Tobruk, 23, 24, 35, 36, 50, 52, 53, 55, 56, 59, 61, 65, 66, 68, 69, 74, 81, 85, 88, 90, 93, 102, 108 *et seq.*, 124, 137 *et seq.*
Tom of Lith, 257
Torteval, 196, 199

Tostedt, 277
"Totalise", Op., 221
Touffreville, 204 *et seq.*
Touques, River, 223, 226, 227
Tracy Bocage, 195, 196, 199, 215
Trevor, Maj. W. A. B., 87, 96
Trigh Capuzzo, 67, 68, 71, 81, 85, 87, 88, 91, 92, 113
Trigh el Abd, 67, 81, 84, 85, 93
Tripoli, 49, 99, 100, 143, 145 *et seq.*, 282
Troarn, 203 *et seq.*
Trumper, Sgt., 138
Tsmama, Wadi, 146
Tummar, 28, 29
Tunis, 11, 13, 156 *et seq.*, 282
Turnbull, Maj. J., 217
Turner, Brig. C. E. F., 125, 291
Turner, Gnr., 73
Turpin, Brig. P. G., 297
Twistringen, 273

UDENHOUT, 260
Uniacke, Lt.-Col., 110

VAUCELLES, 204 *et seq.*
Vaughan-Hughes, Brig. C. B., 125, 252
Vaux, Capt., 107
Veghel, 255 *et seq.*
Verden, 273
Verney, Maj.-Gen. G. L., 215–218, 221, 223, 225–232, 233, 235, 237–239, 241–244, 248, 252, 255, 263, 291
Verney, Lt. P. V., 15, 16
Verrières, 192, 207 *et seq.*
Vesuvius, 168, 178
Vie, River, 223, 225, 226
Villers-Bocage, 192 *et seq.*, 212 *et seq.*
Vimont, 203 *et seq.*
Viney, Capt., 107
Vire, 211
Vire, River, 188
Volturno, River, 168, 171 *et seq.*, 282

WAAL, River, 254
Wainman, Lt.-Col. W., 52, 69, 84, 177, 196, 234, 271, 282
Wainman, Capt. (R.A.M.C.), 224
Waldfeucht, 266
Walker, Capt. E. W., 229
Walker, Lt.-Col. W. R. G., 292
Walker, Maj., 78

Wall, Lt.-Col. N. M. H., 184, 232, 291
Wallace, Col. Q. V. B., 292, 297
Walsh, Brig. J. J., 292, 296
Walsrode, 275
Warden, Capt., 41
Waterloo, 299
Watkins, Brig. H. R. B., 19, 293
Watson, Lt.-Col. T. G., 30
Watt, Maj. J., 266
Wavell, F.-M. Earl, 21, 24, 25, 29, 31, 33, 37, 49, 51, 53, 58, 60
Webb, Brig. G., 221, 301
Wedlake-Lewis, Lt.-Col. E. P., 249
Weert, 262, 269
Wells, Capt., 207
Wesel, 269, 270
Weser, River, 272, 273, 275
Weser-Ems Canal, 273
Wessem Canal, 261
Wetteren, 244, 245, 247
Whigham, Lt.-Col. I. H. D., 14
Whistler, Maj.-Gen. L. H., 166, 171, 181, 275, 294
Wildeshausen, 274
Wilkinson-Cox, Lt., 262, 274
Williams, Brig. E. S. B., 19, 293
Williams, Capt. M. D., 220
Williams, Brig. S., 107, 292
Willis, Maj. G., 115
Wilson, Lt.-Col. C. P. B., 69, 84, 92, 94, 95
Wilson, Maj. J., 79
Wilson, F.-M. Lord, 21, 36, 50
Wilson, Lt.-Col. R. N., 168
Wingfield, Brig. A. D. R., 15, 257, 273, 294
Wingfield Digby, Rev. S. B., 179, 264, 293
Withers, Maj. H. C., 41, 44
Withers, Lt.-Col. H. H., 125, 292
Woodhouse, Rev. S. M. F., 60, 293
Woods, Maj. H., 124
Woolcombe, Maj. M. J., 42
Wright, Maj. J. P., 196
Wyldbore-Smith, Lt.-Col. F. B., 171

YOUNG, Lt. E. A. I., 244
Young, Maj., 226
Younger, Maj. R., 71, 78

ZAAFRAN, 84, 88
Zanten, 269, 270